Something
Meaningful for God

The
Mennonite Central Committee
Story Series

The Mennonite Central Committee Story
Volume 4. Biographies

Something Meaningful for God

Cornelius J. Dyck, Editor
With Robert S. Kreider and John A. Lapp

HERALD PRESS
Scottdale, Pennsylvania
Kitchener, Ontario

1981

Library of Congress Cataloging in Publication Data (Revised)
Main entry under title:

The Mennonite Central Committee story.

    Vol. 4 also has title: Something meaningful for God.
    CONTENTS: v. 1. From the files of MCC.—v. 2.
Responding to worldwide need.—[etc.]—v. 4. Biog-
raphies.
    1. Mennonite Central Committee—History—Sources.
2. Mennonites—Charities—History—Sources.
3. Mennonite Central Committee—Biography.   I. Dyck,
Cornelius J.   II. Kreider, Robert S.   III. Lapp,
John Allen,   IV. Mennonite Central Committee.
V.   Title: Something meaningful for God.
BX8128.W4M46   361.7′5   80-10975
ISBN 0-8361-1229-6 (v. 1)   AACR1

Contents

Preface

When the idea of writing a history of the Mennonite Central Committee (MCC) was first raised with several of us who have been close to its life and work our response was not positive. Who would read a big volume about an agency that has become an institution and is simply taken for granted among Mennonites, and perhaps others? Besides, we do have *A Ministry of Goodwill, A Short Account of Mennonite Relief, 1939-1949* by Irvin B. Horst (Akron, 1950), and the larger volume *In the Name of Christ* by John D. Unruh (Scottdale, 1952), as well as other writings about the life and work of MCC. There seemed to be no shortage of available information.

In reflecting further on the question, however, it became clear to us that most of this literature was *about* MCC and that the readers had little opportunity to see for themselves how MCC worked, how its decisions were made, or how it all began. And so a proposal grew among us for the preparation of several smaller volumes which would tell the MCC story in a firsthand way and become a resource for other writers, for study groups in congregations and schools, as well as for private enjoyment.

For the present this has led to the preparation of five modest volumes, with the possibility of one or two more being added later. Of these five the first three form a unit which might simply be called "From the Files of the MCC." Volume four (which you hold in your hands) contains fifteen biographies of persons who have played a central role in MCC over many years. Volume five, which is still in preparation, might be called "What Would You Do If. . .?" because it presents specific situations from MCC experiences around the world in terms of crucial ethical and other issues and choices faced by MCC persons in their ministries.

The decisions about what and whom to include were difficult. In the first three volumes the rows of file boxes filled with interesting documents were almost overwhelming. Only a few could be selected, hopefully representative of the issues considered, and placed into context by brief introductory notations. Spelling and punctuation errors in the documents have been left as they were and have not been identified with the standard [sic] to avoid excessive cluttering up of the manuscripts. Whom to include in this small collection of biographies proved equally difficult. It is hoped that it may become possible to compile another volume eventually of the great contributions made to MCC by non-North Americans. Only two of these biographies are included here. The selection of issues and choices faced in sixty years of global activities was equally difficult, from the death of Clayton Kratz in Russia in 1920 to the involvement in Vietnam in the 1960s and 70s. To ask "What would *you* do ..." in specific difficult situations can lead to spiritual growth and, perhaps, to words of counsel to MCC and persons serving with it.

The primary committee appointed by the MCC Executive Committee to guide this project consisted of Robert S. Kreider of Bethel College, North Newton, Kansas; John A. Lapp of Goshen College, Goshen, Indiana; and Cornelius J. Dyck of the Associated Mennonite Biblical Seminaries, Elkhart, Indiana, who, in his capacity as director of the Institute of Mennonite Studies was responsible for the implementation of the project. His debt to the wisdom and help of the other two members of the committee is here gratefully acknowledged. A larger committee was convened once for consultation, but written counsel was also received and appreciated. Its members were Paul Longacre and William T. Snyder of MCC, to whom special recognition is due for their strong support and encouragement, but also to Clarence Hiebert of Tabor College, Kenneth B. Hoover of Messiah College, J. M. Klassen and Dan Zehr of MCC (Canada), and Ted D. Regehr of Saskatoon, Saskatchewan.

Beyond these recognitions deep appreciation is expressed here to the many others who helped in one way or another, including Vernon Neufeld of Mennonite Mental Health Services for facilitating the selection of documents in that field, to Leonard Gross and Sharon Klingelsmith of the Archives of the Mennonite Church at Goshen, to typists and researchers Lois Janzen, Jennifer L. Dyck, Shirley B. Souder, and particularly to Suzanne Keeney Lind and Sue Yoder for exceptional skills in research and in typing respectively. The writers of the biographies deserve their own special praise for erecting monuments in tribute to those whose lives they shared with us. The project could not have been undertaken without the financial and moral support of the MCC itself, through its executive committee and annual meeting, which is here gratefully acknowledged.

May all that has been done be "In the Name of Christ," in his spirit, and to his honor and glory.

Cornelius J. Dyck
Institute of Mennonite Studies

Something Meaningful for God

1.
Nasri
Zananiri

By
Marion
Preheim

"Look up Nasri," former MCC director Ernest Lehman told Harry Martens. Martens was being sent to Jordan as a new influx of refugees flooded into that country in 1967. As soon as he arrived, Martens located Nasri and set him to work.

The life of Nasri Zananiri, a Palestinian Arab, had thus far taken shape from key Middle East events coupled with Mennonite response. The first such major event happened when the United Nations partitioned Palestine in 1948, setting up the state of Israel.

The Palestinian Arabs and surrounding Arab nations disagreed with the division. Tension mounted and border incidents occurred despite a written Armistice Agreement. Jerusalem became a particularly sore spot with both sides claiming the right to occupy the holy city. The United Nations divided the city between the two sides.

Nasri's family lived in the newer part of Jerusalem, the part given to Israel. Because of the danger there during the summer of 1949, his family decided to visit an aunt living in the Old City, the Palestinian Arab part. They left their house for what they thought would be a one-week vacation.

The time extended to one month, then two, and finally six. The Israelis forbade Arabs who had fled to return to the new part of the city. They could not even visit their homes. In 1950, Nasri's family moved to

Jericho. With some shock the Zananiris discovered that they were labeled "refugee." In time, as other events brought new groups of refugees into Jordan and other Arab countries, they would be known as "1948 refugees."

Nasri was fourteen when they arrived in the dusty town of Jericho. They had only enough money for three weeks. They lived in rooms owned by the Coptic Church and received United Nations ration cards for securing food.

Nasri and his five brothers set out to find jobs. One of them peddled kerosene for people's cookstoves. They all tried selling vegetables and fruits—eggplants, cucumbers, tomatoes, bananas, oranges, and grapes—but this didn't provide much income. Nasri did some construction work for a time. The job he finally settled on would set the tone for the next number of working years, although he had no way of knowing that then.

Walter Rutt of the Mennonite Central Committee (MCC) hired Nasri to help rebuild the streets of Jericho. He earned ten piasters a day (30¢). The second week Rutt added a piece of clothing from the MCC Clothing Center as part of his pay. Nasri worked mornings and went to school afternoons.

More and more refugees filled up the West Bank of Jordan. Nasri began to help with clothing distributions. He loaded the heavy bundles on the truck and unloaded them at distribution sites. For this work he earned eight dinars per month ($24.00). After six months he received a raise, making his salary 12 dinars.

Most of the Palestinian Arabs yearned to go back to their homes and businesses, shops, or farms. Discontent grew as they realized they might always be refugees and in 1956 this frustration erupted in a refugee strike. In the disruption, refugees burned the

MCC warehouse. The loss discontinued the clothing operation. Nasri did not have a job for a year. As soon as the clothing distributions resumed, the MCC director looked up Nasri and hired him.

To Amman

Ernest Lehman was the MCC director working out of Jerusalem at that time. Not long after Nasri started working, Lehman asked him to move to Amman, Jordan. He wanted him to work for the Near East Christian Council, an Arab Christian relief organization for which MCC furnished some personnel and material aid supplies.

Nasri made the move and worked in the large refugee camps that sprang up around Amman. Some of the refugees found work right away because they had skills they brought with them from Palestine. But others could not find work. Many of the men had been farmers. The camps, located in unproductive parts of the country, did not provide a means for them to farm. Some of the refugees were women who had lost their husbands in the conflict and needed to remain with young children.

Nasri wanted to help those refugees less fortunate than he. "How would you like to live without water nearby, without electricity, without much hope?" he asks. "None of us would. That's why I work for those refugees. I do not as a refugee have to live as some do, but still I feel with them."

The refugee problem thus became one of finding food, housing, and work for the people. The Jordanian government, the United Nations, and private organizations set out to solve these problems. Nasri worked at the emergency relief effort with the Mennonites.

By 1957, the Israelis and Arabs had agreed upon the

long disputed Armistice Agreement. Both sides agreed to stop border incidents and peace came for several years to the Middle East. The following year, Nasri agreed to work for the Bedouin Relief Service, a service under the Near East Christian Council (NECC). Food and clothing for the distributions to the nomadic Bedouins came from MCC.

The Bedouins, who traditionally crisscrossed borders to find good grazing conditions for their flocks, found themselves barred from certain areas right after the 1948 partition of Palestine. As the years went by their situation grew worse. Nasri worked in food distribution among them. It often took him to remote areas where nomads tented down. One time, caught in a snowstorm, he slept for three nights on top of his truckload of figs and ate the figs for his meals. Another time, when caught on the road too late to return home, he slept on flour sacks stacked in the truck.

Nasri proved to be helpful in translating from the Bedouin dialect into Arabic and English and in explaining their pattern of thinking. For example, in obtaining information about the number of persons to be served in a distribution, the answers the people gave were sometimes confusing.

One time he asked a father, "How many children do you have and what are their ages?"

"I don't know," the man said.

"You mean you don't know how many children you have nor what their ages are?" Nasri exclaimed.

Then he realized the man did not want to answer because he was not the muktar, the village leader. The muktar would decide what number of persons to assign the man within the larger family.

In 1959, Nasri again worked only under NECC. That year he married Sou'ad Samara. Although he didn't tell his new bride until some time later, a loan from MCC enabled him to get married at that time. He paid back the loan over the next few years.

Refugee Among Refugees

Nasri's work involved the refugee camps that ringed the city of Amman; mostly he distributed new and used clothing. In order to distribute it most efficiently, the MCC team tried a number of different methods. They made up packages for families, but people sometimes complained about what they got. They tried allowing people to choose, but those who came first took the best and the ones who followed complained. The team then devised a point system. For example, men's pants were worth eight points. They assigned ten points per person and gave families up to the amount of combined points they had. This system had its problems and they turned to weighing the amount of clothing each family received.

A few times, when people became uncontrollable, the distributors closed up the clothing distribution and went back without giving out anything. Despite the problems, Nasri felt it was worth the effort to help people.

As the emergency needs subsided, MCC turned to more long-term projects. Harry and Olga Martens had started some innovative projects after the 1967 emergency: The preschool kindergartens and sewing training centers which they began are still in operation.

Nasri located two large tents for the first kindergarten classes. Children came in three two-hour shifts per day in order to take as many children as possible into the program.

In the sewing training center, young women took a nine-month sewing course that trained them in various skills. MCC extended the course to eleven months in

1970. These graduates were often in demand as factory workers and wives. Olga Martens worked with the sewing training center and also initiated plans for a Self-Help Needlework program similar to the one in Jerusalem. The program employed Palestinian refugees who had skill in embroidering.

Virgil Claassen came as MCC director in 1968. His wife, Louise, worked with the Self-Help Needlework program. During their term, MCC built permanent asbestos structures for the kindergartens and women's sewing training center. Nasri purchased supplies and materials such as tables and chairs for the kindergartens and sewing machines for the women's sewing center and looked after the MCC buildings.

The Arab and the American

In all his activities, Nasri had not only to learn to work well with his own people, but he also had to adjust to the ways of the Americans with whom he worked. He gives the following story as a sample of how he learned American ways.

One day a workman installed an electric cord in the MCC director's house and it hung somewhat crooked. Nasri inspected the work, noted that it hung somewhat serpentine, but said to the worker, "That's all right," using the oft-repeated Arabic word *malish*, which means, "Never mind."

He had just told the electrician he could go home, when the MCC director walked in and saw the installation. "Nasri," he said. "I don't want anything *malish* in my house. We want things to be done right." Nasri thought a minute and then said, "You are right." From that and other incidents Nasri learned that Americans are different from Arabs in some ways.

Another difference he noticed was that of ideas about

time. "I'll tell you that I'll come and see you tomorrow," Nasri says in explaining the difference. "Don't wait for me tomorrow. My tomorrow may be five days from now. The way you people say tomorrow, tomorrow is tomorrow, and eight o'clock is eight o'clock. My five minutes may be twenty minutes or one day."

"One morning I told the MCC director I would be gone twenty minutes," Nasri said. "He told me, 'Nasri, please don't do it in your twenty minutes. I need you.' He knew my twenty minutes might mean I would be back at two o'clock that afternoon. If they want me back at a certain time, they will say something like, 'Be back at ten o'clock *English* time.' "

Nasri, Assistant to the Director

In 1970, the mounting Palestinian commando activity within Jordan prevented the new MCC director from living there. Urbane and Gwen Peachey and their three children lived in Beirut, Lebanon, and Urbane commuted to Amman. Nasri assumed the position of assistant to the director and began working full time in MCC projects.

He worked out a system whereby Peachey would know whether he should come to Amman for the week or not. Urbane would telephone on Sunday. If Nasri said, "I'm very busy," this meant the commandos were active and it was too dangerous for him to come. If he said, "I'm not busy; I'm at home a lot," Peachey could come and they would probably be able to work.

During this time, Nasri's wife, Sou'ad, helped with the layette program in which mothers made an outfit of clothing and learned child care prior to their babies' births. After the birth of a child, each mother received a ready-made MCC layette. Sou'ad worked with this program for two years.

When the commando threat subsided in 1971, the Peacheys moved to Amman. Mrs. Gwen Peachey became director of the kindergartens. She worked with the Arab teachers in preparing their lessons and wrote a manual for them, which the Arab staff translated into Arabic. The manual was published and was the only publication of this sort in Jordan. The National Ministry of Education and private kindergartens use the manual as a major source book for their programs and for teacher training.

Nasri often interpreted the kindergarten program to the people. Particularly the men did not always understand the program's value. They would say things like: "We can keep our child at home and have him play." Or, "He can draw at home." Or, "I can buy pieces of wood downtown and let him play with them." Nasri would explain to them what the teachers wanted to accomplish through play, drawing, and block building. He would say, "Do you want your child to be dumb? The teachers are teaching him how to think."

In 1969, under the leadership of Virgil Claassen, MCC had begun a Self-Help program which granted loans from $100 to $500 to persons establishing a small business such as a tailor shop, grocery store, barbershop, or goat production. By 1970-71, MCC had aided 70 needy families through this program and Nasri played a major role in it until the end of 1975 when MCC transferred the program to the National Ministry of Social Affairs and other voluntary agencies.

Since the 1950s, the work in West and East Jordan had been mainly in relief, education, and needlework. Relief projects were practically terminated on the West Bank before the 1967 war. The influx of displaced persons and refugees to East Jordan as a result of the 1967 war, and the separation of West Bank from East

Jordan, made it necessary to establish an MCC office in Amman, Jordan's capital. Nasri had a major role in the emergency services carried on by MCC in Jordan from 1967 until 1972 when all the relief efforts were terminated. The economic situation in the country had improved sufficiently so that MCC was able to concentrate first on self-help and then on rural development and agriculture.

People who were helped in these projects often saw a dramatic change in their lives and felt grateful to MCC for the aid. Nasri remembers one man in particular. The Ministry of Social Affairs had referred him to MCC because he was having difficulty with the government and could not get a loan for his chicken business. MCC gave him a loan of 200 dinars ($600). He paid his bills with this, bought some small chicks, and by careful management increased his flocks to 5,000 and then 10,000. Finally he had six chicken houses, all run by his wife, his children, and himself.

The man responded in deep gratitude to MCC. "I'm going to put a sign up at my place like you have at project sites so people will know MCC helped here," he said. "I will never forget how MCC helped me." When Nasri and Urbane Peachey went to see him, he wanted to give them 50 chickens. "No," they told him, "but we will come and eat a meal of chicken with you."

In 1976, when MCC started a poultry project near this man's village under the leadership of John Hubert and Harry Harder, he let them put small chicks in his houses for two weeks without charge and offered them a third week if they found they needed it. The poultry project benefited 35 villages. Helping this one man with a loan in turn helped many other people through his generosity.

Nasri's primary contribution after 1971 was in the

implementation of irrigation and domestic water supply projects. In the Jordan Valley an irrigation system and a service station were rebuilt. The water pumps and irrigation networks were in the farmland of refugees who had lived since 1948 in Karamah Camp, population 25,000. The camp and the surrounding area were 75 percent destroyed as a result of the Israeli raids into the Jordan Valley in the spring of 1968. This served as a kind of pilot project, giving MCC experience for expanded work in open ditch irrigation and domestic water supply.

For drinking water, villages often could hook up to a main line to secure a good water supply. For such projects, Nasri measured the pipes needed, bought them, and supervised their installation. The National Water Authority provided engineering assistance. Nasri usually got clearance with officials through the Ministry of Social Affairs. "When we work with the government," Nasri says, "we are much further ahead than if we try to do it on our own."

Providing farmers with water for their crops also requires planning with the local leaders and government officials. Often Nasri needed to explain to the people the need for the cemented irrigation ditches. "Bringing water to the field in dirt ditches is not good enough," he would explain. "The water in the canal starts out six inches deep up in the hills, but we will end up having only one inch of water down here because most of the water seeps into the ground." Then he would make plans with the people to cement the ditches. In rocky mountainous areas, Nasri sometimes rode on a donkey to inspect a water source and possible canal location. Building materials were often transported to the canal sites by donkey.

Nasri worked well with local village leaders and

people in the villages. Urbane Peachey, who served for nine years as MCC Personnel Director in Akron, says, "He was a better personnel man than I was. He possessed an intuitive sense of people's feelings and reactions. His personality style in the office or on a project was warm, jovial, and vigorous, but not domineering."

Nasri received in-service training for community development work under the leadership of Urbane Peachey. The transition from relief to development programming was difficult because people had been accustomed to receiving assistance from the government and from voluntary agencies for so many years.

Peachey emphasized to Nasri and the other staff that in community development work we do not raise people to a higher level of living by giving them the whole ladder. Peachey emphasized, "We will provide one or two rungs of the ladder to enable the people to get started, but the villages must supply the rest." This brief anecdote was told over and over again in many villages throughout Jordan in order to help people visualize what participation in a development project meant for them.

Often the villagers would say, "We don't have money, our people are poor, we have seen so many wars, we only get one good wheat crop in seven years, etc." In the earliest projects, MCC paid the lion's share of the project costs. But it is interesting to observe how that changed when development projects were undertaken and neighboring communities heard about what was being done. Interest and participation increased rapidly so that, on an average, development project costs are now being shared 50-50 between MCC and the receiving communities.

But traditional Arab communities are full of delightful bargainers, and it was quite natural that the villagers should try to get as much as possible from what they thought of as a "rich foreign organization." Nasri tried to help bridge the gap. In nearly every project MCC staff had the opportunity to explain that the assistance was coming from the churches of North America and not from a rich government.

Nasri's superb bargaining skill was essential for MCC. It may seem rude, but on several occasions when village leaders complained that they didn't have money for a project, Nasri would point to several men in the circle and tell them how much money they had in their pockets. On one occasion he pointed to five village leaders and said, "I believe you each have five dinars on you right now and you have more in your houses."

In another case where MCC had made a loan, the man refused to pay. "I shocked the man," Nasri says. "I asked him how much money he had in his pockets right then. He pulled out his money which amounted to 300 dinars ($900), which was the amount he owed MCC. I felt somewhat sorry for him because he had so much on him, but he did pay."

On another occasion, a distinguished sheikh did not want to pay. "I am an important sheikh," he said, hoping the MCC team would be in awe of his authority. "If you are a big sheikh," Nasri replied, "then you can afford to pay." The man paid.

Sometimes the people balked at carrying through a project to the end. In one project the people had agreed to cut down some of their trees to make way for a canal and the road leading to it. Nasri understood how valuable trees were to the people, but water was also a necessity for them.

Nasri halted work on the half-finished canal and talked with the people. "Having more water means you will have more trees in the future than you have now," he said. "You must cut the trees. I understand it is hard for you to cut the trees. It takes a long time to grow a tree. But we must cut them now to have more trees in the future."

Sometimes the MCC team would call in an intermediary, a traditional Arab custom. Usually it is someone of authority like a sheikh, a muktar, a governor of a district or a subdistrict, or personnel from the Ministry of Social Affairs. Since MCC developed the policy of working with all leaders involved when implementing a project, it follows naturally that they can call on one of them when difficulties arise.

Whenever there is a local way to solve a problem, Nasri helped MCC do it that way. In some cases, Westerners might call on a lawyer and go to court. In Jordan, Nasri knows they can call on a governor or some other official to serve as an intermediary and settle the matter by negotiation. For MCCers, this also seems like the biblical way.

"Of course," Nasri says, "when it is just a small matter, we try to take care of it ourselves." One small way is to say the MCC team will not drink tea or eat with the people until a matter is settled. Nasri is often able to sense at what point they need to call in a governor or a person from the Ministry of Social Affairs.

MCC Is My Business

Nasri has served the Mennonites and the Near East Christian Council for 26 years. "I don't feel like an MCC employee," he says. "I feel like I'm a member of the Mennonite Central Committee."

He recalls one time when he discovered the MCC cashbox missing from the office. He hunted for it all evening. First he asked the office personnel if they had seen the box. He checked with the kindergarten staff. Near midnight, he finally learned that an MCCer had taken it out to a project that day. "It was like money from my own business," he said.

Nasri never asked for a raise because MCC seemed like his own. "But the chances came for a raise by themselves," he says, grateful for the security he has found in his moderate salary over the years.

When shopping for MCC, he tries to find the cheapest items without sacrificing good quality, even if it means going to ten places before making a purchase. In the project operations, he works at figuring out the most economical practices.

One thing does bother him, however. Some of his fellow Arabs feel that anyone who works for an American organization is automatically against the Arabs. Americans aided Israel during conflicts with the Arabs. When Nasri worked in distribution, for example, some would accuse him of being a Jew. They would say, "The Americans give us Arabs a piece of clothing, but they give the Israelis airplanes." Nasri explains to his fellow Arabs that some Americans are different. Despite the complications in his life because of the Middle East conflict, Nasri does not feel enmity toward the Israelis. "I prefer peace, not war," he says. "I would go back to my home now even if it was unsafe there."

Nasri did get a chance once to visit his old homeplace in Jerusalem. "The people living in the house we rented still use my parents' furniture that we left in 1949," he remarks. "They served me coffee. I was only thirteen when I left, but I wanted to drink coffee in my house."

Because of Nasri's spirit of peace and reconciliation, co-workers and others often turn to him when they have conflicts. Once a secretary said she was going to quit. "You resign today and come back tomorrow," he advised. "Rest up this afternoon." That's what she did, taking the afternoon off to recuperate.

"Recently I found one of the fellows in the office asking a secretary to type a letter of resignation for him," Nasri said. "I asked him what the trouble was." He told Nasri he had too much work to do. "Especially you give me a rough time," he said to Nasri.

"I didn't say much," Nasri relates. "I could tell he was tired. I told him he could go home at two o'clock."

That evening Nasri went to the man's house with a piece of paper. "I'm bringing you this paper with a resignation written up so you can sign it," he said, "but first I want to eat supper with you." While waiting for the meal, they talked. Nasri admitted assigning him too much work in one instance, but basically it became clear that the employee did not want to do the work in the job he was holding.

After they had eaten together, they talked some more. Then at one point Nasri said, "Here's the paper. Tear it up. Don't sign it. Tomorrow you can come to work. We don't agree on your resigning." They talked until late evening, although Nasri had told his wife he would be back at 7:00. "I would have stayed up all night to settle the problem if I had needed to," Nasri says.

Nasri arrived back home around 10:00. Soon he received a phone call from his co-worker. "How come you made me agree to go back to work?" he asked. At 10:40, however, the man and his wife showed up at Nasri's house. The man said he was sorry and assured Nasri he would be at work in the morning, which he was.

In addition to dealing with office situations, Nasri often helps solve problems with the sheikhs and muktars, the leaders of Arab villages and groups. When the kindergartens wanted to raise the amount the people

Nasri Zananiri (left) with kindergarten teachers.

paid for having their children in school, they could not get the muktars to agree. A policy of some payment existed from the beginning of the program, but the muktars of the area did not want to ask the people to pay more.

Nasri invited the head of the muktars to his house. He served him tea and cakes. They visited and drank tea and more tea. Then at an appropriate time, Nasri said, "If you don't help me, we will have trouble in this area." Not long after that, all the muktars agreed that they should increase the payments.

Having Nasri as a part of the MCC team really aids in project decisions and relations with the people. "When we go in to start a project," Nasri says, "we talk and make friends first. Often the people want us to eat with them. This is an Arab custom. Before a person knows who I am or where I come from, he is expected to prepare food for me as a visitor. When I'm hungry I can ask for food, especially among the Bedouins. We don't often do that, but if one does have a need the host must feed him."

But the MCC team soon learned they could not accept every invitation to a meal. If, for example, they ate at the first place they stopped in their working day, it would take so much time they would not get the rest of the day's work done. Eating with people is also an unspoken agreement to do something for them. So MCCers often turned down a first invitation saying, "We don't eat until after we decide on the project." Or, "We will finish the project and then we will eat."

The people would press them hard to get them to eat with them. "If you can't stay for lunch, eat breakfast with us now," some would say. As Nasri and the director made their way to the car to leave without eating, the people held onto their hands or held them by the chin.

Nasri explained the meaning of the Arab actions. "If you hold a man's chin as an Arab, it means something," he said. "I'll tell you what that means. Say I would kill a person and go to a sheikh's house or a Bedouin's tent. If I would hold his chin, it says, 'I am in your house; take care of me.' He will do everything for me then and nobody will touch me. Grabbing by the chin means everything will go nice and smooth."

He also used his knowledge of Arab customs to help the people who were involved in a project. In one village where MCC had a project, a dispute over a marriage kept the people from working well together. The sheikhs could not settle the matter. The father of the boy, a sheikh himself, held Nasri by the chin and asked his help.

On the next visit, Nasri visited the father of the daughter, also a sheikh. The sheikh prepared a meal for Nasri. Nasri held him by the chin and said, "I will not eat your food nor continue the project."

"What do you want?" the father asked.

"First of all you must settle the problem of your daughter's marriage," Nasri said. The boy and girl had waited five years to marry, but the girl's father thought the boy was not rich enough. "One always deals with the father of the girl in a marriage problem," Nasri noted.

"So I would not eat with the girl's father," Nasri says, "until he said he would do something about her marriage. Bedouin love is too bad. They kill each other over it. So I just held his chin and told him to let his daughter marry the boy. He agreed and then I ate the meal."

The next day, the father of the boy came to visit Nasri in Amman. He gave him a big box of chocolates because the other father had now agreed to let the two marry. "So the boy is married now," Nasri says.

The sheikhs, like any leaders, are anxious to benefit their people. They try to get projects approved sometimes even when they do not seem feasible. Nasri helps greatly in working through project decisions.

One day, Nasri and Peachey went to see about building an irrigation canal in a new location. After looking the situation over, they both agreed the place did not suit for a canal and that this project would not be in accordance with MCC policy. They told the local sheikh this. He studied the situation for a few minutes. Then he said, "Once my people were hungry. We only had *wawee* (fox) to eat, but my people do not eat *wawee*. Someone said, 'Don't call it *wawee*, call it *we-we* (a made-up name with the same pronunciation).' "

When the sheikh finished the story, he said, "Don't call it a canal. Call it anything you want, but put it there." They did not approve the canal, but left making the sheikh feel he had made a noble attempt.

In another situation, a man told a story to convince

them to do a water project despite the cost being too high. He told this story to convince them:

"One day a man wanted to get quickly to another location. He took his donkey with him to the main road and stopped a truck. He asked if he and his donkey could ride in the back of the truck. The man knew the driver would charge him for the ride at the end of the trip. When they arrived, he asked the driver how much he wanted. The driver said he charged one dinar ($3.00) for the man and one dinar for the donkey. 'But I rode on my donkey in the back of the truck,' the man said. 'I owe you only one dinar.' " Nasri and Peachey showed appreciation for the man's efforts to get approval for his idea, but again they graciously declined to do the project.

In addition to mediating between people and negotiating with them, Nasri has been valuable in cutting through governmental red tape. One incident which substantiates this happened when the city cut off the water supply to Nasri's own house. He tried in vain to get the water turned on again. After twelve days, he called the water department and said, "This is the minister for the Mennonite Central Committee. I would like my water." Within an hour, a worker came and delivered the water. Nasri called back to the water department. "Why is it you came when it sounded like I was a minister of some department? I'm just Nasri Zananiri and I needed water."

Visit to the United States

During the summer of 1976, Nasri and Sou'ad visited the United States for an in-service educational experience. During the month-long stay, they stopped at Akron, Pennsylvania; Henderson and Beatrice, Nebraska; Newton, Kansas; southern Manitoba; and the Kitchener-Waterloo, Ontario, areas.

At Akron, they went through the large Ephrata Material Aid Center. They had felt a connection with the center all through the years when Nasri worked with clothing and other material aid. They also saw the material aid centers in Kansas and Ontario and some of the self-help shops that have sprung up in Canada and the U.S.

Their visit coincided with four regional retreats of former Middle East workers. The Zananiris met again some 75 people with whom they had associated over the years. They also attended an MCC executive committee meeting in Akron and felt a part of MCC at that level. Ernest Bennett and Gwen Peachey presented them with a gift from MCC.

At other sites, the Zananiris visited children's institutions, psychiatric hospitals, welfare agencies, and farms. At Kansas State University they saw experiments in grazing animals where vegetation is limited. On various farms they particularly noted chicken, cattle, and crop development. In Nebraska, they saw irrigation systems and the processing of grain from the combine to the grain elevator. When they returned home, Nasri and Sou'ad felt they could now better explain the MCC work of which they are a part.

I Like Easter

In all the trials, terrors, tensions, and red tape of Middle East life, Nasri finds his faith is what tempers the times for him. He thinks back to how he became and has maintained being a Christian.

"My mother more than my father helped us to be Christians," he says. "My father was a Christian, but my mother used to pray and pray—when we ate, when she woke up, when my brothers went out in the car, she prayed."

"I followed the church," he says. "I prayed, but especially after we were chased out of Palestine, I prayed more. In Palestine, we thanked God for food and for our nice life. After we left, we asked often for him to help us return. My wife comes from the church also. We are both Christians."

When asked about special celebrations in his Greek Orthodox Church, Nasri said, "I like Easter more than Christmas. We believe Jesus had a hard time for us—being killed and hanged—and so that's why we love him and remember Easter more. The evening before Easter Sunday they start about 10:00 and pray until Easter morning.

"In our Arabic Bible is one part that says even if I were rich and spend money for others and there is no love, that doesn't mean anything. We must love others. That's how I feel. I hope I'm right."

Nasri often witnesses to his faith spontaneously. In most any project, he says, the name of Allah comes up. Once when he was working in a village water project, someone expressed his gratitude for the project by saying, "We thank the King and Mohammed."

"You forget to thank the right person," Nasri said. "You don't need to remember the Mennonites, but you must not forget God. God sent the project, not the king. The king doesn't even know we're here. Mohammed doesn't know we're here. You forget God and the Mennonites."

Once a refugee buffeted by events beyond his control, Nasri of Jordan is following his Lord by providing a refuge for others caught in the crisis of life in the Middle East. No wonder people say, "Look up Nasri," when they need help.

Henry A. Fast

2. Henry A. Fast

As Told to
Maynard
Shelly

Not long after I had come back to Kansas I, Henry A. Fast, was asked to speak to a Founders Day meeting on "My View of Bethel College After Ten Years." I had graduated from the college in 1917.

At that time, I was pastor of the Bethel College Mennonite Church in North Newton. I don't know whether anybody remembers my preaching, but I assure you, I remember what the church did for me as a young pastor.

In those days, a young man assuming a pastorate was on trial, particularly if he had just come out of seminary as I had.

Bethel College, too, worked under a cloud of suspicion. The modernist-fundamentalist controversy was creating tensions. Some people felt the school was treating the faith once delivered to the saints too critically. Bethel College even employed teachers who had gotten their training at the University of Chicago, which was regarded as the seedbed of liberalism. Mistrust had been engendered by Moody Bible Institute and by its president, an ardent fundamentalist and supporter of World War I.

In looking back on my college days, I recalled to that Founders Day gathering my happy experiences as a student. I talked of J. F. Balzer, under whom I had studied Bible and Greek. I mentioned other teachers and said they had contributed much to my viewpoint, had given me a vision, and had ordered my life.

By their attitude as well as by their words, they taught me reverence for truth wherever found. They guided me to a faith that sustained me and challenged me to adventure in the business of living and serving. Some of these faculty members had later been forced out as a result of the theological controversies brewing during those years.

"Those men," I said, "ought never have been allowed to leave here."

Orderly Management for a Boy Forlorn

I came to Kansas from Mountain Lake, Minnesota, in the fall of 1912, to enroll as a college freshman. That summer must have been exceedingly dry because the grass was yellow and the trees almost bare of leaves. I came to college about as green and lonesome as they ever come.

My boyhood days had not always been easy. With two sisters and two brothers all quite a bit older, I just did not fit into the fun and fellowship of either my sisters or my brothers and their friends.

You can imagine how forlorn I felt as a young boy when so often I was told and made to feel I didn't belong and wasn't wanted. To get away from me when they were going swimming, my brothers often resorted to various devices to lose me somewhere along the way. But sheer desperation soon taught me to run always fast enough to keep up with my next older brother.

My parents named me Henry when I was born in 1894. The middle initial in my name I added later so the letters from my girl friend did not reach my pious uncle

Henry Fast, Sr., before I could read them. Later when I had to report for induction to Camp Funston, Kansas, the receiving officer insisted I give myself a name to indicate what the "A" initial stood for. The first name that occurred to me was that of a favorite uncle on my mother's side. So by military order I am now registered as "Henry Abram Fast."

I was fortunate that I could get a running start on the twentieth century. In 1898, America embroiled itself in the Spanish-American War. When the year 1900 arrived, my mind had already been stimulated by pictures of that war and the conversations between my parents, both of whom had been teachers for a few years prior to my birth. And father, as a young man, went to Rochester, New York, to a Baptist seminary to study under Walter Rauschenbush, who awakened people to be sensitive to human need.

Our home was not ideal. With seven children, all very human, how could it have been? Father was strict and had plenty of temper. I had the feeling he controlled more temper in one week than most people did in a year.

Father, and mother as well, strongly believed in the importance of order in the life, work, and planning of our homelife. As children, we were taught the importance of orderly management, of promptness, and responsible performance. Every week, I had the duty to sweep the halls and gangways of the barn. A task, pleasant or unpleasant, was to be handled promptly and responsibly without dawdling and without complaining. You finished what you started.

In our work on the farm, father insisted that we observe order in the care and placing of tools and machinery. Feed for livestock was conveniently placed and restocked as needed. I'm glad to admit, we did learn to appreciate such practices. But sometimes we really chafed under the pressures and felt rebellious when father's demands appeared arbitrary and unrealistic.

Father followed crop rotation simply as part of intelligent and good land use practice even before agricultural colleges began to promote it in our area. The planting of crops and garden followed a plan. Father carefully picked the seed grain for the next year. Before the seeding season, he used a good homemade fanning mill to sift and clean the seed grain so that only good quality grain was used in our seeding. I know, because I was his favorite chore boy to turn the fanning mill on many occasions and in many seasons.

When I graduated from high school as valedictorian in a class of five, I had to contribute an original oration as part of the graduation exercises. My topic was: "Labor, the Price of Attainment."

Resisting the Wooing of the Spirit

Revival meetings came to our community during my early teens. In their zeal for converts, these preachers and their supporters exerted heavy personal pressure on those present. I attended those meetings faithfully and listened carefully. On several occasions, some workers became quite personal and urgent in pressing their appeal to me.

For some reason, I never went forward in response to the call to come to the altar. And for this, I was made to feel guilty as one who resisted the wooing of the Holy Spirit. I was indeed concerned about responding to the call of God and it did bother me that I did not feel free to respond as others did. I prayed about my problem more seriously than some who had walked so readily to the front and assumed everything had been settled.

I haven't always understood myself or the mysterious

leading of the Spirit. But this I know: from my earliest childhood, I had responded in trust to Jesus and I always wanted to follow him and accept him as Savior and Lord. But I did not want to take this step because I was pressured into it. I wanted this to be a free, deliberate, and glad declaration of my own commitment.

And I did this later in a wholehearted way at the age of nineteen at the close of my first year at Bethel College. I owe a good deal to Bethel College.

During my younger years, I was also one of the concerned Christian young people who were impatient with the social injustices and immoralities prevalent in our time which were corrupting all our human relations. We were restless, much like some of our own concerned Christian young people are today. We, in our time, came to be branded as advocates of the social gospel—a bad word, then.

My Father's Woodpile Thesis

I was tremendously timid as a young man. I still am. I was afflicted by a sense of inferiority that was terribly depressing. But now I can almost thank God for it because I might never have discovered how insufficient I was in myself. I was compelled to seek strength greater than my own and discovered how God on many occasions magnified himself through my weakness.

What a struggle I had to come to certainty about my vocation. From early boyhood, I had felt an inner urge to enter the ministry, but I was so timid and tongue-tied that it frightened me. I was tremendously attracted to medicine but my hands were not steady. How could I become a good doctor with such a handicap?

I had to do something. So I went into high school teaching and liked it so much that I was strongly tempted to stay in it.

My first teaching experience was as principal of the high school in Whitewater, Kansas. I was coach of athletics and director of a girls glee club. That was interrupted in the spring of 1918, when my draft board ordered me to report for induction to Camp Funston. When I was discharged a year later, father asked me whether I would help him get settled in town; he was retiring from the farm. That fall, the high school superintendent in Mountain Lake called me to his office. When I left, I had signed a contract to be coach of athletics in my hometown.

Well, that was a switch. Father had been so antagonistic to high school athletics and had written rather vehemently against it. "If boys need any exercise," he would say, "let them split wood." He always had a big pile of wood at home for us, but not every boy had such an opportunity.

I didn't say anything about my contract. After awhile, the news got back to father that I was coaching athletics. When he asked me about it, I said, "I know what your attitude is, but I know what kind of an influence a coach can have on young men in these years. And I know how easy it is to get the wrong kind of a coach. I think I can do something with the boys and that's the reason I accepted it."

That's all there was. He accepted that as a valid reason.

No Accident on Bluffton's Icy Pond

I had a good experience as coach that year and had the offer of a raise the next year if I'd come back. But by that time, I had become interested in doing seminary work, and I went on to Garrett Biblical Institute in Evanston, Illinois. J. W. Kliewer, who was president of Bethel College, had graduated from Garrett. One of my fellow students at the seminary was Harold Bender. We took Greek together—an exegetical course in First Corinthians.

Later I went on to Witmarsum Theological Seminary at Bluffton, Ohio, where I got my degree in 1922.

The summer after I graduated, J. A. Huffman, who had been head of the New Testament department at Witmarsum, resigned in order to accept a position in the Winona Lake Bible School. The faculty at Witmarsum asked whether I would accept the New Testament teaching position if they gave me a chance to carry on additional studies toward a master's degree in New Testament during the coming summers. I had taught some courses in Bluffton College while I was a senior at Witmarsum, so they knew what I could do.

It was during my time in Bluffton that I experienced God's guidance in finding my life's companion. I had had a number of mild romances before that time, but why didn't they ripen into engagement and marriage? I don't know. I do know that I traveled from Minnesota and Ethel Schindler came from Iowa and we met in Bluffton, Ohio, on a skating pond. Some may think it was an accident, but I believe God had a hand in it.

We were married in 1923 and our subsequent experiences together through the years thoroughly convinced me that a blessed providence helped us to find each other.

Heavy Lies the Thresher's Hand

I accepted the call to the Bethel College Church in 1925 for two reasons. I felt that if I were going to continue teaching in a seminary, training young men for the ministry, I ought myself have some experience in the pastorate.

And I had inner conflicts about the ministry that I

had to resolve. I felt, a little like Moses, that I had a heavy tongue. But from early boyhood, I also had the feeling that I was called to be a minister.

That feeling goes back as far as I can remember. I can still recall a day during the threshing season when I was perhaps six or seven. A good friend of father's and a veteran thresher in his own neighborhood called on us while our crew was busy in the field.

Uncle Wall noted my fascination and shared in my thrill at all the things transpiring before my eyes. Well, it was exciting.

A fireman stoked the firebox in the big steam engine with a continuous stream of straw. The long heavy belt from the engine to the threshing machine flapped and chafed. The men on the grain stacks threw one bundle after another into the fierce, slashing mouth of the machine while straw poured onto the stack and grain flowed from a chute to be bagged and carried away.

The older man started a friendly conversation and I warmed to his interest in me. When it came time for him to leave, he put his hand lightly on my head, and said, "You're going to be a preacher someday."

I never forgot that remark. But others who remembered my parents as teachers saw things differently. After some friendly meeting, they would look me in the eye and say, "We think you'll be a teacher sometime."

Strange to say, both prophecies have been fulfilled. My life's work has been divided almost evenly between a ministry to teaching and one of preaching.

Reconciliation Needs an Easy Discipline

Coming to the Bethel College Church, when I was about thirty years old, I followed President J. W. Kliewer who was not only an outstanding educator but also a wonderful preacher and a good thinker. I felt a bit brash to succeed a man who had served so magnificently. But he was most helpful; he had the wonderful tact and good judgment to push me rather than to stand in my way.

The church ran into some discipline cases, the kind that really needed a veteran minister. Some involved membership in the Ku Klux Klan and some were problems of sex. Some had to do with young people, but the more serious cases were those that involved older people, because they had reputations and families.

At that time, the practice was to have those people appear before the congregation and make a public confession. I looked on that as humiliating and self-defeating. Instead, I asked the persons involved to meet with me and the deacons and in a more private conversation talk the whole thing through and try to be redemptive and conciliatory. Well, that seemed too easy going to some of the older veterans.

I used to teach some Bible classes in the college while I was pastor of the church. That helped me keep the relationship between church and college alive and meaningful. During the latter part of my ministry, a movement started among the students looking for something more mystical than the wrestling with the problems for the Christian in society which marked my preaching.

I tried to understand these young people. What did they mean by mystical? I examined my sermons and asked myself whether I was tending to be too intellectual or sociology-minded.

After five years in the church, I sensed some critical attitudes on the part of some. So I invited some of these people to meet the deacons and me to openly share what they would like to see done. That helped. Some were honest and tried to be objective. But some got pretty antagonistic and vindictive.

Such strong feelings coming from people who I thought were my good friends was a bit horrendous for me. I told the deacons that perhaps I ought to resign for the good of the church and my own.

Wayside Tales from Critics of the Church

Just then the office of dean of the college became vacant and I approached President Kliewer for a chance at that. I offered to continue graduate work in preparation for it. Well, he was most sympathetic, but he said, "I'm afraid we've gotten along too far in our negotiations with P. S. Goertz to make any change."

I also felt the need for further study in Bible. I felt particularly my insufficiency in the Old Testament field because my study up to that time had been largely in New Testament. So I made arrangements to go to Hartford Theological Seminary.

In Connecticut, I had to find outside employment to support my family, so I took on the pastorate of the Buckingham Congregational Church in Glastonbury. It turned out to be a happy relationship. Actually, I was free to preach most anything I felt led to preach. The touchy part in New England was not theological liberalism but economic liberalism, especially since those were the depression years. A minister had to handle with care any liberal thoughts he had on justice for the working class.

I made it a point during the summer to supplement my income by working for an Italian fruit and vegetable grower who also had a large hatchery and chicken business. One summer I worked on the road, just doing handwork, not running the grader or anything like that.

Sergeant's Short Critique of Graduate Theme

My graduate study was on the principle of nonresistance as found in the teachings of Jesus in the synoptic Gospels. My work began with an investigation of the teaching on nonresistance in the Bible. I was one of the first American Mennonites to do graduate doctoral research in the field of biblical studies.

Few sayings of Jesus have so perplexed Christians throughout the centuries as those dealing with nonresistance. When Jesus speaks in Matthew 5:38-42 and in Luke 6:29, 30, his demand that we resist not evil appears so absolute and unqualified. It doesn't seem to take into account important problems in practical ethics.

One of those ethical problems had absorbed my full attention less than a year after I graduated from college. The United States had just entered World War I, and a year later my draft board ordered me to report for induction to Camp Funston in Kansas on May 23, 1918. I was principal of the high school at Whitewater at the time, but I had to leave a week before school ended.

How would I handle my concerns of conscience when I would arrive at camp and would confront the order to accept a gun and train for combat duty? I decided I would rather state my concern at the very beginning and then face the consequences.

When I registered at the reporting desk and had answered the routine questions, I told the sergeant in charge that I was a conscientious objector and would like to be assigned to hospital service in the camp. The moment he heard the reference to conscientious objector, he blurted out an angry, "Damn C.O.!"

His blast was so loud and clear that every person in that large room must have been jolted wide awake. Every head turned in my direction to see what such a person looked like, a person, presumably, too cowardly to fight for his country.

Most unpleasant methods were used to force conscientious objectors into line and to break down their morale. These experiences of testing and of later service in the camp represent a critical, but also a maturing, period in my life.

Army officers tried to induce us to renounce our convictions or force us to fall into line through devious ways. These included ridicule, intimidation, discrimination, and physical and mental abuse. Occasionally, an officer tried to "kill with kindness," intending to undercut any reason for objecting to military service.

Sometimes it worried me that our Christian testimony appeared so negative. But the highly motivated *no* of conscientious objectors in World War I was heard all the way to the highest circles in Washington.

Good Will That Melts Ill Will

When I came to Hartford to study nonresistance, I found that the Gospels do not give merely a collection of sayings from Jesus. They present a picture of a matchless person who lived with people, served them, and taught them. Jesus is the key to his teachings. His attitude on nonresistance cannot be fully or correctly understood except against the background of his life, death, and resurrection.

My findings on nonresistance received wholehearted acceptance from the Hartford faculty. They were sympathetic but I had to prove myself and show that I knew what I was doing.

The results of my investigation on "The Principle of Nonresistance in the Synoptic Gospels" were later published, with adaptations for general reading, by Herald Press in 1959 under the title *Jesus and Human*

Conflict. The way to overcome evil is not to fight it with a greater evil, but to melt the ill will by a good will that has its source in God and wins by enlisting the inner consent of the wrongdoer, by allowing the deep in ourselves to appeal to the deep in others.

As Romans 12:17-21 shows, nonresistance has positive as well as negative aspects. This passage does not allow a spirit of retaliation but urges that it be replaced with a spirit "noble in the sight of all."

Following World War II, I visited the home of Johannes Hodel, in the Karlsruhe area of Germany. The community where he lived had been bombed by the American air force. This venerable and gentle Mennonite told me something about the raids that his family and neighbors had endured. How had he been able to void the bitterness that such senseless destruction often leaves with the survivors? Johannes Hodel was a marvelous example of a person who forgave those who had injured him. But many people couldn't.

The kingdom citizen should engage in acts of unwearied, generous, and thoughtful concern. That will lead to reconciliation and restored relationships.

When I was a child, my older sisters caught me in a perfectly stupid prank and threatened to tell mother. My pleading restrained them, but for months (or was it years?) they held this threat over my head when they wanted to force some compliance from me. Finally, in desperation, I confessed it to mother myself and mother was so gracious in accepting me that I discovered something of the peace and reconciliation that forgiveness can bring.

From Church to Church in North America

In 1936, just as I received my doctoral degree from Hartford Seminary, the General Conference Mennonite

Church needed a field secretary to visit all its churches and present the needs of the conference enterprise. The conference executive committee asked me to take the job.

I was to represent the work of our various boards and our young people's committee. I was to inform the churches of the activity, needs, and opportunities. I was not sent out as a solicitor of funds, though undoubtedly it was hoped that my efforts would result in increased contributions.

Beginning in October 1936, I had visited some 125 groups by the middle of 1939. I was almost constantly among the churches, often for periods of six weeks, two months, or three months at a time. It's a mission that has never been repeated.

I used to visit about two churches in a week. I spent about three or four days in a church and met with various smaller groups such as boards of deacons, women's groups, and young people's groups besides speaking to the congregation.

In talking about the conference, I compared it to a tree with roots and branches, illustrating my message with a chart on which a tree had been drawn. The branches represent the variety of missions and services in which the church engages. But each witness comes out of the same root—the spirit of Christ that dwells within each of us and drives us to serve, to teach our children, to develop Sunday schools, to do relief work, and to build hospitals and homes.

I presented the total work of the conference and that included the work of the Mennonite Central Committee. People would often say, "We had no idea the conference was doing work like that."

It was tremendously heartening to find a church that had an active interest in Christian service outside itself and had something of a vision of the larger needs in the world.

From House to House in South America

I became a part of that outreach when in 1939 I was sent by the General Conference to visit Mennonite congregations in South America. I was asked to take greetings to them, irrespective of whether they were Mennonite Brethren, Evangelical Mennonites, or General Conference.

And I did that. I never told them what conference I represented unless they asked. In Brazil and Paraguay, I went to every Mennonite village. Taking one of the church leaders along, I started at one end of the village and stopped at every house for at least ten or fifteen minutes.

The people would say, "How is this possible? You're from North America and you stop at our house? Other visitors when they come, they visit only the ministers. But you visit us."

In Paraguay, I visited all the homes in the Fernheim and Friesland colonies. Menno colony wasn't open to such visitation, but I did call on a few of their leaders and found them friendly enough.

The Fernheim people had come to South America around 1929, having fled from Russia and the growing oppression of the Stalin era. Some came by way of Europe and some by way of China. For the former group, President Hindenburg had been helpful in opening the door into Germany where they were cared for in certain refugee camps. From there, the Mennonite Central Committee took on the task of finding homes for them.

The United States wouldn't receive them without physical examination and most families had illnesses that would exclude them. Canada was more lenient, but only Paraguay would take them without asking any questions.

So MCC bought land in Paraguay close to where the Menno colony people from Canada had settled in 1927. This was in the Chaco, a vast unsettled wilderness north of Asunción and west of the Paraguay River. To go there with bare hands and empty pockets and to try to dig in was a most discouraging experience. They couldn't find water that was sweet enough to drink or grass fit for raising cattle.

They had to reorder their whole style of farming. They had been wheat farmers, but here wheat wouldn't grow. They couldn't raise tomatoes and they couldn't raise onions. By the time I visited them, they had succeeded with the help of MCC in raising some citrus fruit. But all that stock had to be carried into the Chaco, which was a sandy and a thorny hell—that was what they called it.

Because the situation was so unfavorable, they began to quarrel among themselves. The struggle had been so hard and the climate so unfavorable; sickness came in; some said they should never have come. So they split and a group of them left and settled east of the Paraguay River where there was more water in a place they called Friesland.

Politics and the Practice of Peace

We got into some lively discussions on politics, especially as they involved Hitler and all the events in Europe in 1939. These people felt a strong attachment to Germany, so they were ready to shut their eyes and explain away the more unpleasant and much criticized sides of German politics.

These attitudes caused many to waver over the principle of nonresistance. They agreed that it was wrong to kill, but they felt that if a government in crisis demanded it, they would do so because God would expect them to be obedient to government.

I also visited the Mennonites in Brazil. Here too the people were desperately poor. They had settled in a mountainous region in the Kraul River valley. And it was a backbreaking and spirit-breaking task to clear the land. Then they had to deal as well with their difficult community and church problems when everybody was physically tired and mentally exhausted. In those situations, they said some sharp things to one another. The feelings that developed were hard to get rid of.

Just before I left Brazil, we were riding in a buggy, four or five of us, and the most irreconcilable and bitter on the wagon was one of the leading ministers. They were really pulling each other to pieces. I took it about as long as I could.

Then I began to talk to them like a Dutch uncle. "This is intolerable," I said, "that you, being leaders of your people and preachers of the Word and the gospel of forgiveness, should talk like this." Obviously, I was scolding them. But they listened and quit arguing. It helped to put a bit of a damper on the bloodletting.

War Shock Propels Peace People

While in Paraguay in 1939, I came to the village of Friedensfeld in Fernheim where I spoke to a gathering on September 2. At the close of the meeting, Hein Friesen, one of the preachers, told me the news that had come by radio telling of the outbreak of warlike hostilities between Germany and Poland. What a shock! Everybody was shaken to the foundation.

"Oh, if God would only intervene to stop this human insanity," I said.

When I got back to the United States, Emmett Harshbarger, chairman of the General Conference Peace Committee, asked me to serve as executive secretary of the committee. I was to do some writing for peace and also do some fieldwork.

The committee wanted me to help young people shape their convictions on the war issue and if possible to organize some projects to promote peace. The Western District Peace Committee volunteered to begin my support which was to be a salary of $1600 per year and travel costs.

In that connection, I attended a training session sponsored by the Quakers at Pendle Hill, near Philadelphia. It was an intensive and concentrated study. What was most valuable to me was that it brought me into contact with the American Friends Service Committee and I learned to know its leaders.

In the summer of 1940, the United States Congress began work on a conscription bill. The Mennonite Central Committee asked me to go to Washington as the Mennonite representative to work with delegates from the Quakers and the Brethren. We were to secure acceptable provisions for conscientious objectors to war as the conscription act was taking shape.

We helped to organize the National Service Board for Religious Objectors through which we made our contacts with government. Raymond Wilson and Paul French of the American Friends Service Committee and I were always in close contact. Church of the Brethren leaders came in and we consulted with them.

The Quakers had the most experience in dealing with government. They sometimes treated the Church of the Brethren and the Mennonites as being innocent and inexperienced. They felt they had better take the lead.

Paul French had been a newspaper reporter. He knew how to approach people in high office. He observed to me once that Mennonites were afraid to talk to men in government.

"Yes," I said, "we are shy."

Then he told me how he made his contacts. "I'm not afraid of these men," he said. "They are important and have important work. But I have an important work to do, too, and I have come to talk about important things." That helped me a lot in my contacts with government people.

We worked out a schedule for approaching key people about the forthcoming plans for conscription. We sought out those with open minds and to whom we could talk frankly about our concerns as peace churches. I visited our Kansas representatives. Senator Brookes Hayes from Arkansas was a person who listened to us. We had contacts with Attorney General Jackson, a very able man, who later became a Supreme Court justice.

We talked about our experiences in World War I. We found that the people in Washington knew about our witness. They often confessed that the conscientious objector problem had been poorly handled in the past and that they surely didn't want to repeat that experience.

We had our proposals. We wanted conscientious objectors to have the opportunity to do civilian service either under government control or under the direct control of private agencies. In either case, we asked that the government pay the wages of the men in service. But President Roosevelt strongly opposed our plan, especially if the government needed to provide support for conscientious objectors.

We had to compromise. It soon became clear that the

church would have to pay the wages of the men doing alternate service. We faced the heavy burden of subsidizing this program which came to be known as Civilian Public Service (CPS).

But the National Service Board for Religious Objectors could not assume this burden. It represented only the peace committees of the several churches and had no authority to solicit such large sums of money. So for the support of the Mennonite camps, we had to turn to the Mennonite Central Committee. Of course, MCC needed to get the approval of its member groups. It was an important and most decisive moment when we faced the whole question and then got a mandate from our churches.

To the Front for CPS

And then I was chosen to administer the Mennonite camps. I operated out of the MCC offices at Akron, Pennsylvania, and always kept in closest contact with Orie Miller, MCC's executive secretary.

How they happened to pick on me for this job, I don't know. I came from the so-called liberal Mennonite group, and I'm sure they often didn't quite trust me for that reason. But, by and large, I must say that I got fine cooperation and understanding from all groups.

It was perfectly amazing what happened. We had to deal with so many young fellows in the CPS program. We needed leaders, so we tried to get men and women of experience like teachers, ministers, and people from all kinds of occupations. But so often, the church or school would say, "We're sorry. We can't spare them." So we had to pull in some young fellows who were just out of college. We said to each one, "Here are 150 boys. You serve as director of this camp."

These fellows measured up, sometimes in dramatic

ways. We encouraged them, stood by them, and inspired them with some confidence. They knew where they could go if they had problems, and they proved to be very able fellows. The same thing was true of the women who served as camp matrons and dieticians.

But not everything ran smoothly; we did have problems. For example, we had a camp director in one of the Western states who was not very popular with the boys. Things started out bitter and got worse. Finally, they tarred and feathered the director.

I made a quick trip to that camp. Our standing with the government would have been damaged if we had lost control. The camp director told me who was involved. We called the ringleader into the office. When he came in, I was standing.

I said, "Sit down."

The man, who was a big fellow, said, "I prefer to stand."

"*Sit* down," I said.

I'm not sure what I would have done if he hadn't.

Our inter-Mennonite rivalries were, of course, a major problem in administering the CPS program. We were so jealous lest some group get an advantage. We had to make sure that we got proper representation in leadership as camp directors, business managers, cooks, and educational directors.

Who would visit the camps as ministers and to whom would they minister? And when ministers would offer communion, would it be to only the members of their own groups or would others be allowed to participate?

We all had our stereotypes of one another. You mention somebody who is a Mennonite Brethren and you have one kind of image. And if you are from the General Conference, that stirs other feelings. They were a little bit afraid of G.C.s at that time because the stereotype said that G.C.s were worldly, activists, and liberal minded.

We had to be very sensitive to the conservative groups. Eastern Mennonite College was quite a center of conservatism at that time. There were some fine men among them—C. K. Lehman and John R. Mumaw were fine to work with. But I never once got a chance to talk to the college assembly.

When I went to visit the Amish, I was conscious of the fact that I had some adornments. I had a wedding ring, for instance, and a gold watch and chain. Now, what should I do? When I go among them, should I take it off? Should I put my watch in my hip pocket?

In all these cases, I thought I better just be myself, honestly and openly. I did better that way than to take my ring off and then when I was out of sight, put it back on again and they discover it anyhow.

During those CPS days, we were always looking for opportunities to serve human need more directly. We were in forestry service and soil conservation. We would have liked to have been more involved with people because it was a time of terrible human suffering, tension, and disorganization.

Such opportunities came to us in bits and pieces at first. We were given an opportunity in the dairy herd testing program to get out of the camps. Then came the opening to general hospitals and later on to mental hospitals. I interviewed the administrators of state institutions; they were fearful. They had so many problems already. "What will happen," they asked, "if we add conscientious objectors to our staff as aides?"

Our present Mennonite Disaster Service got its start in our CPS camps. When there was a flood at Council Bluffs, we sent a large group of men from Camp Denison to strengthen the river dikes. We did that in other places when there were storms and disasters. We had the men in our camps and we could assign them with the approval of our work camp directors.

Our later voluntary service programs also grew out of the CPS experience.

CPS as Variation on a Theme from Russia

One question often asked about the Civilian Public Service program is whether the church should have cooperated with the government in the operation of these camps. If we were to repeat the 1940 experience in days like these now forty years later and the options were the same, I wouldn't go as far in cooperation with the government as I did then.

But you had to weigh with good judgment and with inner commitment and ask, "What are the options? What is possible?"

And what were the options before World War II? Either you simply accepted the military draft and went all the way or went into noncombatant service which might mean hospital service. The only other option was to say a complete no and that meant prison.

Some of the first draftees did that and they did go to prison. But that seemed to be a bit out of reach for the rank and file. You couldn't say to your boys who were 21, you must make the kind of decision that might mean prison while the people at home kept on farming and reaping the profits of war. So we had to search for other options and find other things that our young men could do and still maintain a witness against the whole war business.

Were we really ready to take an absolute stand against the war system in a positive, aggressive way and say we will have nothing to do with war or even any form of conscription? The Quakers were almost ready to take that step. But Mennonites would not have gone that far.

As I had traveled among our people in Canada and South America who had lived in Russia, I heard over and over again of their experiences with compulsory military training where they arranged to give a noncombatant type of service. If they had been able to work it out in a somewhat satisfactory way in Russia, I thought, then maybe we ought to see what that held for us here.

Thus, when the CPS program became law, we were willing to accept its requirement that conscientious objectors do "work of national importance" under civilian direction. We were grateful to the government for its recognition of our position, and we were willing to do such work under conscription as an alternative to military service.

College Prayers Caught from Mother

President E. G. Kaufman of Bethel College called me to succeed Amos E. Kreider as professor of Bible and chairman of the division of Bible and Christian education. I had always hoped for that kind of opportunity and I didn't feel I could turn it down when it came. So I turned over the administration of CPS to Albert Gaeddert at the end of June 1943, after serving from the beginning in 1940.

During the seventeen years that I served at Bethel College, I also worked at various times as dean, religious counselor, director of public affairs, alumni secretary, foreign student adviser, and as secretary of the faculty.

As director of chapel services, I had the opportunity on many occasions to lead the school community in prayers of thanksgiving and to pray on behalf of the school, its students, faculty, and friends. I hope I was able to share with them my feeling that prayer does indeed have vital meaning, a conviction that I caught from the trustful and sincere prayers of my mother.

We had devotions daily in our home, both morning and evening. My parents were wholeheartedly and sincerely Christian in life and thought. Their religion was not something gushy; it was something deep—so deep and precious that they talked about it and lived it.

The years at Bethel College seem like a capstone to my career. But they did not end my service for the Mennonite Central Committee and for the church. The opportunities to serve seemed to multiply. About the time that I came to Bethel, I was elected to the Emergency Relief Board of the General Conference and made its chairman. Through that office, I became a member of the Mennonite Central Committee and then its vice-chairman and a member of its executive committee.

Spirit Awakes Concern for Mental Health

In 1945, as World War II was drawing to a close, I felt convinced that we as Mennonites ought to make use of the experience we had gained by serving in mental hospitals under CPS. After my visits to Mennonite congregations in both North and South America, I had an increasing awareness that we had a mental health problem in our Mennonite circles.

This concern for the mentally ill among us was not new. Our people who had lived in Russia still remembered Bethania, the mental care home that they had built there. From all the reports I ever heard, it was really a forward looking type of program, less structured than the type of mental hospitals that we had here before World War II.

I raised the concern with the Emergency Relief Board. Should we take responsibility for starting a mental health ministry or would we do much better if we presented this need to the Mennonite Central Committee? Mental health, after all, was a problem not confined to the General Conference. Each group had it and each was too small to undertake its treatment separately. Why shouldn't we face it together?

I brought this concern and proposal to the floor of the General Conference at its meeting in North Newton in June 1945. The conference then proposed that the church cooperate with MCC to establish a mental institution. This proposal got a good reception in MCC circles, particularly from Orie Miller, who, in my mind, always had a fine sense of opportunity.

He took the issue to the MCC executive committee. But the committee, especially Harold Bender, wasn't sure that MCC had that kind of mandate from its supporting churches that would allow it to build an institution. We were basically a relief agency. While we had taken on the CPS program, this was something new again.

We decided that we had better take the mental health issue to our constituent groups. And when the returns came in, we heard the churches say they would like to do this together. That was a turning point in our history. We discovered that if we followed the Spirit of God we could do more things together than we had thought possible.

I was happy to have had a share in the development of the Mennonite mental health program, which now has institutions in Canada and the United States and whose high quality of service is widely recognized. I was the first chairman of the Mental Health Rest Home Advisory Committee, the predecessor of Mennonite Mental Health Services, which started our first program at Brook Lane at Hagerstown, Maryland.

Guns—No Caliber Is Safe

In 1945, the Mennonite Central Committee asked me to visit the Mennonites in South America once again. Because of the war, they feared they might lose their Privilegium—their exemption from military training. Since I had had some experience dealing with government officials and in working in the CPS program, I hoped I could be helpful to them.

Some of the Mennonites who had come to South America had been involved in the *Selbstschutz* (Self-defense force) in Russia, when Mennonites felt conditions demanded that they arm themselves. And now in Paraguay, some of them still felt that the colonists needed guns for their own protection.

In Friesland in east Paraguay, particularly, they had to make these long trips by horse and wagon to the river port. They passed through Paraguayan settlements along the way where they felt they were exposed to the possibility of robbery.

The oberschultz (colony master) of Friesland took me to Concepcion on one occasion. He was carrying a gun, and we argued considerably about it. "The only reason we're safe," he said, "is that they know I have a gun."

Well, having just come out of the CPS program, that was a challenge I couldn't let pass. I had a conference with Cornelius Kroeker and Mr. Hildebrand of the Friesland cooperative. We talked about the practice of their leaders carrying guns. They readily admitted that they believed they were safe from abuse by the Paraguayans only if they carried a gun. One of a caliber less than 38 was not effective.

They really didn't want to carry guns, they said, but they saw no other way. They believed they'd never have to use their guns. The very fact that they had them induced respect.

I pointed out that that was exactly the reasoning of the world. As followers of Christ, we had been taught another way. And how inconsistent it was to apply for special privileges as nonresistant Christians when everyday practice belied their claim.

The Mennonite Central Committee, I told them, could not approach the Paraguayan government with clear conscience until this matter was cleared up. How could we, when colony leaders showed their lack of faith in the way of love and the protection of God?

They got the point unmistakably, and said, "*Dann müssen wir doch wohl zur Zeit diese Sache sein lassen*" (Well, then, we probably better drop this matter for the time being).

Self-Respect for Refugees Resettled

Having been in South America when World War II began in 1939, I found myself there once more when it came to an end. On August 19, 1945, I attended a service of thanksgiving for peace in the Colegio Church in Asunción which was attended also by the American embassy staff, the British Council, and United States aid representatives.

The change in the Mennonite colonies in the six years from my previous visit was simply astonishing. They had begun testing programs in agriculture and had made contact with the American assistance programs. They were also working with the agriculture ministry of Paraguay and were developing their vegetable and citrus crops.

They had set up a cotton gin. Their hospital was in much better shape with the help of Dr. John and Clara Schmidt, whom MCC had sent. The relationship between Fernheim and Friesland had improved. They had learned to live with one another.

In resettling this group of refugees, MCC's insights had been sharpened. We began to see that these people needed not so much charity as understanding assistance which would safeguard their self-respect, build the spirit of brotherhood, and keep alive a vivid sense of vision. Great care was taken not to dampen local initiative and responsibility.

Scenes of War's Insanity

Because still other Mennonite refugees were being gathered together in camps in Europe, MCC commissioned me to go to Europe in 1947. We were concerned about what to do about these refugees, particularly those in Denmark. While in Europe, I also visited the other relief programs of the Mennonite Central Committee there.

When I got to Bremen in Germany, I saw for the first time something of the horror and terrible effect of the war bombings. But its full meaning did not sink in until I came to Hamburg which had been 75 percent destroyed. Then I felt the utter insanity that is war. It was utterly depressing to drive through the miles and miles of rubble and past the empty shells of scorched houses that had once been Hamburg.

"Where will all this rubble be left?" I asked. "And who will build on these sites even after they are cleared of debris?" The most pathetic thing to see was children growing up and playing in such a scene of havoc and decay. It made me sick at heart to see it.

Obviously, the children and older people needed supplementary food during those days. I saw many children with very spindly legs, though others looked all right. I saw one girl nine years old who looked like five.

Thus I was glad to see the feeding programs that MCC had begun. Most interesting was the kindergarten feeding at Gronau; it was fun to see 120 children eating. In another place, twin boys shared a bucket of soup very brotherly and innocently: One drank out of the tin can and licked his lips and then the other boy took his turn.

All relief agencies liked to feed the children and that was right. They were the innocent victims. But the old people were equally pathetic. Many had lost contact with their families.

The summer of 1947 had been extremely dry. All that many people could harvest were little nubbins of potatoes. The fruit dropped from the trees before ripening. The old people went into the fields after the grain was cut and picked up individual grains of wheat. And that was their meal for the next day.

These were the forgotten people. Others had assumed that they would know how to care for themselves. We gathered them together in homes and in settlement places like Enkenbach and Neuwied.

How Deep the Wounds of War

But in those postwar years, MCC was doing more than giving relief. It was also working to heal the inner and spiritual wounds of war, even within the Mennonite Church itself.

Before the war, the French and the German Mennonites were simply not on speaking terms. That was the aftermath of earlier wars. The MCC presence helped to bring them together so that they could study the Bible together and cooperate in sponsoring the Mennonite World Conference in 1952.

Almost the deepest hostility I ran into was among the Dutch. They were outraged at what the German armies had done to them. They had tried to shelter the Jews and had hidden them in their attics and in all kinds of places.

We tried to encourage the development of peace groups within the Mennonite churches. Domine Hylkema was one of their leaders, but there were others working side by side with him. That helped to soften the antagonisms, but even when we had the Mennonite World Conference in North America in 1948, it almost came to blows between the Dutch and German Mennonites.

Through MCC's ministry, we could bring the various groups together for Bible conferences in Basel and in other places. Well, that wasn't relief work in the form of giving food, but that was trying to heal the wounds of war. That was serving in the name of Christ.

Mission to Europe's Homeless People

For many years, my special missions for the General Conference and the MCC took me away from my home and family for long periods. Whenever I left, Ethel and the children were brave although they knew full well the meaning of separation. I thanked God for a family so brave and self-forgetful, especially for Ethel's brave heart and spirit that made my work possible. I always prayed that God would compensate both her and the children for their sacrifice.

Then in 1951, Ethel and i had the glad opportunity to go to Europe together with Richard, our son, to live in Basel and give leadership to the MCC program in Europe.

Considerable need still continued, especially in Germany and Austria, and especially among the refugees. In our work with children and with older people, we discovered anew every day that man needs much more than housing, work, and bread, indispensable as these are. We saw that relief work itself was no cure for the mortal sickness of the world. Jesus Christ alone has the cure for this and we must be more active in witnessing to his saving power and love and in proving its validity in our life and service.

Someone once characterized those days as the years of the homeless man. That shocking and haunting statement wouldn't let us rest, not after we had seen these homeless people, looked into their eyes, and heard their stories and not after we had seen how they lived in their crowded camps, in tomblike bunkers, or in some terribly cramped quarters. Sometimes we found them crowded together in large vacant rooms of some abandoned factory where they slept on dirty gunnysacks on the cement floor, row on row, with blankets but without bedsheets or pillows.

At that time, Germany alone contained 12 million such homeless people, and some 8,000 of them were Mennonites, mostly from West Prussia. And they were scattered over vast areas of the country. We had a resettlement project, but we could care for only 600.

The young men of Pax Services helped families build their houses. We helped to organize and build large resettlement and housing projects. And in the process there developed an inevitable spiritual ministry which was inescapably connected with every type of work in which MCC was engaged.

Short of Money, Long on Grit

We continued to search for the Mennonite refugees. We were finding them in East Germany and bringing them across the border, finding them in Berlin and trying to gather them in places where we could minister to them. We had difficulty getting into Salzburg, Innsbruck, and Vienna, which had refugees too.

With all these problems, we had another crisis to face. Contributions from the churches at home had slumped to such a degree that the European budget, already low, had to be cut twice in one year. And what was worse, the Akron office was not even able to meet this drastically reduced budget.

As a result, our operating funds were so low that there was no cushion left. We had no alternative but to close some programs, reduce our staff, and cut project allowances almost to the crippling point.

Yet it was amazing what was accomplished during those years. We worked among refugees in northern Greece who had just come from Yugoslavia where they had been kept during the war years. They really had to start from scratch again, using their old tools that simply scratched the soil and depending on whatever rain and water they could get.

We sent some young men to the village of Panayitsa as part of MCC's expanding Pax program. It took a good bit of pioneering on their part to get a start there. We had to build a house where they could live and we followed the MCC pattern of identifying ourselves with the people; we did not want to establish our little colony off by ourselves and distance ourselves from the people. We placed our living quarters as close in as we could so that we could become friends with the people.

Salvaging a Rushed Retirement

After our term in Europe, I returned to teaching at Bethel College. It seemed only a short time after that, in 1960, that I was told I had reached the time for my retirement from teaching. It was something of a shock to receive this kind of notice because retirement at age 65 caught my generation a little by surprise.

Then I, like other older people, had to wrestle with the question: how does one retire with a sense of dignity and without losing one's feeling of usefulness and purpose? How does one make the most of the "plus" time of one's older years?

For me, these years have had their share of rewarding experiences with opportunities to serve the church in many ways: as executive secretary of the Board of Christian Service of the General Conference for three years, as director of senior Voluntary Service for MCC for a year, and as associate pastor of the Eden Mennonite Church, Moundridge, Kansas, from 1967 to 1971.

It seems to me now that I have always gotten better than I deserved. Knowing myself, my limitations, and my weaknesses, I've often been amazed and puzzled, wondering why this responsibility or that opportunity came to me. I certainly wasn't smart enough to plan it that way or to push my way in. I can only attribute it humbly and gratefully to God's wisdom which had a purpose of love in guiding my course, even as he seeks to do for every other person.

There was plenty of struggle, frustration, uncertainty, groping for the light, discouragement, closed doors, sickness, and bereavement in the family circle. Six or seven times, I was under the surgeon's knife. Always I have been poor. The organizations I served always helped to keep it like that. There were times when I felt crushed but I was never left prostrate.

Pressing the Pointed Question

I've been placed many times in places of large responsibility. I can't understand why; I don't know myself.

Recently, I heard that J. J. Thiessen, a Mennonite leader from Saskatchewan who served with me for many years on the MCC executive committee, said, "H. A. Fast is a good administrator—a bit sharp; but he has a great love for people."

I'm not sure what he meant by that. I do love people.
I'm grateful for that. Some of my greatest satisfactions
in life have come from that kind of root and motivation.

But I have also a capacity for impatience and in-
dignation. If I'm irritated for too long, I'll snap back.
Maybe I'll feel sorry for it afterward, but when one gets
impatient, one also tends to say impatient things. One
has some misgivings about it later and feels sorry. I
thank God for the occasions where I was not ashamed
to say, "I'm sorry. Please, forgive me."

Something Meaningful for God

What remains is that God has given me the opportunity to serve his people and the people that I love.

I am thinking of a children's Christmas program in
my home church, one of the first that I can remember. I
sat with father on one of the front benches. The church
was beautifully decorated with its tall Christmas tree. A
festive spirit was in the air, as a large crowd filled the
church.

The Sunday school superintendent asked the congregation to sing, *"Welchen Jubel, welche Freude
bring die schoene Weihnachtszeit."* The people picked
up the song and sang it with such fervor and with such
a ring of joy in it that I instinctively sensed something
important was happening.

Later in the program, the superintendent, clear out of
the blue, called me by name and asked whether I had a
verse I would like to say. Well, mother had taught me a
short verse from the Christmas story but it took much
urging from father to have me step forward.

When I appeared on the platform standing all alone, I
looked so small that the superintendent was afraid the
large audience would not be able either to see or hear
me. So he put me on a chair and, standing close by me,

he said, "Speak very loudly so everybody can hear you."

I took a deep breath and gave it all I had. And the audience apparently heard me to the last man. The response was so spontaneous and overwhelming that I never forgot it. I felt relieved when I returned to father, but I had the warm happy feeling that I had contributed something meaningful to the service.

The work given to me to do I would never have sought out on my own initiative. A great crisis arose, perhaps, or a great need, and the church needed someone to head up a program or organize a service.

Why they thought of me is still a puzzle. But once I got into the work, I discovered to my amazement how all my training and experience had prepared me for the task that had seemed too big for me.

I also made the blessed discovery that when God says, "Go, here is your task, your duty," he truly goes with you and gives the enablement.

3.
Norman
A.
Wingert

By
Clara
K.
Dyck

It was 1948. Norman A. Wingert was working in his study at Beulah College, Upland, California, when the phone rang. It was not a local call but Orie Miller, whom some people referred to as "Mr. MCC," calling from Akron, Pennsylvania, to invite Norman to a year of service in Germany. "Yes, the war is over," Orie said, "but you know the shambles it left in Germany. We need someone like you to help us there." Norman asked for time to think it over.

God had indeed been good to him, Norman thought, as he reflected on his past experiences. He thought of his marriage to Eunice on Christmas Day, 1927, and of the birth of their two children, Lois and Norman Olan. He realized how much he enjoyed his college teaching in Bible, sociology, and psychology. He would miss that if he went. Orie had mentioned something about working with students and retreats. Was he qualified to do that? Norman wondered. Perhaps his teaching of the subjects he did would help, as well as his earlier work with the Brethren in Christ mission in Pasadena and later with the Illinois Childrens' Homes and Aid Society in Chicago. It might be that even his work on Skidrow in Los Angeles as a student would prove to be a valuable preparation for what he was being asked to do, he thought.

That night when they talked and prayed about it as a family, it seemed clear that this was indeed a call from God and that he should accept it if the college would release him. They agreed that Eunice would go with him to a Youth for Christ convention in Switzerland and then return home. It would mean a family separation for one year. When his request for a leave was approved by the college the answer was final. Preparations were soon completed, suitcases packed, and he and Eunice were on their way.

Students and a Castle

The French Military Occupation Forces in South Germany had requisitioned Kropsburg, an ancient castle in the Palatinate, and agreed to let MCC use it for student rehabilitation programs. The owners of the castle were asked to stay on to do maintenance work and the cooking. MCC agreed to provide food, bedding, and other necessities, as well as the staff.

Being a member of this staff was Norman's first assignment. Three days after his own arrival at the castle fourteen male and six female students chosen from the 6,000 students at the University of Mainz arrived. Eleven of them were Protestant and nine were Roman Catholic. Nearly all came shabbily dressed, desperately poor, and very hungry. They were to stay for one month of recuperation.

The view over the valley of vineyards gave them no trace of the bombed out cities they had left behind. Instead, on a clear day, one could see the mountains beyond the Rhine and some twenty towns with red tiled roofs. Seeing this idyllic setting, an MCC sponsor might well have protested: "So that is where our dollars go—to provide a time of easy living for students!" But if such a critic had been present on the last evening of the students' stay at Kropsburg and heard their parting comments, the criticism would undoubtedly have turned to joy.

Alphonse, a medical student with limited arm leverage and a big hole in his elbow, declared quietly: "Four years ago today I was shot by an American, but today I have no ill feeling toward Americans. How could I, after Kropsburg!"

Karoline, the oldest of the group, was a philosophy student preparing to teach. She had worked thirteen years as a stenographer to save 9,000 marks with which to attend university, but the currency reform had wiped out nine-tenths of her savings. "Many hours in life pass into oblivion and are forgotten," she said. "Only a few remain in one's memory and constitute the riches which one possesses. You and your American friends have made the days at Kropsburg unforgettable. I wish I could do as many lovely things for you as you have done for us!"

Ulrich, a pharmacy student with an artificial limb as a result of the war, remarked: "It was very good for me to see and to learn from you how to live a real Christian life."

Joachim, whose home was in the Russian zone, who had been in the German Air Force and a prisoner of war in Russia, agreed: "We never believed it possible that men of two nations could live together like we are doing so shortly after a terrible war . . . we will try to pass on all we have received in the name of Christ."

Although only twenty years old, Friedrich, a Lutheran theology student, had seen two years as prisoner of war in Siberia. His father was still there, and they had no word from him. Aged beyond his years, he would repeatedly pour out his heart at the piano in such deep concentration that he would not hear when someone spoke to him.

And Gisela, a philosophy student whose parents had died of malnutrition, yet who was still the cheeriest of the group, prayed: "... we have become friends and have been bound together in Thee ... give the fullness of thy blessing to our friends who have given us the wealth of their love. Amen!"

This month at Kropsburg, Norman wrote later, was a fitting introduction to the many thousands of displaced persons, refugees, and suffering persons I was to meet over the rest of the year in Germany.

Winners and Losers

His next assignment was to direct the distribution of food and clothing in Kiel. In his diary he wrote of his first impressions:

> *Although I had seen ruined cities, I was not prepared for the experience of living in the midst of rubble right at Hamburg and Kiel. I once stood on a spot in Hamburg where for four blocks in every direction I could not see a two story building. It was a sea of debris. Some 50,000 people had died in two weeks of concentrated bombing.*

He had similar experiences when he came to Kiel. Its population before the war had been 240,000. Because it was the major German submarine base during the war, it received particularly heavy bombing raids. Seven of every ten houses had been either totally or partially destroyed. Though he had come to help, there was no room for him anywhere, and no food rations, so he was assigned to live in the British Army Officers Mess. His diary records that he was not comfortable living well among so much misery:

*From my Officers Mess I could see the long, unpainted
sheds where a whole family existed in a single room.
Though only a stone's throw apart, that distance between
mansion and shack was the measure of the chasm
between the winners and the losers of the war. The hurt of
the war is not only the original destruction; one must live
in the postwar atmosphere for a while before it begins to
burn into one's consciousness what it means for an
enemy people to come into one's country and take over.*

Making a Hard Winter Bearable

Some four hundred tons of MCC food and clothing
were already in a Kiel warehouse when Norman arrived,
and additional shipments came during the winter.
Soon a group of MCC and local workers were busy providing 8,000 loaves of white bread weekly to refugees
and old people, outfitting 1,300 grateful families with
clothing, and providing a hot meat soup daily, except
Sunday, to 500 undernourished children. After one
month the average weight increase among the children
was seven pounds.

But even this major effort seemed to be no more than
a trickle in a vast sea of misery. It was believed that
there were over 35,000 refugees from Russia and the
Baltic states in Kiel. There was Peter who lived with
MCC, helping to keep their cars and trucks in repair. In
their flight from Russia he had become separated from
his wife and children. Month after month he waited for
her to come but she never did. Was she dead, or in a
slave labor camp in Siberia?

There was Gert, aged 72, who had taught school in
Russia for 30 years. He told of his miraculous de-
liverance from a firing squad, of his brother-in-law who
died of starvation in Siberia, of his two sons who were
still in Siberia, but that he and his wife had finally made
it to safety in the British zone of Germany only to fear

that the Russians had found his hiding place, forcing him to flee further west again. "Theological and Bible school students believe that God is and that the Bible is true" he told Norman, "but I *know.*"

Norman's diary continues the accounts of suffering and of MCC efforts to help. "Last night a man who had been in a Russian prison for seven months told me about his neighbor who had been in a Siberian concentration camp in which 600 of the 760 inmates had starved to death." The entry of another day reads: "We must get the university tuberculosis student project started, as well as the student clothing distribution and the old peoples' soup feeding." And again, "Today was a high-water mark at the distribution—125 families. And they were big families too, one with eleven children. On the whole they were *very* poor. How the children rejoiced at the colorful clothing!" Another incident of a more trying kind was entered later: "Miss Johnson of the English Salvation Army told me today her secretary saw a woman hand her husband a fur coat in front of our building, enter, and later come out with one of our coats on her back. One can expect something like this once in a while."

Clothing and food distributions continued throughout the winter as MCC shipments arrived. One of the frustrations of the workers was that the MCC warehouse seemed to be empty so fast. The need was great. During one particular clothing distribution 16,500 pieces of clothing and bedding were given to 3,733 individuals in 1,303 families. Each individual received one major piece and three smaller items. Most of them, Norman recalls, were deeply grateful for what they received, though a few were "choosy, complaining, regardless of real need." "But fortunately," Norman wrote, "there are very few of this type."

Brahmsee Is Born

One day Norman met a young man named Siegfried. As Siegfried began to share his experiences the tragedy of the legacies of war almost overwhelmed and numbed Norman. Siegfried went on:

> *I had a very good childhood. My parents owned their own farm and it was well stocked. For six years I attended elementary school. Two years later I was confirmed in the Evangelical church, and after two more years I was apprenticed as an electrician. But, when I was seventeen, I was drafted and left home. I never saw it or any of my relatives after that. I learned indirectly that both my father and mother had committed suicide when the Russians came into our home. They attacked my sister and then shot her dead. I eventually landed in Italy and was captured there by the Russians in 1945.*

As they continued visiting, Norman asked, "Tell me, Siegfried, what happened to your front teeth?" "I was knocked unconscious several times" Siegfried replied, "and one time, when I regained consciousness, I found that my front teeth were missing." The young man fell silent again while searching for something in his pockets. Finally he drew out a small photograph. It was that of his sister. "It is the only thing I have left from my home," he said. On the back of the photo Norman read the words "*zur Erinnerung* (in remembrance). *Gertrude.*"

That night Norman could not sleep. It seemed to him as though Siegfried was sitting on the edge of his bed asking, "What are you going to do for us?" Norman knew well that there were hundreds of young "Siegfrieds" in the area, men who had just returned from prisoner of war camps, who had lost their homes and loved ones and, with it, all purpose in life. Next morning he wrote to the MCC director recommending that a program similar to Kropsburg be started in this north German area. The reply soon came: "Let's do it, if we can find a suitable place."

It was a providential decision. A few days later the Evangelical Lutheran church gave MCC a youth center, located on beautiful lake Brahmsee for one month. A German relief agency offered to pay the rent. The British Occupation Forces administration gave their enthusiastic support, donating clothing and promising to send their barber to give the boys free haircuts. City officials, the city mission, the Swiss Relief Team, and other organizations joined the project. City Manpower, in collaboration with a Mennonite contractor, promised to give jobs to the boys after their stay at Brahmsee. This was beyond expectations, for of the 240,000 people in Kiel 35 percent were without work. "Thus" Norman wrote, "under the blessing and guidance of God, was launched—Brahmsee!"

As the young men began to arrive Norman realized again, as he had at Kropsburg, that these beautiful physical facilities were only the necessary context for a much more urgent personal and spiritual ministry. One by one they began to share their experiences:

In 1944 the Russians overran our community. My father had been taken prisoner by the British. The Russians forced my mother and my brothers and sisters out of our home. Then began for us a period of misery. My youngest brother died . . . I myself was near death. My mother was taken away nights by the Russians . . . and we got practically nothing to eat. In 1946 we came with a refugee transport to Kiel. We lost our goods. Today we are living in a small attic.

My father was a potato merchant in Stettin. I sang in the church choir. On October 16, 1942, I became a soldier. On May 8, 1945, I became a driver in a tank division, and

*from that date until April 18, 1949, I was a Russian
prisoner of war.*

*I do not know my father because he committed suicide
when I was barely four years old. My mother was all
alone then with twelve children. We had lost everything.
Then began the years of starvation . . . since then it has
been going downhill with me. Soon I was on the black
market. In February 1948 I tried again to get work and
went into a coal mine. This lasted four months. I tried
once more to keep myself above water by dark affairs.
Then it happened that I met a young boy who had
already been punished for an offense, and we committed
several punishable crimes. We were sentenced to prison
terms. Because I was sixteen, I got only six months. After
serving this sentence I was invited by the MCC to
Brahmsee, where, as a thankful guest I find myself now.*

And so the stories continued. "By the second day," Norman reported, "the hard lines in their faces were already softening. The refurbishing of the first day revealed the human being beneath the incrustations of physical dirt and the deeper grime of bitterness and hopelessness. At mealtime they reminded one of the voracious appetites of pets devouring an advertiser's brand of food on television. By the third day the boys had a ball game going with all the gusto of youth who never had a care."

When the Lutheran church offered MCC a month's extension of the use of the youth center, a second group of twenty young men was invited. Norman's daughter Lois joined her father for his last three months in Europe, and served as part of the staff at Brahmsee. "It is significant that during both months, not once were there any "improper passes" made toward the girls," he reported, for he had warned Lois of international tensions and possible dangers.

As at Kropsburg, so at Brahmsee the mental transformation was as remarkable as the physical.

Freedom from army and prison regimentation, which they had experienced for so long, coupled with the love and understanding they were receiving achieved remarkable results. One man wrote: "Since I had been back in Germany only a few days before coming to Brahmsee, and still had fresh memories of the hard times in the prison camp, it was a dispensation from God that I could spend four wonderful weeks at Brahmsee and, beside the rest and the quiet, could eat all I wanted." Another wrote: "I have found an inner hold . . . . I wish that we would never have war anymore." Still another one said, "I am extraordinarily happy. I would never have thought that it is so wonderful to believe in God and to love in the manner taught here."

Saying Farewell

Norman's year of service had come to an end. The mayor of Kiel and his wife invited him and Lois, as well as other workers, to tea at the new courthouse. "We will always remember an incident of this social event," Norman wrote in his diary. "Lois was horrified when her teacup slipped out of her hand and crashed to the floor. Quicker than it takes to tell, the hostess' cup, too, slipped from her hand and added more broken pieces on the floor. 'These thin cups are terribly fragile' she apologized. What instant thoughtfulness on the part of our hostess!" His diary entry on July 29, 1949 reads: "Tomorrow will be the last day in Kiel for Lois and me. How wonderful and marvelous God is! And how unworthy I feel about the lavish way God has blessed us in our short stay in Europe. Praise his name!" After he had returned to America he soon recorded: "I found I was facing a new problem; it was how to keep refugees from mixing with the students in the classroom. You see, the refugees had come along home with me."

Burton Buller

Norman A. Wingert

Continuing to Serve

Half a year after his homecoming from Europe
Norman felt compelled to return. At first Eunice de-
murred, but soon also caught the vision and decided to
join him. This time the assignment was in Austria,
again working with material and spiritual resources in
refugee camps and other situations. By 1953 they were
serving in Osaka, Japan, and then in Hong Kong. One of
Eunice's unique contributions was the accompanying

of Korean orphans to their foster parents in America. In 1960 Norman undertook a seventy-day photographic mission, filming social and relief situations in Asia, the Middle East, and Europe. This led to his film *Lines Go Out* which they subsequently showed 331 times, primarily in America. In 1962 they began relief work in the new central African nation of Burundi under the sponsorship of several Protestant relief agencies, including MCC. On their return home in June 1964, they settled in Reedley, California, to serve as managers of the MCC center located there. "Now," declared Norman, "instead of opening bales of clothing and cartons of meat overseas, we were packing and shipping them, visualizing some of the places where they would be opened." At the same time they were promoting the work of the MCC in West Coast churches.

Civil war broke out in Burundi in 1972. On hearing of the suffering and mass murders, Norman and Eunice felt they ought to show Christian concern and decided to go back on their own. After three months of work, however, it seemed best for them to return. To his earlier books *I Was Born Again, A Book of Conversion Stories* (1947), and *Twice Born* (1955), Norman now added a third *No Place to Stop Killin'* (1974) to alert Christians in America to the needs of Africa.

In summing up their relief experiences Norman noted in his diary: "So you see a quarter century of contacts with the underprivileged and suffering in the world has left its marks on us ... as we look back we can see so plainly how God has revealed his plan for us step by step, situation by situation, country by country. We thank God for giving us this wonderful privilege and for the undreamed miracles along the way."

4.
Irene
L.
Bishop

By
Christine
Wiebe

Every Saturday, after Irene dusted the gray head and brown wings of the china hen on the bureau, she carefully lifted the hen off its woven basket and read the narrow column of paper cut long ago from the *Gospel Herald.* And each week Irene dreamed.

The little piece of paper told about her mother's cousin Clayton Kratz who had gone to Russia in 1920 after World War I to help the Mennonites who were suffering from famine. He had been a college student when the Mennonite Central Committee called him to go to Russia. When he reached Russia, he had begun making plans to help the hungry people, but in the chaos and confusion of the war he had been captured and taken away. Although many people searched for him, he was never heard from again.

Irene wished she, too, could go to a distant country. She did not want to be captured or be in a war, but she wanted to help feed people who could not find food. More than anything else, she wanted to be a relief worker. But she was sure only people with a college

Irene L. Bishop

degree and much talent could go overseas. She was just a farm girl who lived on a dairy farm on Hilltown Pike in Perkasie, Pennsylvania. Besides, she was too young.

Although she was only sixteen, she worked hard at home. At 5:00 in the morning she got up to help her father get the milk house ready for milking the cows. And she loved helping her mother cook and can.

Because Irene had always enjoyed grown-up activity, she gladly stayed at home after her mother died in 1939.

She cooked and cleaned for her father and two younger brothers, Lloyd and Paul. She canned vegetables from the garden and picked apples from the big tree in the backyard. She loved to cook Sunday dinner when company came. Irene was happy and busy, but she still dusted the china hen each week. And she still dreamed.

In 1942, when her father remarried, Irene was twenty years old—and free. She was so happy at home that she did not want to leave. But since she no longer needed to stay at home to keep house for her father and brothers, she decided to go to Hesston Academy in Hesston, Kansas, to take her senior year of high school. During this year at Hesston she studied hard and wrote and listened.

She listened especially to a speaker at one of the daily chapels. M. C. Lehman, who had just returned from doing relief work in Europe, told of his experiences with refugees who came from Russia. He told of the many people who did not have enough to eat or shoes to wear because World War II had destroyed so much. The refugees worked outside in the cold all day and lived in unheated barracks.

As he talked, a picture of the china hen popped into Irene's mind. She thought again of her relative Clayton Kratz. I can be one of those relief workers, she thought, just like Clayton and M. C. Lehman. I can go to Europe.

A Dream Comes True

Irene did not rush off to Europe immediately. She knew she was not ready yet. First she finished her year at Hesston and then went to Messiah College in Grantham, Pennsylvania, for two years, where she earned an associate in arts degree. She spent the two summers during college working at mental hospitals in a special program which prepared workers for foreign relief work. While attending Goshen College the next year she even enrolled at a nursing school, but when Mennonite Central Committee accepted her for service after World War II ended in 1945, she decided she did not need the nursing degree. The director of the nursing school hoped Irene would not be sorry for not finishing her schooling, but Irene believed she could serve well with the skills she had.

In November 1946, Irene left with four other MCC workers on a boat for Europe. Irene and the other workers were eager to start giving food and clothing to the people they had heard about whose homes had been destroyed by the war. The five workers arrived in Amsterdam, Holland, where Irene waited for nine weeks for permission to go into Germany. In Germany Irene had to wait another four weeks before she could go to her assignment in Luebeck. Orie Miller, the director of MCC, had warned Irene and the other workers about the periods of waiting ahead of them. So Irene did not get discouraged when the weeks dragged on.

She enjoyed going to museums and watching city life. Day and night in the center of the city she heard the never-ending stream of traffic—rattling carts, heavy trucks. From her window she saw thick featherbeds airing in a neighbor's window; a well-tended flower box in a small attic window; patched old laundry on a washline in a backyard. Down the street an old woman carried a bundle of branches on her head past two old men sunning on the bench at a corner. And always a few people searched garbage cans for something to eat, use, or sell.

When she was finally assigned to a child feeding program in Luebeck, she was ready to work hard. Because the young children they fed were still growing, they desperately needed the extra food they did not get at home. When MCC soup and bread came to the feeding stations each morning, the children were given soup made from carrots, potatoes, beans, purina, milk, and chunks of beef canned by Mennonites in North America.

Each morning the MCC workers made sure trucks were backed up to the veranda outside the MCC kitchen. At about 8:00 the kitchen helpers began to load the trucks with full paper sacks and big metal cans. Inside the sacks were huge white rolls. Inside the cans were thick soups—so thick a spoon could stand up in them.

One day something strange arrived in the boxes of supplies sent from America. "We can make something special with these," Irene said as she took a bag of raisins to the kitchen. "Wouldn't these taste good in hot cereal?" The next day many schoolchildren ate the strange looking "soup."

"Oh, Mutti, it tasted so good," one five-year-old boy told his mother when he came home from the feeding station. He had never seen raisins before. "There were even little Mennonites floating around in the soup!"

Besides "Mennonite soup" and vegetable soup, each child received a crusty roll. If they could not eat the roll at the distribution point, they could take it home, but first the workers had to break it open. White flour was so scarce that rolls were sometimes sold by the parents instead of eaten by the children.

Irene was glad she was helping to feed children who had little to eat at home. As she visited refugee camps she began to see other people who needed help. In an old people's home she found many people with only a few blankets huddled in one corner of their bed to keep warm. She took them a case of meat the next week so they could make some good soup, but she wished she could do more.

In the Name of Christ

Soon she was asked to do much more. MCC asked her to oversee all of the MCC material aid distribution in a larger area of Germany. She packed a little Volkswagen to the brim with supplies—clothing, bedding, soap, and canned meat. On the side of the car white letters spelled out "Mennonite Central Committee." Then she traveled to children's homes, boarding schools, homes for old people, and for soldiers wounded in the war.

As she traveled, she saw buildings toppled on their sides, just as they were when bombed. Craters from bombs made it impossible to drive on certain roads, so she detoured along winding roads through wooded mountains dotted with red-roofed houses. Everywhere she went she told people that the clothing and food were given "In the Name of Christ"—MCC's motto.

"Are you sure all these things are for me, Miss Bishop?" asked one little girl in a children's home. The girl had come with the other children to the home for several weeks of good food and fresh air, because there was not enough food at her home.

"Why, yes, Elsa, they are all yours," Irene said. "They are sent to you from the Mennonites in North America because they love you and they love Jesus, too."

Elsa smoothed the folds on her new dress. She cautiously held the soap to her nose to smell its clean sweet smell. "Now I have a Christmas present for my mother," she said.

"Christmas is several months away," said Irene. "Will you save the soap until then?"

"Of course. Last Christmas Daddy asked Mother what she wanted for Christmas and she wanted a piece of soap. Daddy looked and looked but he couldn't find any soap to buy. Now I can surprise her!" Elsa grasped

Irene's hand and pumped it vigorously. "Thank you, Miss Bishop. Thank you for the soap."

Irene met many people in her travels, both children like Elsa and adults who would bear the painful effects of the war for many years. Many people became her lifelong friends.

The "Daughter of Jesus"

When Irene arrived at the castle in which a Christian workers' conference was to be held, she discovered that Mrs. Gertrude Friedrich-Lenz was assigned as her room partner. The simplicity of the woman intrigued Irene: She wore her hair parted in the middle and pulled straight back in a bun. Mrs. Friedrich-Lenz explained to Irene that she was teaching religion in a village school near Bad Oldesloe. She had returned with her three boys to this village, the community in which she had grown up, after her husband did not return from the war in Russia.

As Irene listened to the woman, she felt she could learn much from her courage and unassuming faith in God. At the end of the conference Irene was sorry to say good-bye to her.

"This conference has been more than worthwhile," Mrs. Friedrich-Lenz said, "even though I had to walk three hours to get here."

"You walked here?"

"Yes, that's right. There was no other way to come."

"Well, you are not walking home," Irene said. "Here is my car." They climbed into the black Volkswagen and in forty-five minutes arrived at Mrs. Friedrich-Lenz's home and school.

"Thank you very much for bringing me home," said Mrs. Friedrich-Lenz. "I only wish I could see you again."

Irene smiled. "I'm going to come back," she said, "but

next time I will bring some supplies for your school-children." She knew Mrs. Friedrich-Lenz was someone she could trust to hand out food, clothing, and other material aid.

Several weeks later Irene returned to the school and jumped out of her car. A few boys from the school helped her unload many bundles wrapped in brightly colored towels.

Irene stood at the front of the class behind a little podium. "I love Jesus," she said. The children became quiet. "Because I love Jesus, I love you, even though you supposedly are my enemies. The children of the Sunday school classes in North America who love Jesus have made these packages just for you. They want to help you."

In all of their lives the children had probably never heard the name Jesus used so many times in one short speech. They carried the precious packages home like newborn babies. One little girl took the bundle home and told her mother about the visitor who had given out the Christmas bundles. As the mother opened the towel and took out a dress, sweater, soap, pencil, and paper, she gasped. It had been years since she had seen such beautiful, new things.

"What kind of visitor brought this? Who was it?" she asked.

"The daughter of Jesus came today," the girl answered.

Naked and You Clothed Me

In February 1949 the "daughter of Jesus" went home to Perkasie, Pennsylvania, for a four-month furlough. When she came back she was assigned to supervise mass clothing distributions in Berlin and the Schleswig-Holstein area of Germany.

"Who's next on our list?"

Irene and Elizabeth, another MCC worker, were visiting homes in Kiel, Germany, to see who needed the most help. They invited the most needy to the monthly distributions.

"The Reschats," Irene said. "Down these stairs here."

They picked their way down the narrow, rotting steps, trying to avoid the cobwebs on the sides. Irene's firm knocks brought a "Come in," in a Slavic accent. Irene pushed open the creaky door and Elizabeth followed, carrying a large box. Through the dim light they saw flowers sitting on the high window ledges of the basement room. Picture post cards flowed across the walls in graceful lines.

"Come right in. I'm just feeding my husband," said a stooped woman. At the end of the room she was spooning some peas to her bearded husband who lay in bed, wearing a cap to keep warm. Irene was sure the damp basement air did not help the man, who was obviously not well. "There, finished. Now what would you like?" the woman asked her visitors.

"Mrs. Reschat, we brought you a few things from our supplies at Mennonite Central Committee," Irene said. Elizabeth gave her the box.

The old woman's eyes widened as she took out packages wrapped in brown paper. "You are too kind." She slowly unwrapped first a jar of lard, MCC beef, then a can of milk, a can of apple butter, some noodles, and a box of oatmeal. "Thank you—you don't know how much this means. Our daughter had been supporting us until she got sick. Now we are alone."

"How do you pay for this apartment?" asked Elizabeth.

"We have kind neighbors. The people upstairs were neighbors for thirty years before our house was bombed. Now they let us live in their basement."

"Here is a requisition slip so you can come to our next clothing distribution," Irene said. "If you hand in the pass on September 26 we can give you a blanket and perhaps a few other things."

Before Irene and Elizabeth left, Mrs. Reschat hugged them both.

"We'll see you at the distribution," Elizabeth said.

When distribution day came once a month, long tables were set up in an empty building—usually a hotel or hall no longer used because it had too many holes and broken windows from bombs.

Mennonite women of the area helped Irene unpack the bales and sort the clothing. Then on the set day the people came. They stood in a long line until it was their turn. The local women helped them pick out one big thing for their family—a blanket or a heavy winter coat—and one small thing for each member of the family—a dress or a pair of pants.

Some people simply took the things without looking at Irene or the other helpers. Some even criticized the goods handed out.

"This is such thin material," said one woman angrily. "Don't you have something heavier?" "I'm sorry," Irene answered. "This is not a store. We can only give out what was sent to us." The woman picked up the dress, stuffed it in her bag, and left. But almost everyone else thanked them sincerely. They were worried about the cold winter coming, and were delighted with the warm quilts made by Mennonite women in North America.

Sick and You Visited Me

Besides organizing distributions, Irene also worked as a welfare officer in a refugee camp. Her job was to guide the hundreds of refugees through the mass of red tape necessary to get them out of Germany. She wrote out reports for unmarried mothers who wanted to migrate to Australia. She signed permission slips so that people who wanted to go to Canada could have passport pictures taken at the expense of the welfare organization. She went to the jail and wrote reports so people could be paroled. She visited sick people who were waiting to get well before going to the United States.

Staying in Germany was difficult for refugees because they were not officially recognized by this country. Therefore they could not get work, but could not go back to their native country for fear of death or imprisonment. For some people, Irene arranged a place to sleep while they waited to leave.

Christmas and Christmas Bundles

Irene and the other volunteers were thrilled when the Christmas bundles arrived at the end of November 1954, giving them ample time to prepare for four distributions. Cupboards and desks in the MCC office were moved aside to make room for 900 bundles which needed to be sorted.

For the final distribution on December 24 they invited thirty refugee guests to the MCC unit house. A tall candle-covered evergreen tree lit the living room. Windowsills and cupboards were covered with more evergreen, candles, and gifts wrapped in gay prints. The guests listened to poems, songs, and finally the Christmas story portrayed by children.

Quietly the children came forward as their names were called to get a bright towel-wrapped package. Everyone extended a hand to say *"Danke schön."* The boys bowed and the girls curtsied, as all German children were taught to do. Everyone waited till each had a bundle.

Then, "You may open them now," Irene said. Squeals and "ahs" and "look what I have" filled the room. Tinkertoy projects were soon under construction; puzzled faces worked over puzzles; and balls whizzed through the air. Soap wrappers littered the floor; the children had immediately torn them off to smell the bars, which were much nicer than the plain soap they normally used.

In all the excitement Irene did not forget the coffee and cake for the grown-ups and the bag of candies for the children. Finally the long, happy evening was over.

In the fall of 1955 Irene went to Austria to be MCC material aid director for that country. She was ushered into a high-ceilinged apartment in Vienna with a spacious foyer and majestic staircase. Although the apartment, which had been subleased to MCC by the occupying army, showed signs of wear, it was elegantly furnished.

Irene did not feel right about having such a huge apartment for herself and her co-worker. Right away she decided she would set the dining room table at least once a month and invite the MCC Paxmen for an evening of good food, singing, or listening to records. Many workers enjoyed the Persian rug, chandelier, and grand piano with her.

Russia Invades Hungary

In October 1956 thousands of Hungarians, suffering from a revolution in their country, fled across the border to Austria. Irene and the other MCC workers often went to the border marked by Austrian red-white-red flags to watch the refugees come in. They were tired, hungry, and sometimes sick. They needed work, a place to stay, and eventually help in emigrating.

Immediately Irene and the other workers began to

give out the MCC goods which were stored in a bombed-out school. Three temporary homes for refugees were set up. Countless hours were spent listening to the Hungarians tell the story of their flight and helping them adjust to the new country.

Three months after the revolution letters began to come from Hungary asking for help. Even though it was impossible to know if there really was need, Irene and her staff sent used clothing, soap, and food to the people who requested it. Eventually Irene was able to make a trip to Hungary and saw that the supplies were actually going to people who needed them.

Irene continued to do the work she had done in Germany—organizing distributions, visiting hospitals and refugee camps and other institutions, then sending them a shipment of supplies through the Austrian Evangelisches Hilfswerk, with whom they worked. The director of a children's boarding school wrote:

Dear Miss Bishop,
   Our heartfelt thanks for the many lovely things. The patchwork quilts make our rooms look like they have never looked before — cheerful, gay, and neat. The clothes are also all, without exception, usable and the children are overwhelmed with joy at the colorful variety.

Irene received many letters of thanks from the places she visited. When she was planning to leave Austria in 1960 the director of a Bible bookstore urged the MCC director to reappoint her to Austria. She had been a tireless, energetic, and cheerful worker. But MCC had other plans for Irene.

When Irene arrived in the United States, she decided first of all to finish the one year of college left to get her degree. She returned to Goshen College, Goshen, Indiana, and majored in sociology. Then John Hostetler, a

Mennonite sociologist, asked her to help him research the Hutterites, because she knew the Austrian dialect this religious group spoke. For four months she traveled to Manitoba, Alberta, and Montana to live with them. She ate with them, talked with them, and dressed like them in polka dot kerchief and long aproned dress. It was a fascinating time for her as she observed how Austrian their dress and speech had remained since their exodus from Europe.

After her research assignment was over she came home to Perkasie, to spend a few months with her father, who was not well. Her stepmother had died while she was attending Goshen College. Before Irene left for her next MCC assignment, this time in Algeria, her father told her, "You will always have a home, Irene. My home will be yours when I die."

And Then to Algeria

Irene was not worried about a place to live when she flew to Algeria in 1963. There were too many other things to think about. The war for Algerian independence had ended only the year before at a tremendous cost to Algeria. One million people had been killed and the upheaval had caused food and clothing shortages. Irene was to organize clothing distributions with the help of three other workers, but first she had to learn French.

As she drove to the site of the first clothing distribution with Gerda, one of her co-workers, she wondered what she would find. Algiers, the capital city, was full of white buildings that reflected the intense desert sun. The fields outside the city were covered with some orange trees and an occasional palm, but for the most part they were quite barren. As they climbed up a narrow mountain road they saw other roads, like narrow brown ribbons, wrapped around surrounding hills. Hundreds of feet below, clusters of mud houses with mud roofs sheltered people who lived a simple existence.

Two MCC workers had already arrived at the distribution site, a former Koran school which was by now both doorless and windowless. The men had nailed plastic to the holes and the distribution had already begun. Hundreds of people sat outside the school, the veiled women on the right and the men on the left. Only a few people were allowed inside at a time, because otherwise the distribution became chaotic. Algerian officials stood near the school in case the crowd got out of hand.

Irene noticed that the people who came often had only rags or pieces of leather for shoes. She was glad they were giving out clothing and warm blankets, for the mountain air was very bitter at times. "Saha, saha"—"Thank you, thank you," was the constant refrain, until almost 2,500 people were served in that first distribution. Thousands of other people were given blankets, shoes, clothing, and other supplies while Irene was in Algeria, but she felt as if it was only a small gesture compared to the sweeping actions needed in that area.

Although the intense heat in summer sent everyone else inside for afternoon quiet periods, Irene often did not stop traveling around to iron out the details necessary for distributions. In Al-Asnam she proposed and set up a sponsorship program for students who could benefit from an education but did not have the money. She arranged for supplies to be given to missionaries, Catholic sisters, schoolteachers, and hospitals.

Shortly before Irene was to leave Algeria, her father

died. She flew home for the funeral and then back to Algeria to close out the material aid program. Irene was alone now, for all the other workers had left. She wondered what she would do when she was home again. At least she had a place to live, for her father had done exactly what he had promised—given his house to her in his will.

There is Always Work for Those who Love

She did not have to wonder long when she reached home in 1967, for Plumstead Christian School desperately needed a teacher. She taught there for one year before going to Quakertown Christian Day School where she was both teacher and principal for five years. She did not know what she would do after she resigned, but she felt the Lord wanted her to do something else.

The "something else" so far has been travel. A tour company asked Irene to go to Europe to make bookings for them. Later a second company asked her to lead tours through all the European countries in which she had worked as an MCC worker. She has had a delightful time going back to the places and friends she knew in earlier years.

When she is at home she hosts international visitors and the many North American friends she has made. The cozy, 140-year-old log house her father gave her is filled with dishes, pictures, and souvenirs from her travels.

But the china hen still has a prominent place, with the newspaper clipping about Clayton Kratz tucked inside. And sometimes, when curious visitors ask, Irene tells them about the little girl who dusted the gray head and brown wings each week, and relates how the dream of being a relief worker came true.

5.
Peter
(P. C.)
Hiebert*

By
Wesley
J.
Prieb

His parents did not expect him to live. He was a very sickly child, but somehow he escaped a severe epidemic of diptheria which caused the death of four children in one week in a neighboring family. Peter C. Hiebert, born on April 5, 1878, never visited a doctor until his adult years. This weak and timid child became a strong man and dynamic witness in education, in the church, and in peace and relief services of the Mennonite Central Committee. "Thou shalt guide me with thy counsel" was P. C. Hiebert's motto.

Kansas Prairie Pioneers

Peter's father, Kornelius Hiebert, came from South Russia to Kansas in 1876 and purchased a farm near Gnadenau Village, southeast of Hillsboro. He was also an ordained minister and helped organize the Ebenfeld church, the first Mennonite Brethren church in America. He helped establish a chair at McPherson College and encouraged the development of Tabor

---

*This story is part of a full-length book about the life and work of Peter Hiebert now in preparation by the author.

College. Kornelius often told Peter, "Son, if you and your generation are not better than I and my generation, you are a failure."

Peter's early life was shaped by the rugged simplicity of the Kansas frontier. His bare feet knew the scratch of wheat stubble and the touch of newly turned furrows cut through the rich black soil with a walking plow. He knew the songs of the meadow lark, the turtle dove, and the mocking bird. He enjoyed the thrill of jerking a catfish out of the Cottonwood River. His mouth watered when his mother baked bread in large black pans in a wood-burning oven in the summer kitchen. His day was measured by an old-fashioned German timepiece, reaching from the ceiling to the floor, the weights and pendulum of polished brass. He saw the Mennonite settlers make adobe bricks with mud and straw. During the mulberry season his hands and face were stained purple by the juice of the delicious fruit. Occasionally he accompanied his father on the buggy to the trading center to exchange farm products for the simple needs of domestic life. He was familiar with the old gristmill powered by a large Dutch windmill in the Gnadenau Village. He saw the sorghum mills produce thick sorghum molasses, which was spread on bread. He also saw the cruelty of nature in prairie fires, clouds of grasshoppers, electric thunderstorms, and runaway horses. The images of the frontier world became a permanent part of Peter's imaginative mind.

When Peter was four, he saw his younger brother die. Five years later his mother died, leaving seven children behind. In four more years his stepmother died, leaving eight more children behind, including five from a previous marriage. His father's third marriage brought five more foster children to the dinner table—a total of twenty. "We were quite a beehive," Peter recalled later.

Peter (P.C.) Hiebert

"There were three Johns in the family, two Peters, two Lizzies, two Katherines. We learned to get along with one another, and I remember no real strife or quarrels in the family group. Father was a great pacifier and we followed his example."

Committed to the Lord

The Bible was the family textbook. It was kept in a small shelf built into the masonry wall at the end of the dining room. "I will never forget," Peter testified, "the worship around the breakfast table. No matter how busy the season, winter or summer, we all assembled around the breakfast table where father read a passage of Scripture, made some explanations, and applications, whereupon the whole family would kneel and father would pray in his habitual posture with his head thrown back and his eyes wide open as if he saw the great God himself. Neither seedtime or harvest abbreviated these family worship hours. I recall how mother taught us simple prayers when we went to bed."

Peter's spiritual pilgrimage began in a chickenhouse on his father's farm: "I knelt down and prayed and something which I had never experienced struck my soul." At the age of seven, when tempted by his friends to adopt bad habits, he overcame the temptations in a grove between two mulberry hedges. "There was strife in my soul. I decided to go the way which was right before God. I made a pledge there and committed my way unto the Lord."

When a revival broke out among the young people, Peter attended a cottage prayer meeting. He noticed that some of his friends called upon God for forgiveness. "I also tried to pray but my mouth seemed closed and sealed. I wished that somebody would speak to me and encourage me, but nobody spoke."

A week later at another cottage prayer meeting Peter overcame his fear: "With tears flowing down my cheeks I called on the Lord to forgive my sins." While walking home after the meeting the assurance of salvation came to Peter: "I was now a child of God. My feet hardly touched the ground, so light I felt."

Sometime later revival meetings were held in the little red schoolhouse in Hillsboro. The Hiebert family traveled the five miles on a spring wagon, but Peter, who was too young, was not permitted to go along. "My hunger was so great that one evening I climbed into the spring wagon and hid under the rear seat and thus as a stowaway came to the little red schoolhouse where we heard the people praise God and pray and ask for forgiveness and thank the Lord for pardon."

When Peter felt he was ready for baptism, the congregation remained for an after-session on Sunday to hear the testimonies of several young people. After Peter gave his testimony, he was interrogated: "Why, Peter, you are so young and small. Do you think you can stand and be faithful?" Quickly Peter responded, "Why, Jesus said, 'I will be with you always, even unto the end of the ages,' and if he is with me I know I can stand."

Although he was a frail child, Peter walked to a rural school. "During those cold winter days I often suffered. We were poor; we didn't even have overcoats and we had very little underwear." He learned easily and advanced rapidly. In six years, at the age of thirteen, he graduated from grade school and then worked on his father's farm for three years. During the evening he found time to study. At the age of sixteen he took the Marion County examination and received his teaching certificate. His father advised him to attend Hillsboro High School, four and one-half miles away, for one year. Peter rode a pony to school. "I got up early in the dark, milked the cows, made and ate my breakfast. Many a cold day when the winds were blowing and the snow was heavy, I suffered quite a bit on my little pony."

Teaching School at Seventeen

After completing one year of high school, Peter taught for two years in a school near Eldorado, Kansas. The schoolhouse, surrounded by blue-stem prairie grass, was shaped like a shoe box with windows evenly spaced on each side. Four rows of old-fashioned school benches stretched across the room, leaving space near the center for a round-bellied cast-iron stove. Above the heater was a tin drum designed to distribute heat, and then a black flue projected upward, arched near the ceiling, and then extended along the room toward the chimney. A hall across the front end of the school building contained a water bucket, a common drinking cup, tattered coats hanging on nails, muddy overshoes on the floor, and dented dinner pails placed in a row on a shelf. Water was delivered daily from a nearby farm.

For $30 a month Peter taught 35 pupils of five nationalities, ranging in age from six to twenty-four years. Once when a little Bohemian boy, Alfred Cash, wasn't learning his lessons, Peter became impatient and annoyed and said to the class, "I wish that they would have at least taught him to speak before they sent him to school."

The next morning an angry father threatened to whip the young teacher. He approached the schoolhouse, taking long strides with his heavy farm boots. Peter heard him step onto the small wooden porch. There he knocked the frozen ice and grass from his boots. As he opened the door he seemed stunned. Before he had a chance to speak Peter said, "Why, good morning, Mr. Cash; I am happy that you came to school. I always like to see people visit the school. Won't you come right in and take a seat?"

Without saying a word, Mr. Cash sat down in a chair close to the stove. Peter continued his class recitation, not knowing what to expect. Sophia, daughter of Mr. Cash, had her lesson well prepared. Peter complimented her. Then it was the boy's turn to recite. He stammered and stumbled but tried hard. He was complimented for his effort. Before dismissing the class for recess, Peter turned to the father, "Mr. Cash, won't you get up and say something?" Cash said, "Oh no, no, I can't speak in public; I cannot do that at all, but you have a very nice school." The two shook hands, exchanged a few more friendly words, and then the siege was over.

After attending the academy at McPherson College for one year, Peter taught three years in the Gnadenau school where he had been a pupil. Peter was known as a strict teacher who loved students. "Live to please God," he told the students.

The five years he spent in rural teaching were some of the happiest in his life: "We would work hard during study hours, and during recess and at noon I would play with them the games they liked. I never had a serious case of discipline."

Training for Ministry

Driven by a thirst for knowledge, Peter enrolled at McPherson College where he completed the AB degree in 1906. While attending college he often spent weekends serving various churches. Once he attended a union meeting sponsored by the M.B. churches of Kansas. During the morning service, Abraham Schellenberg, a leading elder of the M.B. Church, asked Peter to preach a short sermon during the evening service. Peter prepared some ideas based on 1 John 3:1.

When the last speaker of the afternoon preached a sermon on the same text, Peter ran into a nearby field and secluded himself along the banks of a creek. Here he prayed till he was led to preach on the text in Philemon: "If he hath wronged thee, or oweth thee ought, put that on mine account." This was the beginning of a Paul and Timothy relationship between Schellenberg and Hiebert. Peter learned much from the elder who helped shape the growth of the M.B. Conference.

During 1904-1905 Peter attended the Baptist seminary in Rochester, New York, in specialized training for the ministry. Here he learned the discipline required for solid scholarship. He learned that spirituality cannot be separated from hard work.

In 1906, he was officially elected as a minister of the Ebenfeld church. He married Katherine Nikkel, whom he learned to know at McPherson College, on January 1, 1907. Two weeks after their wedding Peter and Katherine were ordained. The church commissioned the couple "as servants of the Lord to go out and preach the gospel." On their honeymoon the couple visited Mr. and Mrs. Henry Lohrenz in McPherson, where Henry was attending college. They shared their dreams of starting a school, shook hands, and pledged to work together to build the educational work among the Mennonite Brethren churches. "We parted and I went to the West Coast to do evangelistic work and he continued his education and started promoting the movement that should build a college."

A few weeks later the Hieberts traveled by train to Dallas and Portland, Oregon, where Peter had accepted a pastorate for two small churches. The young couple lived in a little farm hut. A cow, some chickens, a garden, and a salary of $500 a year provided a means for a living. For nearly two years they served here. Then the call came to help organize Tabor College.

P. C. and Tabor College

In the fall of 1908, thirty-nine students enrolled at Tabor College. The catalog listed three teachers: H. W. Lohrenz, president and instructor of German, natural sciences, and mathematics; P. C. Hiebert, secretary-treasurer, instructor of English, language and literature, ancient languages, and history; P. R. Rempel, instructor of historical and Biblical subjects. During the year, three more instructors were added as the enrollment increased to eighty-four. "The teaching load, of course, was heavy," recalls Hiebert. "We taught from six to seven classes a day. This, together with the preparation needed for the classes, plus additional work of administration and that of ordering books and collecting tuition, and handling the necessities of the school to keep it running, made the program quite heavy."

Hiebert took a leave of absence in 1911-1912 and earned his master's degree at the University of Kansas. Foregoing the opportunity for professional advancement, he dutifully returned to Tabor. The enrollment slowly increased to about two hundred, and the faculty to fifteen members. All progress, however, was suddenly halted. On April 30, 1918, the Tabor College building was destroyed by fire. The total loss was valued at $24,000. "I could hardly believe it. All our hopes for the immediate future seemed to be dashed ... nothing but a pile of smoldering ashes." At a chapel meeting in the church the Spirit of the Lord seemed to prevail. Encouragement was found in the fact that the spirit of Tabor was not dead. The fire that destroyed a building probably saved a college. The crisis led people to new visions of sacrifice and service. The constituency of Tabor College became alive again! Again Lohrenz and Hiebert refused to give up their dream. A new $100,000 building was nearly completed two years later.

The college expanded until the "dirty thirties" when the economic depression and the dust bowl nearly destroyed the college again. When President Lohrenz resigned, Peter Hiebert also resigned to accept a teaching position at Sterling College in Sterling, Kansas, as head of the department of education. Here he taught for thirteen years.

Peter Hiebert gave twenty-five years to develop a conference educational program. While he amplified the lives of many students, he sometimes offended people. Some accused him of being too progressive; others thought he stressed nonresistance too much. Some of his students disliked his rhetorical eloquence and his dramatic emotional appeal. Supporters of the college were sometimes offended by his aggressive solicitation for funds. Peter Hiebert was aware of his imperfections and often expressed regret for his mistakes, but he never allowed criticism to unnerve him.

There Is Always a Way to Go

The genius of Peter Hiebert's teaching ministry can be expressed in a few concepts which gave unity and purpose to his teaching. He demonstrated, first, *a sense of duty.* As a teacher he had confidence in the ability and potential of a student to develop into a responsible and productive agent in society, especially a person who honored God as the source of all wisdom and human achievement. He loved people not only for what they were, but for what they could become. His love was not an indulgent love, but rather love that is reinforced by expectation and discipline. He expected a lot from his students, and this sense of expectation and confidence motivated his students to excel. There was never a touch of pessimism, defeatism, or irresponsibility in his life. He radiated a sense of duty and a love for difficult challenges. "Son, there is always a way to go," he said frequently not only to his family, but to his students and associates. He seemed to have a pipeline to God: "We have to go God's way," he said.

This sense of duty and obedience drove him to accept the most difficult challenges, such as returning to administrative duties at Tabor College at a time when the family was happy at Sterling College. Because he had a mortal fear of not completing a job satisfactorily, he usually got up at 5:00 a.m. and seldom retired before 10:00 p.m. So intense was his sense of duty that he found it difficult to relax during moments of leisure. Many of his students caught the inspiration of a disciplined and ordered life from his example.

Serving and Witnessing

The intellectual process was never an end in itself for Peter Hiebert. He regarded education as a means *to develop character.* Being was even more important than knowing. In fact he questioned whether a person could possess knowledge until it had become a part of the tissue of life. Responsibility and integrity were stressed. "Straight-furrow living," was a phrase he liked to use. It was, of course, his deep conviction that character development can best be achieved when a person allows the Lord of life to rule human aspirations and actions.

Peter Hiebert attempted to work out a Christian concept of *liberal arts* education. He had a biblical worldview, but he was quick to accept truth from any quarter. He saw no conflict between faith and reason. He sought to relate all knowledge to the person of Jesus Christ and believed that the fragments of human knowledge can best be harmonized in terms of a Christian philosophy. In Christ he had freedom to explore the whole range of human thought without fear. He was a defender of intellectual freedom and demonstrated intense curiosity in his search for truth. His love for the great literary classics, history, and philosophy reflected his desire for an expansive rather than a restrictive search. His appreciation for Greek thought and culture is reflected in the beautiful Greek architecture of the Tabor College administration building, which has one of the most impressive Greek fronts among college buildings in Kansas. Peter Hiebert helped determine the styling of this building, and in the design was suggesting his concern that the ideal setting for education is a place where Christian thought and Greek philosophy can be studied together.

The key word that characterized Professor Hiebert's relationship with his students was *love*. He taught and practiced the principle, "Love one another." He had a deep concern for children and infinite patience. "The boy will find himself; don't speak too quickly." He gave children the liberty to disagree with him, but he always made his position clear. He knew how to let the ropes go with young people. He was a master of counseling and guidance and had the ability to develop incentive among students indirectly. Love was not without discipline, which sometimes included the woodshed, but he seldom disciplined a child in anger. If emotions got too strong, he would walk out of the room to cool off. Peter Hiebert cared for people. For him teaching was essentially caring enough for people to help them become better people. This was a form of cross bearing, getting under the burdens of other people. He also understood something of the persuasive force of love. He could break down natural resistance and win the confidence of his opponents. He believed that "a soft answer turneth away wrath." Love, for Peter Hiebert, was not pacifism, but a redemptive and active way of helping people resolve difficulties in an ambiguous world of good and evil. He believed sincerely that the highest expression of love was to help people discover the God of love: "For God so loved the world that he gave his only begotten Son."

Finally, he believed that *service*, not self-advancement, is the legitimate end of the learning process. True greatness, Hiebert felt, expresses itself in giving of self, in sharing a cup of cold water. He believed that the victorious Christian should reflect strength in faith, belief, and action. "Live so that people know what you believe," he said. He had no patience with false piety and mushy meekness. He encouraged Christians to take the offensive. He stressed positive Christian action and a high level of consistent living in service vocations. He was a practical evangelist who believed that each Christian has to work out his Christianity in the sermon of life.

Throughout his life Peter Hiebert was an active churchman. With his versatility and administrative skills he served the M. B. conference well, holding a variety of offices. He served as secretary of the Board of Home Missions for nine years and as chairman for another nine years. He helped organize the mission work with the Mexicans in Los Ebanos in southern Texas. He served as chairman of the church hymnal committee, which compiled the 1953 edition of the *Mennonite Brethren Hymnal.* He served as moderator of the Pacific District and the Southern District; several years he served as secretary of the Southern District and the General Conference. For forty years he was chairman of the Mennonite Brethren Relief Committee, later called the Board of General Welfare and Public Relations, which collaborated with the MCC. Three times he represented the Mennonite Brethren Church at the Mennonite World Conference. For over sixty years he served as a traveling minister in the United States, Canada, Europe, Russia, and South America. Always willing to accept a call to proclaim the "good news," Hiebert was a minister who enjoyed preaching.

As a master of the pulpit Hiebert talked with, rather than at, his audience, as if the listeners were his friends. His affectionate smile, his sympathetic eyes, and his earnest voice captured his audience. He sensed quickly the quality and the needs of his listeners and easily established rapport, never allowing his notes to separate him from his audience. He was a dramatic preacher with a clear and vibrant voice. He could be eloquent, but he could also speak in a calm conversational tone.

He preached with a Bible in his hand, frequently raising it above his head with arms outstretched in a dramatic gesture. He fingered his well-worn Bible rapidly and with certainty while reading many supporting passages during the course of a sermon. His messages, so clear that children could understand them, were enriched with illustrations from history, literature, science, nature, and domestic life. He sought to make his sermons relevant and contemporary. He enjoyed using proverbs, sayings, and images of the countryside. Since he could preach with equal ease in both German and English, he had the folklore of two languages at his disposal. Sometimes he would slip into the Low German for the sake of humor or informality.

Hiebert's sermons reflect a consistent message. Certain themes and convictions gave unity to his preaching and life. His world-view was deeply influenced by the Anabaptist movement in the sixteenth century and the evangelical movements of the nineteenth and twentieth centuries. He sought to harmonize the basic convictions of the Mennonite faith with the evangelical witness. His unique ministry revolved around the following themes:

Biblicism

The ultimate authority for Hiebert's ministry was the Bible. The founders of his church were known as the people with the "bulging coat pocket" because they frequently carried a well-worn Bible. The Bible, which he carried with him nearly always, was his law; he studied it with daring freedom, personal conviction, faith, and humility: "The Bible is the most fiercely attacked book today," he said, "but that should not surprise the Christian nor should it in any way disturb his faith. The Bible will stand through all attacks, and always come out better established after friend and foe have questioned its verities. It is hardly necessary that we defend the Bible; rather lean on it when we are assailed and need help, for it will stand firm." For him, the Bible superseded all closed theological systems. The Bible was his absolute, but he never insisted that he understood it absolutely: "Approach the Bible with an open mind, and avoid the attitude of looking for proof of your beliefs. The most effective key for understanding the Bible is a surrendered heart, a consecrated life, and a spiritually inclined mind."

Hiebert believed that a willingness to obey the authority of the Bible is the best way to study it. The door to an understanding of God's Word swings on the hinges of obedience. "You have to experience his truth by doing what he tells you to do."

The Cross

The cross is not a tragedy, Hiebert believed, but a glorious expression of divine love. Christ's voluntary and atoning death was the greatest redemptive act in history. When man was at his worst, Christ was at his best, not retaliating with wrath and judgment, but offering mercy and grace: "Father, forgive them; for they know not what they do."

Hiebert described the cross as a bridge between sinful man and a righteous God—a kind of link between two incompatible worlds. The cross represents the point of tension between these two worlds, a tension created by a confrontation between good and evil. On the cross God, through his Son, confronted evil with a new weapon—the power of love. "Imagine," said Hiebert, "responding to evil with love and forgiveness. When this happens, love has to die, but evil is overcome, and love lives again in a new resurrection."

In a sermon entitled "What Do We Know of Jesus," Hiebert said, "The elimination of Christ's death from the Christian religion would take away its uniqueness. Christianity is not merely a system of ethics; it is the history of redemption through Jesus Christ, the person Redeemer."

Conversion

Accepting the Bible as God's objective revelation, Hiebert also stressed the importance of a personal encounter between God and man called conversion, a deep spiritual experience which involves accepting Christ as Lord and Savior. Salvation comes entirely as a free gift through grace. It is the result of God's love for man.

When man accepts God's love manifested in Christ, something happens—man becomes a new creature. Hiebert referred to this change as the beginning of a new life, a radical switch or conversion, a wrenching of man into conformity with the will of God, the starting point of a life of discipleship.

True conversion is a two-dimensional experience. Hiebert accepted the Reformation emphasis upon justification by faith, but he insisted that true repentance and regeneration must result in a new life patterned after the teachings and example of Christ: "Let no man deceive himself, a profession of becoming a Christian without a change of life is not regeneration."

Without newness of life, faith is hypocritical. Faith in Christ must be linked with following Christ (Nachfolge Christi). Hiebert agreed with Hans Denk, a leader of the Anabaptist movement in South Germany, who said, "Christ cannot be truly known by anyone, except he follow him in life." Hiebert stressed the all-sufficiency of God and pointed men to the cross as a means of salvation, but he also stressed the demands of discipleship. This new life demands holiness, purity, separation, and a positive nonconformity. It leads to a new ethic and meets evil in the world with love, self-sacrifice, and suffering. It places great moral and social responsibility upon man as a free moral agent.

Peoplehood

The church, Hiebert believed, is a voluntary brotherhood of adult believers, the visible extension of the incarnate Christ in the world and in history. Baptism signals the voluntary integration of a responsible convert into the brotherhood of believers. Baptism is a "covenant of a good conscience toward God," the pledge of a complete commitment to obey Christ.

Joining the brotherhood is a serious choice. The prospective member must renounce all allegiance to the world and affirm his loyalty to the church. Each member is accountable for his behavior to all the others, and all the members are accountable for his behavior to all the others, and all the members are accountable to the outside world for the behavior of any one of them. Brotherhood involves a whole fabric of common concern and mutual responsibility under the guidance of the Holy Spirit. Baptism indicates that the believer is not only in a right relationship with God but that he is willing to accept a responsible position and maintain a Christian relationship within the brotherhood. Within the gathered church, the believer can be nurtured through Bible study, worship, prayer, and fellowship.

Nonconformity

Hiebert believed that a man seriously committed to following Christ will be a nonconformist in the world. Nonconformity is not a choice between individual rights and group rights; it is simple obedience to the highest authority in the life of a believer, and this obedience to Christ often involves the believer in a tension between Christ's and the authority of the social norm or the state.

In his counsel to a small group of Christians in the city of Rome (Romans 12:1-2), Paul encouraged conformity to Christ rather than to the city. He did not counsel them to retreat, to move to another country, to isolate themselves in a rural community, to preserve purity of biological descent, or to maintain ethnic cohesion. To Paul, nonconformity simply meant complete obedience to Christ. Paul further expected the small group of Christians to mold the city of Rome rather than be molded. In other words, Paul expected the believers to be responsible agents in "proving" or demonstrating in an urban society the validity of the gospel. Hiebert underscored Paul's witness again and again. It is from Christ the Head that the body derives its life and it is by this Head that the believer is to be controlled.

Cross Bearing

The real test of Christian maturity and responsibility is the believer's willingness to suffer, to take up his cross in order to help his brother or his enemy. Though the cross of Christ offers love and salvation, the Christian cannot expect Christ to carry the load alone. The call to discipleship is an invitation to join Christ in meeting evil and in bearing the burdens of humanity through suffering love and self-sacrifice. Jesus said, "If any man will come after me, let him deny himself, and take up his cross, and follow me."

Hiebert understood that the cost of discipleship is great. It calls us to abandon the attachments of this world, and it warns us that suffering is the badge of true discipleship. When Christ calls a man, he bids him come and die if necessary to further his cause.

To bear the cross, said Hiebert, is not a tragedy or an accident. The believer is never forced to bear the cross. It is a volitional and deliberate choice to get involved in the ministry of reconciliation. It is a deliberate choice in response to a command: "Bear ye one another's burdens, and so fulfill the law of Christ" (Galatians 6:2).

Cross bearing, therefore, is a life-long vocation; it is planned compassion that goes out seeking the distressed in order to help them. It is the basis for nonresistance, social reform, the healing ministry, mutual aid, disaster service, evangelism, and missions. It is a radical method of meeting evil and getting under the burdens of our brothers. It is binding upon all believers: "Greater love hath no man than this, that a man lay down his life for his friend" (John 15:13).

The Great Commission

Hiebert regarded the Great Commission as a matter of obedience and cross bearing: "Go ye therefore, and teach all nations, baptizing them in the name of the Father, and of the Son, and of the Holy Ghost: Teaching them to observe all things whatsoever I have commanded you: and, lo, I am with you always, even unto the end of the world" (Matthew 28:19-20).

This missionary mandate calls us to encounter the world with a prophetic voice, calling people to repentance and to a life of discipleship. The purpose of the mandate is to evangelize the world. It answers the eternal question of man, "What must I do to inherit eternal life?"

Hiebert recognized that the Great Commission does not stop with converting people, for conversion never takes place in a vacuum. The convert must relate himself to a complex social order. The Christian witness, therefore, must relate itself to man's economic, political, and social involvements. Hiebert expressed this two-dimensional witness in his compassion for the hungry, the sick, the poor, and the homeless. He also stressed the importance of extending the Christian witness into the ambiguous areas of church and state, economics, racial relations, colonialism, militarism, capital punishment, etc.

Hiebert believed that a genuine encounter with Christ will change life. A Christian will change, and he will seek to change his family, his friends, and his community. No other single power has brought about such radical changes and reform movements as the gospel of Jesus Christ. The best way to help mankind is to proclaim Christ. There is no greater agitation for a better life than the hunger which comes from a soul that has been liberated from sin through Jesus Christ: "We make no mistake when we say that evangelism is the first, and in a sense the supreme, mission of the church."

Hiebert's life was a ministry of love and cross bearing. Although he believed in nonresistance, he was no naive pacifist. Nor did he share the easy optimism of many theologians who thought the application of a little love and sympathy would resolve the ambiguous problems of human relations. He was a realistic Christian who believed that the ultimate call to discipleship was the call to bear the cross. For him nonresistance was not a philosophical problem; it was simply a matter of obedience to the supreme authority of his life.

Hiebert's optimism was based on a cataclysmic rather than an evolutionary kingdom of righteousness. He strongly believed that man is unable to save himself, and that the gospel of self-reliance is suicidal. He believed that the only hope for man's salvation was divine intervention. His hope for the future rested in the coming of Christ, who will judge the world righteously and establish His kingdom of peace and righteousness. This conviction did not breed pessimism or irresponsibility. Seldom has a man worked harder to achieve peace and reconciliation among men. He had great faith in people who allowed Christ to become the Lord of their life. On the basis of this faith, Hiebert never ceased to proclaim to the world, "For God so loved the world . . ." (John 3:16), and then quickly added, "I am my brother's keeper." This was the amazing secret of his faith—a commitment to Christ as Savior and Lord and love for his fellowman.

Honored with the Order of Merit

A small group of friends gathered in the Hiebert home in Hillsboro, Kansas, June 30, 1953, to pay tribute to Peter Hiebert. The following resolution was read by the Honorable Hans P. Schweigeman, representing the German Consulate in Kansas City: "Dear Dr. Hiebert and friends. It is indeed an honor and a privilege for me to be able to come here and present personally this declaration that the German government has bestowed upon Dr. Hiebert. The comparatively small community of Mennonites has done a tremendous amount of relief work in Germany and the relief has been received with gratitude. Many a family, as recipient of these activities, has gotten new hope instead of utter despair after this war. In recognition of the activities of the Mennonites and as a symbol of the gratitude of the German government, the President of the Republic has bestowed upon you, dear Dr. Hiebert, the Grand Cross of the Order of Merit."

The resolution had been passed by the German Reichstag, signed and approved by President Heuss and Konrad Adenauer, the prime minister. It came from a nation which had been left in smoldering ruins after World War II, a nation that felt not only the military fist of America but also the open hand of the Marshall Plan and the services of MCC. The Grand Cross, an award comparable to the American Congressional Medal of Honor, was placed around Peter Hiebert's neck.

P. C. (Peter's name tag used by friends) had served as chairman of MCC for thirty-three years. He accepted the medal of honor on behalf of the member Mennonite churches. Fragments of his MCC experiences flashed through his mind.

The following highlights of his pilgrimage as peacemaker was recorded in his *Memoirs* during his retirement years. He thought about many of them on this special day. He remembered:

Memories ...

(1) A visit with a Mennonite boy in the guardhouse in Leavenworth, Kansas, during World War I: "The young man stepped out, looking more dead than alive with a uniform forced on him, only partially buttoned up. His face was greasy with soot and dirt and he looked sick. We hardly recognized him. He came and sat down near us, briefly telling us the story of his suffering, especially the fact that he was ill with the flu and had to work hard crushing rocks. He added that he had been forced to put on the uniform. We gave the boy a few oranges and other articles to eat, brought him the greetings from his mother, and told him that we had consulted with Colonel Cook and that he would be taken care of the next morning."

(2) A hasty trip to Fairview, Oklahoma, where an angry mob tried to hang a German-speaking Mennonite who had removed a U.S. flag placed in the window of his house by patriots who thought he was a traitor. P. C. met with a group of concerned citizens in the community building. He noticed a large U.S. flag on the wall. He stood beside the flag and declared publicly his allegiance to the flag of this country and expressed appreciation for the freedom he enjoyed: "I said that we were willing to work for our country and even sacrifice, though by our religious convictions we could not participate in taking life. I explained to them that these people used the German language in their worship services because they used Luther's translation of the Bible. In their homes they spoke the low German or a Dutch language and were really low-land people and never lived in Germany. I further called attention to the fact that our ancestors had been persecuted in Germany and driven out so that they fled and got protection in Russia before they came to America." At the

close quite a few persons, especially those who had been opposing the Mennonites, said, "Why we're Dutchmen too, so we're relatives and we're so happy that this is not a disloyal group."

(3) Going to Newton, Kansas, July 13, 1920, to hear a delegation of four Mennonites from South Russia describe the tragic conditions of the Mennonites in South Russia in the wake of political upheaval, drought, and a typhus epidemic. At this meeting P. C. was appointed to serve as secretary on a Committee of Information organized to assist the Russian delegates in promoting relief efforts. A few days later this committee—D. H. Bender, John Lichti, William J. Ewert, D. E. Harder, and P. C. Hiebert—met on the front porch of Hiebert's house in Hillsboro. They saw the need for cooperation of all the Mennonite relief agencies and suggested a general meeting.

(4) The historic meeting of July 27-28, 1920, in the Prairie Street Church of Elkhart, Indiana. Here P. C. served as interpreter for Abraham Friesen, one of the Russian delegates. P. C. was elected to serve as chairman of a temporary committee with Levi Mumaw and H. H. Regier, appointed to draw up tentative plans for the new organization. Orie Miller and P. C. first met at this meeting and established a friendship that enriched not only their own lives but the lives of many people with whom they worked. Many years later Miller recalled: "It was at this meeting where some of us met brother P. C. Hiebert and were impressed with his warmness, his clear vision, deep commitment, and particularly with the courage it must have taken then to accept the chairmanship of MCC as then conceived. This quiet faith and steady courage, so strikingly manifest in the period from 1925 to 1935 in holding MCC together as an organization for possible future

need, deeply impressed us. This Hiebert trait of confident faith and courage, also evident in his moving forward only after unanimous concensus for every step taken, is one of the things that so strikingly impressed us and gave us time and time again full confidence in his leadership of MCC."

(5) The meeting in Chicago, September 25, 1920, when a permanant executive committee was appointed to serve as the new Mennonite Central Committee (MCC). P. C. was elected as chairman, Levi Mumaw as secretary-treasurer, and M. H. Kratz as a third member.

(6) The death of Clayton Kratz, the first MCC worker to lose his life in bringing relief needs to South Russia. The courage of Kratz remained an inspiration to P. C. throughout his life.

(7) The "Famous Sixty-Two." P. C. and Orie Miller worked together in assisting sixty-two Mennonites who had fought with Wrangel's army against the Reds, and were thus forced to leave South Russia when the White Army was routed. P. C. and Orie went to Washington to negotiate successfully with the Secretary of Labor to open the doors of America to these stranded homeless refugees.

(8) Waving good-bye to his wife and four children as he left the depot in Florence, Kansas, on a trip to Russia to make plans for a relief program. C. E. Krehbiel of North Newton accompanied Hiebert on this trip.

(9) Meeting with the Soviet commissioner in Constantinople: "We presented our case, and he seemed very happy that we were willing to enter Russian relief work. He then wrote out a statement quite strongly worded, which would admit us into Communistic Russia. It promised all kinds of favors and privileges and proved to be quite advantageous later on."

(10) Crossing the Black Sea on the U.S. Destroyer

Sturdevant. P. C. was amused by the paradox of a battleship carrying messengers of peace and goodwill.

(11) Preaching in Halbstadt on Sunday morning, April 2. "I never in my life heard anyone pray, 'Give us this day our daily bread' as these people did with tears running down their haggard faces."

(12) The American kitchens designed to provide food for the hungry: "We were able to feed 43,000 children daily, give them one wholesome meal of 778 calories at the rate of $1.00 per day."

(13) The hungry boy who stole food from an American kitchen. He was caught and brought to P. C. for punishment: "How could I punish him? I decided that they should forgive him and put him on the feeding list which was perhaps the greatest gift that I could give to anybody at that time."

(14) J. G. Ewert, an invalid for 25 years, who transmitted $89,000 through the food and clothing remittance plan from his home in Hillsboro to Russia. His legs were both cramped, and his joints were stiff and immovable; his left arm was shriveled. His jaw was ossified, so that all his food had to be administered in liquid form through an opening made by removing his first molar tooth. His neck was stiff. All that he could use was his right arm when suspended in a swing, and on his right hand he could use the thumb and one finger. This man, who should have been the object of relief, became an agent of administering relief to the hungry in Russia. He learned to type. With his right arm hanging in a swing, he punched keys on a typewriter placed on his bed. His brother David, also an invalid, moved the carriage and put new sheets of paper into the typewriter: "For hours at a time and during the days of the food-draft rush, from early morning till often past midnight, these two men would work together. While

Jacob, the elder, would pick away on the keys to fill the line, David would sit motionless near at hand with a small string attached to the cylinder of the machine. As soon as the line was complete, the shift was made with one pull at the string. The very modest home of this invalid with his brother, and a very aged mother, became the Mecca for thousands of those who wished to send help to their relatives."

On March 15, 1923, after the last application had been typed, Ewert finished his work with these words, "I have written the last food draft application. My work is done." A few days later he died.

. . . And Actions

Other noteworthy details of his life included:

(1) A personal interview with President Hoover in behalf of about 1,000 Mennonite refugees stranded in Harbin, Manchuria. Within a year most of these refugees were settled in the U.S., many in the Reedley, California area.

(2) Visiting Paraguay seven years after the first colonies arrived. The purpose of the trip was to minister to them, encourage them, and to assure them that the Mennonites of North America were interested in helping them.

(3) Visiting President Franco in the capital of Paraguay: "We were pleading mainly in the interests of the welfare of our colonies who had settled in Paraguay trying to cultivate the green hell of South America, the Paraguayan Chaco. After we made our remarks, President Franco replied, 'These colonies certainly should have a highway and we are going to build one right to their front door, right into the colonies.' This all sounded very well. We thanked him and after some expression of solicitation, we departed." Several days

later P. C. picked up a paper in Buenos Aires with headlines screaming, "Revolution in Paraguay, President Franco deposed."

(4) The creation of the MCC Peace Committee to deal with conscription. P. C. was elected chairman. On September 16, 1939, the committee met with representatives of the Church of the Brethren and the Friends. By September 20 the joint committee was ready with a "Plan for Action for the Mennonites in Case of War."

(5) Meeting President Roosevelt in the White House to discuss the proposed plan. Rufus Jones, eminent Quaker leader, spoke for the delegation. The president responded, "I am glad you have done it. It shows us what work the conscientious objectors can do without fighting. Excellent! Excellent!" Roosevelt wanted to talk about the Mennonites in Paraguay: "I was down in Buenos Aires, and I asked about the Mennonite Colonies in Paraguay and was told that they were the most successful colonies in all of South America." P. C. replied, "Yes, I was there a little over a year ago, and I found that they had done some marvelous things in seven years." Harold Bender then added, "I was there too and I found that they make ends meet, but they don't have a navy or army." The president laughingly rejoined that under those conditions he could balance the budget too.

(6) The passing of the Burke-Wadsworth Bill, known as the Selective Service Act, September 16, 1940. Section 5G, which dealt with conscientious objectors, was as liberal as the peace churches hoped it would be. One month later Dr. Clarence Dykstra became the director of Selective Service and was asked to designate work of national importance for conscientious objectors.

(7) The formation of the National Service Board for Religious Objectors (NSBRO), October 5, 1940, to

provide an agency through which the peace churches would work in dealing with Selective Service, represented by Lt. Col. Lewis B. Hershey. Thus the machinery was established to set up the Civilian Public Service camps.

(8) The crucial meeting with General Hershey in December when it was discovered that the government could not fund the camps. Early in the morning, prior to the official meeting, a prayer meeting was held, and P. C. asked the Mennonite representatives what the Mennonites might do if asked to finance the whole program: "Do you think we can do that?" P. C. asked. Orie Miller looked at P. C. and said, "Have our brethren ever let us down when we had a real case to present before them?" In the official meeting Hershey asked, "Are your people willing to undertake this job even if it will cost you a great deal of money?" There was silence for a while, and then Orie, with deep and sincere conviction, spoke up, "By the help of God we will try."

(9) The day in May 1941, when the first CPS camp was opened. By the end of the war 151 units were scattered over thirty-four states, Puerto Rico, and the Virgin Island. In addition to forestry and soil conservation, services included experimental research in biology, meteorology, and agriculture. Other projects included community education, recreational and health programs, public health, mental hospital work, guinea pig projects, dairy farm work, and fire fighting. From 1941 to 1947, 11,996 men served their country through CPS. Of this total, 4,665 were Mennonites. The CPS men received no pay, but were given a monthly allowance from the MCC amounting to $1.50 to $5.00.

(10) His favorite CPS unit, the Smoke Jumper Camp, stationed in the midst of the forest to watch for fires. "It was interesting to see the huge parachutes come down.

Even though the hazards were quite considerable, the morale was high because most of the young men felt that they were really risking something and doing a genuine work in the interest of their country."

(11) VJ day in Akron, Pennsylvania, during the summer of 1945. A group of young teenagers, celebrating the U.S. victory over Japan, invaded the MCC headquarters and heckled the conscientious objectors. The vandals threw potatoes through the windowpanes, tore the clothes off one Mennonite boy, threatened to throw a rope around the neck of another, and insulted the workers. When P. C. returned in the evening from a business trip, the situation was tense. During the next few days, through positive leadership on the part of the campers, this incident led to a better understanding between the MCC unit and the community. Responsible citizens of the Akron community expressed regret for the incident, and the Mennonite workers responded by distributing six hundred pounds of fish in the community as an expression of good will.

(12) A trip to Germany in August 1945, to deal with displaced Mennonites in Europe after the war. P. C. was deeply impressed by the work of C. F. Klassen and Peter and Elfrieda Dyck in caring for over 1,000 refugees in a Berlin camp. The saga of the miraculous trip from Rotterdam harbor to Buenos Aires on the *S. S. Volendam* was one of the miracles of MCC services. P. C. was in Buenos Aires shortly after their arrival. Temporary living quarters had been provided for the refugees in a tent city: "We were worrying about how these campers were getting along. So I went there quite early and found the camp flooded. Many of the tents had water in them which compelled the occupants to pile up their clothing and belongings on beds and chairs while walking barefoot. I expressed my sympathy at their hardship

and one man said, 'Why this isn't hard yet, it isn't cold. We have slept in sub-zero weather in the open air when we were fleeing Russia.' A certain stoicism and willingness to bear responsibility was apparent." Warned that they would have to build their own huts in Paraguay, one woman said, "That won't be difficult, we can put up those mud huts ourselves; it won't take us long. Just so we have liberty and freedom and a chance to make a living again."

(13) Serving as chairman of the Program Planning Committee and president of the fourth Mennonite World Conference in 1948, held first at Goshen College in Goshen, Indiana, and then at Bethel College, North Newton, Kansas. In retrospect P. C. said of this conference, "It will stand as a monument of united effort and a united service where people that had never worked together were drawn into one great program and learned to understand each other better and realized that we were all serving the same Lord even though we had different methods of approach because of varying backgrounds."

All these experiences and more were symbolized in the medallion he received from the German government. P. C. expressed deep appreciation for the Grand Cross, but it was another cross that had compelled him to become involved in burden bearing—the cross of Jesus Christ, the supreme expression of love and self-sacrifice for suffering humanity. The Christ of Calvary invited his disciples to "take up thy cross." The disciple's cross, to Peter Hiebert, was not a medal of honor or a badge of merit, but an invitation to join Christ in the ministry of reconciliation: to suffer, to sacrifice, to love, to forgive, even to die if necessary in an expression of redemptive and dynamic love.

He was seventy-five years old now—too old for

strenuous work. His physician advised him not to drive the family car anymore. Katherine drove the green Plymouth when they went shopping, when they went to church, or when they went out for a ride to enjoy the countryside.

Peter Hiebert, however, could not quit. Although his health hampered his activity, he continued to teach a men's Sunday school class, to serve on the church council, and to maintain office hours at the Mennonite Brethren Conference office building. During the last three years of his life, with the help of a secretary, he wrote the *Memoirs*, the basis for this biographical sketch.

Peter Hiebert died on May 27, 1963, at the age of eighty-five in Hillsboro's Salem Hospital, believing that the fragmentary pieces of his human experience would somehow fit, through no merit of his own, into a great design ordered by the Lord of life and harmonized by perfect divine love.

Peter Hiebert's life was deeply colored by the Anabaptist vision of radical Christian discipleship, and he spent much of his life in recovering this vision. Beyond the medallion, which he had received from Germany, he saw two crosses—the cross of atonement for man's irresponsibility and the disciple's cross inviting Christ's followers to responsible discipleship. These two crosses gave unity and purpose to his life.

6.
Edna
Ruth
Byler

By
Marion
Keeney
Preheim

Joe was gone. Up to that fall in 1941 Edna Byler's life had pivoted around her husband, Joe, and their two children, Donna Lou and Delmar. She would always put high priority on being a good wife and mother. Joining the Mennonite Central Committee "family" in Akron as hostess, however, would take Edna in directions undreamed of when she married J. N. Byler, nine years her senior. And she did not know how much he would be gone from home in his role as MCC relief director.

Events that catapulted her into the MCC setting moved swiftly, almost too fast. The Byler family spent summers away from Hesston College where J. N. taught history, economics, sociology, and manual training. A finished carpenter, he earned money during the summer months at that trade.

Usually they went to Colorado, but the summer of 1941 they were invited to Washington, D.C., and decided to go there for a change. In July, Edna and the children went up to Akron, Pennsylvania, to visit Annie

Wolf, mother-in-law to MCC Executive Secretary Orie Miller. Edna's roots went back to Lancaster County. She had many relatives there including Annie Wolf.

Edna visited Main House, the large Wolf family house that Orie Miller had converted into an MCC office, dining, and dorm quarters. Personnel there took note of where J. N. Byler was because they were interested in having Mennonite college teachers aid men in Civilian Public Service (CPS) camps.

In August, MCC asked J. N. to be educational director at a CPS camp in Bluffton, Indiana. Having been a conscientious objector in World War I, he felt the tug to serve. He got a year's leave of absence from Hesston. He and Edna returned to Kansas to settle household affairs and on September 3 the family went to Bluffton.

Just after they drove into camp, J. N. was told he had a call from MCC Akron asking him to go as relief director to the unoccupied area of France, working out of the southern city of Lyon. J. N. went to Akron immediately. The family stayed in Bluffton for several weeks. He came back to get them for the train ride to Pennsylvania. Ernest Bennett, Orie Miller's assistant, met them in a Ford, MCC's only car.

By October 4 Joe was gone. Edna and the two children were living in two rooms upstairs in Main House. Edna Byler was to become somewhat of a legend in her own time in Mennonite circles, but no one knew much about this diminutive 36 year old woman at the time. She was at first J. N. Byler's wife given the typical female role of hostess.

She took that role seriously. The stream of CPS men and office secretaries who began arriving early in 1942, most of whom stayed for the war's duration, still refer to their group as the "MCC family." They credit Edna for the ingenuity she used in welding them together.

Edna's Early Years

Of course, Edna did not emerge overnight with the characteristics that were to become her trademarks. She grew up in a Kansas community that was really Pennsylvania Dutch. Her father, Benjamin Miller, had come from Elizabethtown, Pennsylvania. Her mother, Anna Mary Weaver, had relatives all over Lancaster County.

Born May 22, 1904, Edna early showed signs of having a mind of her own. Around age four she insisted one day she was going to speak only English although she had been only German-speaking up to that time. The family had a lot of fun hearing her attempts. During Edna's early years she played at home most of the time with her three brothers Roy, Oliver, and Paul.

Edna attended a one-room school and a Pennsylvania Mennonite church composed of Amish Mennonites and Mennonites. The church group was innovative in such things as evangelistic services, the Sunday school, a library, and service.

Edna's love of music began early. Her mother had to lift her up on the platform the first time she sang in church. Around the age of six she started playing the family organ. Later Edna's father, known to dote on his only daughter, promised to buy her a piano if she did well on the organ. One day when she was about ten, she came home from school and saw a new piano in the front parlor. As Edna grew older she sang for weddings and church gatherings and on the radio.

Just as music threaded its way through her life, so did illness. Around the age of ten she got very sick. In much pain, she screamed for hours on end. Her parents took her to different doctors, but nobody could find the trouble. Being near death, they had surgery performed to see what was wrong. They found her appendix in the center rather than on the side.

After the operation the doctor told her father she could have anything she wanted to drink. Not liking water or milk, she told her father she wanted a bottle of strawberry pop. He bought her two bottles.

Later on illness was to reappear, but not before Edna spent some happy years at Hesston, graduating from the academy in 1923. It was while she was at Hesston College that J. N. Byler noticed her, an attractive young woman with natural curly brown hair.

J. N.

J. N. had behind him a tragic story. Born in 1895, his Amish father died when J. N. was three, leaving his mother with six children. She remarried a man with eight children and they had three more. J. N. left home early and went to Iowa where he became a Mennonite and took up carpentry.

J. N. looked foward eagerly to his first marriage at the age of 23. The day after the wedding, on their way to visit relatives, the train he and his bride were in wrecked, killing her.

Just at the tail end of World War I, J. N. was drafted. He took the conscientious objector position, but was sent to a military camp. Much to the consternation of the military personnel, he refused to wear a uniform or carry arms. While serving his term someone asked him, "Wouldn't you like to do relief work?" Not knowing that would ever happen, J. N. replied, "Yes. I would like to do relief work."

That would not happen for another 20 years. Instead, J. N. went on to school. He had only had several years of elementary school as a young Amish boy, but his mother had predicted that some day he would do further studies. He did finish high school at Hesston

Academy in two and a half years and then attended Hesston College. He completed a master's degree program at the University of Nebraska in Lincoln. He taught first at Harvard, Nebraska, high school, and then at Hesston College. He and Edna were married in 1925. He was 30, Edna was 21. By 1928 they had their first child, Donna Lou. Delmar was born in 1930.

The Depression: "We Weren't Poor"

The coming of the depression directly affected their family. Hesston College could not pay faculty salaries. J. N. had a job, but no income. They lost the house they were buying because they could not pay the mortgage. Hesston allowed them to live in a house owned by the college in order to give J. N. something of what they owed him. He chopped wood to get extra money or food. In one six-month period he earned only one silver dollar. The rest was barter.

However, the family never really worried about having enough to eat because they were part of a community. "We weren't poor," the children say. "We just didn't have money." They did not have a car for a number of years during the depression. They had a garage which they let someone use in exchange for taking Edna to Newton to shop, where food was cheaper, and to the doctor's.

Medical help for Edna became a necessity during those years as she fell extremely ill. Going to several doctors, one finally diagnosed her problem as undulant fever, an infectious disease usually transmitted through raw milk. The infection caused a cycle of intermittent fever with pain, headache, night sweats, and great weakness. She took all kinds of medicine, but she did not get well. The doctor gave her six months to live. J. N. decided to borrow a car and money to take her to

Mayo Clinic in Rochester, Minnesota. Doctors there discovered she had an allergic reaction to certain foods and prescribed medicines. She got better after her visit to the clinic.

Even when ill, Edna faced life with an indomitable spirit. She taught public school music to help make ends meet. To add further to the family income she kept college students in her home, charging them for room and board. They sometimes brought the Bylers eggs, meat, and produce from their families' farms.

Edna evidenced her hospitable nature despite her illness. If she felt the least bit better, she would invite guests for a meal. One of the ways the community judged a hostess was by whether she could invite somebody on short notice and be able to come up with something creative to eat. Once a family came on a Sunday previous to the one on which Edna had invited them. No one could tell she had fixed a last-minute meal until little slivers of pie appeared for dessert.

Edna's flair for serving the unusual can probably be traced back to her father. He would bring the family various kinds of treats. They especially remember his raw oysters and big, black olives. One time Edna served squab to a bunch of students. Some of the students had caught them in the Hesston College barn. Her children recall her serving other different meats like brain and sweetbreads. She also did up dishes of spinach, asparagus, and dandelion greens that they eventually learned to relish.

Edna developed her baking skills during those years, doing cakes when her arms were too swollen to work a handbeater. Her father bought her an electric beater to make it easier for her and came by one evening with it. She was so excited she stayed up late into the night baking a cake.

Each summer during the Hesston years the family went to Colorado where J. N. did carpentry work. While there, Edna often had people who were away from home into her home. The Byler family had a picnic out every night because the little house they lived in was so hot. They included others in their outings. During the summers Delmar fished and Edna treated the little trout he brought home as if they were a gourmet delicacy. J. N. made his fishing equipment from a pipe found on his job, a string, and a cork.

From 1939 to 1940 the Bylers lived the whole year in Boulder, Colorado. J. N. had been spending some time during the summers working towards his PhD degree. That year he had a teaching assistant position in sociology at the University of Colorado and finished his classwork requirements for a PhD. Despite the sacrifice this meant for the family, Edna stood by Joe in his goals. During his MCC years, Joe often talked about going back to get his degree, but he never did.

For Christmas that year in Boulder they went to the hills and cut their own tree. Delmar told school friends that they had no decorations along with them. One friend said his family had new electric lights and the Bylers could use their old ornaments. They turned out to be beautiful handblown, antique bulbs. That year was hard on the Bylers' budget. Delmar helped out by collecting gunnysacks full of pop bottles for which he got a refund. Sometime in December J. N. decided to stop using the car. He jacked it up so the tires would not rot, disconnected the car battery, and drained the water out of the radiator. Other neighbors did the same thing so the Bylers did not feel too different.

By Easter the family's finances were such that all of Edna's creativity was needed for the Sunday noon meal. Ham was too expensive. Somehow the cheap calf heart she served seemed quite tasty.

Despite hard times during the depression and following while J. N. went to school, the Byler children feel their parents made it a happy time. They remember how their father used his carpentry skills to construct a doll bed and cupboard for Donna Lou and a sled for Delmar.

In Kansas they spent Thanksgiving, Christmas, and New Year's days with the Miller family. For Christmas they had turkey, but for New Year's day Edna's father always brought oyster stew no matter where the gathering was. For those who did not like oysters he began bringing fresh salmon.

When they left for Washington, D.C., the summer of 1941, they had no idea Christmas would not be in Kansas that year. They did look forward to being near other relatives. Edna and J. N. had not been to visit relatives back East since 1926, the year after their marriage.

Clarence Horst, a former student of J. N.'s, had invited him to do carpentry work in Washington. On the way out the Bylers visited relatives in Indiana and Ohio. Edna's cousin, Joe Weaver, was working in Washington for the National Service Board of Religious Objectors. They moved into his basement, putting up a series of drapes to divide the room. Every weekend they went somewhere with the Weavers.

To Akron and MCC

But one weekend Edna took the children up to Akron, not realizing it would be a watershed event in her life. By September the Bylers themselves were living in Akron. They came at a critical time for MCC. Drafted men during World War II greatly expanded its program. Both Edna and J.N. played key roles in Akron.

The influx of Civilian Public Service men at the Akron headquarters began in 1942. The first to come was Otto Sommers. Then followed Emil Thiessen, Esko Loewen, Richard Ebersole, Robert Kreider, and Marlin Lauver.

In 1943 Ray Schlichting, Elmer Ediger, Irvin Richert, William Snyder, Irvin Horst, Royal Snyder, and Roy Miller arrived. Many of the men lived in an old garage fixed up as a dormitory which they called "The Monastery."

MCC hired its first secretaries: Laura Histand, Ruth Brunk Stoltzfus, Helen Lehman, Edna Weber, Donna Yoder, Rhoda Hess, Lillian Wenger, Gladys Derstine, and Berdella Blosser.

Edna grew with MCC. She created not just a place, but a home, so that the group began calling themselves "the MCC family." Edna encouraged them to work hard, but she also cared about how they got along with each other.

Edna did the little extras for meals she had learned to do for her own family. Knowing what young people were like, she figured out snacks they could have when raiding the refrigerator. She catered to workers who had special recipe needs, such as for borscht and zwieback, and picked up Lancaster County specialities like chicken corn soup.

Learning to cope with wartime rationing, sugar substitutes, and scarcity of meat were part of her job. Edna tried to keep the costs down to 12 cents a meal. She always seemed to know where to get things. She would shop around for the best bargains. Regular delivery men came with meat, pretzels, and milk. Often peddlers appeared at the door.

As new workers kept coming she added more tables inside Main House and on the back porch. Guests passing through Akron joined the group for meals. Edna did the cooking at first, but then Royal Snyder, who had been a CPS camp cook, replaced her. This freed her to take care of the increasing hostess duties. She still planned the menus and supervised the buying.

For the household chores Edna organized the group, men and women. They did the dishes. She required all of them to take turns doing the laundry for the group even though some of the fellows objected to doing it. For spring and fall housecleaning local Mennonite girls came in to help, but Edna expected everyone to help.

Once Edna engineered a gift for the men in "The Monastery." Some women who worked in a knitting mill brought a bunch of the mill's products for the men. Included were knit pajamas that would stretch way out and snap back. The men had a lot of fun wearing the pajamas and taking photographs of themselves. Some put their arms in the legs for special effect.

Edna was busy, but she missed Joe terribly. In November 1942, unoccupied France fell to the Germans. Everyone assumed J. N. was captured and would be interned as other relief workers had been. He managed, however, to cross the border into Spain three days before the defeat, borrowed money from a Quaker woman, and found a ship to take him back home.

By the time J. N. returned on November 29, 1942, having been gone over a year, the group was affectionately calling Edna "Mrs. B." J. N.'s report to the MCC Annual Meeting in December read, "During my year's service in the field an average of 7,112 individuals per month were given help of some kind." In 1943, MCC assigned J. N. to work on mental health concerns that were developing.

The Bylers together left the stamp of their special character on MCC life in Akron. Many of the workers came from the Midwest and West. Edna and Joe, having roots in Kansas and Lancaster County, served as a bridge in helping people feel more at home in the conservative Eastern setting.

They felt particularly sensitive about MCC's relationship to the local church, wanting the organization to be accepted. Edna went to women's sewing circles to talk about MCC. J. N. gave talks on relief to the churches. Once plain-coated J. N. was giving a talk at the large Blooming Glen Mennonite Church in eastern Pennsylvania. About 1,000 people turned out. J. N. took along a quartet of CPS men, but special music was frowned on in many churches at that time, and the quartet had no idea whether he was able to arrange for them to be on the program or not. At the end of the service the minister said the benediction. He then announced that an MCC quartet would sing over the loudspeaker system piped into homes of shut-ins and anyone could stay to listen. The quartet proceeded to give its concert.

Edna tried to arrange something that did not turn out so well. Local Mennonite churches were quite careful about whom they included for communion, but she was able to get the Ephrata Mennonite Church to include the MCCers in their communion. Much to her chagrin, one of the girls came to church in a bright red dress. Edna never tried to arrange for communion there again.

The MCC Akron unit had chapel together each workday at 11:30 a.m., taking turns within the unit and using people visiting the Akron office. They did a lot of singing together.

As time went on, Edna's work increased. She had to organize for large groups of people. She planned the food for training schools of educational directors and administrators for CPS camps. Meetings of MCC unit leaders for mental hospitals required her assistance.

Her energy seemed unbounded. She undertook large canning operations to help the MCC food budget. She processed early spring peas through a Maytag wringer with a shield on it to prevent the peas from popping away. J. N. had first devised that for her in Kansas when she began canning for her family.

She had a gift of mobilizing people to work. She accepted bushels of rejected peaches given to MCC and enticed everyone to help can them. One summer Richard Yoder, Ralph Kaufman, J. Winfield Fretz, and John Howard Yoder, each with a doctor's degree of one kind or another, were awaiting passage to go abroad. She had them snap beans, peel potatoes, and do other manual chores.

She discovered that, although Mennonite women in the area were good cooks, many of them bought their bread. In Kansas she had perfected her yeast baking, using a recipe for rolls and doughnuts that had mashed potatoes in it. And so she began giving baking demonstrations to small groups of women in her home and then in churches. She had a large kettle with a paddle for turning the dough. She would require women to return several weeks after the demonstration, having baked twice, and to bring a sample of their products for her to test.

Her main effort, however, centered around the MCC unit and her family. In addition to the normal routine, she planned for holidays. When leap year came in 1944 she helped organize a party for February 29. The girls invited the fellows for dates. Three couples continued the relationship and finally married.

Special events meant a lot to the MCCers, particularly the CPS men. Because army men were highly restricted, CPS men were put under similar requirements. A few of the men married during their lengthy term of service, but the government did not allow their wives to live in Akron. Some lived in Lancaster, ten miles away. The husbands could visit them one weekend a month, but the wives could come to Akron from time to time. They remember the retreats MCC held at a Mennonite-owned cabin in northern Lancaster County.

Karen was born early in 1945 to Richard and Geraldine Ebersole, an MCC couple. Edna went upstairs in Main House and found a beautiful old-fashioned cradle left by the Wolf family. She brought it down for the baby to use on its visits to Akron.

During the war years the Akron unit had little turnover. As the war ended, the longer term CPS men were ready for discharge. Mrs. B. felt her MCC family was breaking up. An era was ending. By 1945 her children were also gone from home a good bit of the time. Donna Lou had started at Hesston Academy in 1942 and Delmar in 1945, coming home for summers.

Helping Others Help Themselves

New beginnings, however, were to open up. In 1947 a group that would eventually be called the Monterey Mennonite Church formed. Edna and J. N. became charter members and a number of MCCers began attending there. The Bylers joined the group while still maintaining good ties with other churches.

That same year another new venture started for Edna. She accompanied J. N. on a ten-day administrative trip to Puerto Rico. It was Edna's first plane trip, and she was afraid to sit back in her seat for fear she would tip the plane. MCCers met the Bylers in an old MCC station wagon, wanting to show them how badly they needed a new one. They put Edna up front and J. N. in the back with the MCCers. The truck broke down on the way to the MCC location, and they had to go the rest of the way by bus. J. N. later interceded and got them a new vehicle.

On that visit Edna became fascinated with embroidered linens the Puerto Rican women made. MCCer Mary Lauver was working with them. The women desperately needed more income to supplement their meager family incomes, and local markets did not buy enough of their work. Touched by their plight, Edna promised to do what she could.

On graph paper Mary Lauver drew the designs available and wrote down the prices. Edna planned to take orders and send them back to be filled. How she would do this she did not know.

Soon after her return she received an invitation to speak about MCC at the Lancaster Associated Sewing Circles. They placed some orders. Soon other women began asking her to their homes and churches. Some who had learned to make her doughnuts and rolls now asked to see the MCC needlework. Women responded to her practical call to help feed the hungry. At the top of production, MCC employed 30 women in Puerto Rico.

Edna began traveling across the United States, sometimes with J. N. when he was speaking on MCC relief in which he was engaged in again. She added embroidery work from Jordan to what she had to offer. She made up a kit of samples to send to churches which she could not visit. MCC did not see this as a project in which there should be investment, so several friends of Edna's gave needed capital. But Edna never wavered in seeing the value of the program and kept up a system of orders which sometimes took up to a year to fill. As the work went on, they standardized the sizes to make it easier to manage.

By the time the Puerto Rico project closed in the early

Edna Ruth Byler

1950s, Edna had sold over $30,000 worth of goods from there. Women in Puerto Rico stopped their needlework activity when they found they could get other more gainful employment. The Jordan work continued.

The Bylers were both becoming more and more world-minded. In September 1949, Edna went with J. N. to Europe. In her diary she wrote, "I saw my first refugee camp. Darkness. Lack of tasty food and comfort. Yet the refugees are pleased with what has been done."

Because of the effect the refugees had on her she wrote later on the trip, "Today I saw a meat market. I wonder if I will ever want to eat meat or ice cream or even fancy cake in Germany."

Edna retained her hostess job until 1951, learning to

relate to all kinds of people. She could, for example, be found approaching MCC administrators for something she wanted one day. The next day she might be entertaining several little preschool girls with her best china.

A change came about in 1951 because MCC asked the Bylers to go to Hong Kong. There Edna taught machine sewing to Chinese refugee women and baking and English to her household servants. Joe's main activity was getting ready for relief to go into Korea after the war. He also was in charge of aid in The Philippines, Taiwan, Indonesia, and Hong Kong itself.

They returned home in 1952 going through India, Jordan, and Europe, where Edna looked into local needlework wherever she could. Back in Akron once again, she picked up what she called the MCC Needlework and Crafts Program. And she began enjoying her grandchildren who eventually numbered eight.

Up to 1954 the Bylers had lived in rented rooms, houses, cottages, and apartments since losing their house during the depression. They bought an unfinished house at 122 North Eleventh Street in Akron and worked on it themselves. Starting in 1958, in a modest way, they began a gift shop in the basement. Joe, having retired that year, helped out.

Edna also branched out into some other activities. She began helping with the Pennsylvania Relief Sale around 1958, several years after its beginning. She coordinated the food and quilt sales. One year she predicted they would make $50,000. No one believed her, but she was right. MCC used the money from the sales for relief.

Yet she not only enlisted others to bring food. She also made things herself, such as a cake from scratch. Early on the sale day, she went around collecting pies from people out in the country and picked up dozens of doughnuts she made sure were done during the night. At the sale's end, she often bought food and treated neighbors and friends that evening and the next day.

Edna continued helping with the Relief Sale until several years before her death. Even then she kept in touch. The spring before she died she gave money to treat all the people selling MCC needlework and crafts.

She also helped with the Black Rock Camp sale each year, chairing their Food Committee. She assigned people to bring food, such as strawberry pies, hamburger, hot dogs, and chicken corn soup. The day of the sale she herself gathered homemade bread, catsup, mustard, or whatever was needed. Providing money for the stands, she kept tabs on them during the sale and collected the money afterwards. Profits made at the sales went for supporting underprivileged city children who attended the Black Rock Camp. Edna kept working at the sale until her health failed.

Toward the end of the 1950s a new church group started in Akron out of the mother church at Monterey. The Bylers joined Akron Mennonite Church, becoming charter members of a church for a second time. Using her gift with food, she helped weld the group together by organizing fellowship meals. Being one of the oldest people in the church, Edna became a "grandmother" for a whole host of children. She often took candy into the nursery. When youth were baptized, she gave them each a gift.

"Making Adjustments"

Life seemed full and good, and then in 1962 Joe was gone. He died of congestive heart failure at the age of 67. The years when he traveled for MCC were perhaps preparation for what she would face in her widowhood.

Edna grieved, but not excessively. Friends found as the years went by that she talked a lot about Joe. He became a personality even to persons who had not known him.

With his death, arrangements were made with MCC for Edna's employment. Her years before that had all been volunteer work, but now she needed to have assurance of some income. Still having a debt on the house, she went about in earnest building up the gift business in her basement while also doing the MCC Needlework and Crafts program.

Those who worked for her felt they were her friends. If she went away on an MCC trip, they missed the activity and excitement she created when she was around. One person said, "If something wasn't doing in her shop, she had something going on in her kitchen."

After a buying trip for her shop, she might say, "Did I go too wild?" But she did have a knack for selecting things that would sell. And she tried to pass bargains on to her customers. A keen businesswoman, she always knew in what financial shape her enterprise was. She did a lot of her business by phone feeling she would get better service that way.

Packing her car for an MCC trip, Edna would drive out to Kansas, for example, stopping at churches from which she had received invitations all along the way and back. She did not seem to mind going alone. She would say, "They want me there," and off she would go.

When at home, she used her place as a gathering point for people. Friends remember some of her favorite expressions. When something bothered her, it would give her "the hoot owls." When something bad happened to anyone, she encouraged them by saying it would help to keep them humble. One bit of advice she often gave was "All you have to do in life is make adjustments."

She had her peculiarities. Whenever she got a call to go somewhere or see someone, she would quickly wash her hair which had turned a silvery gray. Having a car accident once, she bought a white one with red upholstery "so they can see me coming." Although not physically disabled when older, she would use a wheelchair at airports like Chicago to get to her next plane.

Take a Minute

By 1970 the MCC Needlework and Crafts Program had grown from mostly needlework to include woodcarvings, bamboo mats and trays, sweaters, slippers, and many other items. It would eventually change names and become the Self-Help Program. Products were coming in from 11 countries: West Bank, Jordan, Haiti, India, Taiwan, Thailand, Bolivia, Korea, Hong Kong, Tanzania, and Paraguay. The majority of items were made where MCC units were located, and most of the others were connected with Mennonite missions or missions of another denomination.

Edna ordered everything directly from the producer. MCC consciously made a policy of this. Executive Secretary William Snyder wrote on May 19, 1970, "I would like to say with all honesty that everything the public purchases at our Material Aid Center is going to help the individual who produced it. I think this is a policy that we should follow and one with which all of us will be happy for time and eternity."

MCC released a filmstrip called "Take a Minute" in 1970 to depict the Self-Help Program. It shows women overseas doing everyday chores and then sewing on needlework. It describes how Edna Byler became interested in marketing the products and how the enterprise grew. It ends finally by saying, "Many skillful eager hands are idle. Take a minute to think about these hands. Strong hardworking hands. Patient, skillful hands. Sensitive, artistic hands. Take a minute."

Edna Byler retired from MCC service at the end of 1970. At the Annual Meeting in January 1971 William Snyder spoke in recognition of her. He presented her with a certificate of service and a photo of her and J. N.

Edna continued with the Byler Gift Shop, which she never advertised except by word of mouth and had no sign out front to draw people to it. Many came, however, from all over.

The last several years of her life she suffered from failing health. Then came the time when the doctor told her after exploratory surgery that she had a terminal tumor. When she came home, Edna never again went downstairs to her shop. Once a worker got her to the top of the stairs, but she remained firm about her decision. She did not say why she did not want to go down, but those close to her sensed she had accepted what was to happen.

Edna had always said life was an adjustment and she was prepared to make the final one. She still showed her joy in life by buying a piano to fill those last few months with music. Edna Ruth Byler died on July 6, 1976.

7.
Susie
Rutt

By
Marion
Keeney
Preheim

Susie still could not forget the deep concern of three years ago. In 1946, the doctor had predicted that her husband, Peter Rutt, would not survive a rheumatic fever attack. His heart, weakened by the same illness in his teens, was probably not strong enough for this second struggle, the doctor said.

Susie's pastor at the Ephrata Mennonite Church, Ephrata, Pennsylvania, passed word on to other churches in the Lancaster County area for others to pray for Peter's recovery. He did get well. "We felt God healed him," Susie says, "but we knew this did not necessarily mean that everything in the future would be taken care of."

Then in 1949 came the call for someone to work part time at the Ephrata Clothing Center run by Mennonite Central Committee (MCC). Susie already served as a volunteer there, especially during the times when they had extra work. J. N. Byler, MCC material aid director, asked if someone would like to work three days a week in the center. Susie volunteered to do the work, asking that she receive less than a regular salary.

Jim King Photo

Susie Rutt

The Family

Susie thought through carefully whether to work or not. Most women, especially Mennonite women, did not work outside the home at that time. But with the support of her family, her in-laws, and her husband, she made the decision to take the job.

Her husband's parents owned the duplex in which both families lived. The children often went over to the other side to be with their grandmother. The transition for her to care for the three children during the day went smoothly.

Peter not only endorsed Susie's working at the center, but at times helped her with the actual work. He held a job as maintenance supervisor of a fleet of diesel trucks for M. Simon Zook Company in Honeybrook, Pennsylvania, fifteen miles from Ephrata. The trucks hauled molasses from Baltimore to western Pennsylvania. As supervisor he could sometimes take off when Susie needed his help in the material aid work. Peter's Mennonite employer, Mr. Zook, willingly allowed him time off for Clothing Center work. During Peter's illness in 1946, Zook stood by ready to give him his job back when he recovered.

Cans, Sacks, and Bales

With her family's support, Susie plunged into the work in the fall of 1949. At that time the demand for clothing came mostly from three troubled spots in the overseas area: divided Germany, Palestine, and Korea. The political events that brought about these countries' divisions caused hardship for the people. Canned beef, sacks of flour, and bales of warm clothing left the MCC Clothing Center to aid refugees, displaced persons, and orphans.

"In those early days," Susie recalls, "we used to send

everything that people donated. But workers overseas found that they would get too much of one thing and not enough of another. We sent clothes to two children's orphanages in France, Viler and Valdoie. They would get lots of girls' dresses and boys' shirts, but few trousers and underwear. So we realized we had to change this."

Anna Myers, who worked with the Ephrata material aid goods for 30 years and had charge of the mending, remembers how they made the change. "We learned what had enough wear left in it to make it worth sending," she says. "The longer you're at the center, the more you know what should be sent and what should not." Anna also recalls how they used to count every piece, down to calling a pair of socks two items. Anna typed up the hundreds of items in each bale. The list went on the bale for custom officials checking the bales. Eventually, as the work load increased, they found that listing the general contents worked just as well.

Messages attached to donations sometimes amused or perplexed the staff. A package came one day with a pair of handknit men's socks. The giver had carefully darned and patched them. "You could just about tell they were socks and that was it," Susie says. The doner had a handwritten note with the socks saying, "I hope you can send this to someone in the North Pole."

They sometimes received things that would not be suitable to use overseas—an old horse harness, mattresses, furniture, and even a supply of used teabags which someone thought people overseas could use again.

Those early years still hold a certain color that the workers will never forget. People of the area called the Ephrata Clothing Center "the mission." The center allowed men whom the workers called "knights of the road" or "road walkers" to stop by to get clothing. They always had a box full of things in the vestibule that the men could have. The staff took turns having the responsibility of helping those who came to the door.

A man came in one day with long hair and dirty clothes in an age when only tramps looked like that. A volunteer who was working at the center said to the man, "Grandpa, you need a haircut. Can I give you one?" He cut the man's hair and the man kept thanking him and thanking him. "That took ten years off me," he said. Another tramp had a sore foot. Those at the center recommended that he go to the hospital. One of the fellows put Cloverine salve and some of the MCC homemade bandages on his foot.

Some of these visitors wanted eyeglasses. The workers gave them Bible tracts to read to test their eyes. Along with the glasses they gave them reading material to take with them.

They gave away extra items in this way, but Goodwill Industries and The Salvation Army took most of what they could not use. Each Tuesday for years a truck came from Wilmington, Delaware, to get boxes of clothing for The Salvation Army store there.

Susie Rutt, Director

Several years after Susie began work at the center, J. N. Byler asked her to serve as director. At the time they thought it would be an interim arrangement, but the person who had planned to come back did not return, and Susie stayed on as director.

As the MCC work spread from Europe into other parts of the world, the center staff tried to tailor bales going out to suit the culture of the people to whom they would go. For instance, Arabs in North Africa associated dark blue and black clothing with the Spanish and would not wear these colors. In most third world cultures, many women do not wear shorts, slacks, or short dresses.

The material aid people kept feeding information to the Mennonite world, and people adjusted their giving accordingly. *The Women's Activity Letter,* an MCC publication used to inform women's groups, began putting in specific requests. Staff people told groups coming in to help at the clothing center what was needed. The good quality of contributions that followed gave MCC a reputation for the way its people cared for the needy.

Christmas in a Bundle

Special requests sent in by those working abroad helped to clarify what should be sent. A letter came from workers in Germany who were planning a Christmas celebration for children. They had nothing to give the children. Mary Lehman, a volunteer at the center, came up with an innovative packaging idea.

She suggested that people make a bundle of clothing, toiletries, and a toy all held together by a towel and safety pins. The child receiving the bundle would thus be able to use its contents and wrappings.

MCC sent out information to the churches about giving a Christmas bundle. For the girls the bundle included a skirt, blouse, underwear, stockings, a sweater, toothpaste, a bar of soap, and a toy. The boy's bundle contained similar items with the outfit being a shirt and trousers. After several years, MCC eliminated the underwear and stockings from the request. Staff persons felt the reduction in the cost would increase the number of bundles given.

John Hostetler, presently the MCC material aid director, remembers handing out Christmas bundles while he was serving in the Black Forest area of Germany. "We opened all the bundles and sorted them before the children's Christmas program," he says. "I noticed one bundle was from an eighty-year-old woman I knew in West Liberty, Ohio. She got around in a walker, yet she made the effort to send a bundle. Another was from the family of a fellow I knew in CPS days."

They held the program for fatherless children. A quartet sang and an MCC worker told the Christmas story. At the program's end, they gave out the bundles. "Let's face it," Hostetler says. "It was touching. The children were all excited; the mothers were crying."

In Hong Kong, workers rented a gymnasium to hold the large children's Christmas party. With the bundle they gave a comic-style booklet on the entire life of Christ written in the local language.

Stories like these filtered back to those preparing the bundles for sending overseas and made them feel they were part of the process. Susie went around to churches giving talks on Christmas bundles. In 1969, the number of Christmas bundles sent crested at 56,913 bundles that one year. The total given by July 1976, was approximately 950,000. The bundles came mostly from individuals rather than from groups. A few persons made 50 to 100 bundles on their own. One woman in Hesston, Kansas, made 60 each year and a family in Lititz, Pennsylvania, made 100.

Another Inquiry

Susie remembers another special request that also had an interesting ending. Peter Dyck, MCC European director, wrote asking for three bales of warm shirts and wool trousers and three bales of woolen yard goods. His wife, Elfrieda Dyck, and Doreen Harms were working in a program to send packages of clothing to Mennonites in Russia.

Susie didn't know how they would meet the deadline. "A bale contained about 300 garments," she says. "At that time the cheapest wool trousers ran about $8.00 a pair. And we only had about three weeks to get them ready."

She contacted the MCC treasurer's office, but they did not have money for the purchases. The Lancaster County sewing circles only had limited funds, not enough to cover the high price of shirts and trousers. They couldn't reach all the churches soon enough, so they only made contacts locally.

Only two days remained before the shipping date when a van from Maryland drove in loaded with bolts of dark blue and maroon woolen yardage material. They had not heard about the special need, but simply had bought up some yardage on sale.

Another vehicle arrived the following day from Chambersburg, Pennsylvania, a town 100 miles away. In they came with scores of woolen trousers. The churches, Mennonite as well as others, had bought the whole stock for MCC. They had not known about the special shipment, either, nor did they call ahead to say they were coming. They simply loaded up and came.

The requested woolen shirts came from the local people and the shipment left in time. "It was the Lord's doing," Susie says. "It was things like that that kept me going in the work. Sometimes things were rough, but I knew God was working."

Kits for Sewing and School

Workers asking for specifics kept shaping the material aid program. Some wanted yardage rather than dresses so that women could learn to sew and choose their own styles. MCC began to send sewing accessories and material in a drawstring bag. This included various colored thread, scissors, a tape measure, pins, embroidery cotton, and about three yards of material. This particularly appealed to youth groups as a way for them to give something specific.

The kits went mainly to Europe, but also started going to other parts of the world as MCC opened new areas of work. Many Third World women found the Western style clothing unsuitable for their culture and preferred to make the loose fitting dress of their country.

Later on the center designed quilt kits. These went mostly to German Mennonites in Paraguay. They used a large drawstring bag and included enough cut patches to make a 72 by 90 inch quilt, needles, thread, and yardage to finish the edges and make the backing.

Then those in education asked for school supplies. At first the center sent them in large drums only, but then they added the sending of school supplies in drawstring bags for individual children. Each bag contained pencils, a writing tablet, chalk, a chalk eraser, and crayons. Giving school kits caught on as a way for children to give to other children.

Leprosy Bundles

As the program developed, more special projects came into existence. Those working with leprosy patients asked for assorted items geared to meet their needs. The leprosy bundle included yardage suitable for a man's shirt or a woman's dress, a bar of soap, toothpaste, a toothbrush, and a nail clipper. Most of these bundles went to leprosariums, such as the ones in Paraguay and Burundi.

One woman in Lancaster, Pennsylvania, made 50 leprosy bundles each year. An internal revenue man came to check her accounts. His office could not believe that the woman was giving so much on such a small income. The woman was physically ill, but she felt she could serve by watching for bargains and buying for leprosy patients. The government official had a hard time accepting her story. The woman talked with Susie about her problem. Although she had saved her sales slips, she had not saved the receipt from the relief center. Susie gave her another one, and the IRS man seemed satisfied. The next year the Internal Revenue Service checked her again and found everything in order. She had kept her sales slips and center receipt for that year. They never bothered her again.

Relationship with Others

In 1967, the Apostolic Christian Church formed a world relief committee, but initially they had no specific program. When money came in, they looked around for a suitable place to give it.

They called in representatives from MCC, Heifer Project, and CARE. Robert Miller, the MCC overseas director at that time, went to their meeting. Each representative from the three groups told his story. The Apostolic Christians decided to support all three organizations.

Two sisters, Mary Ann and Mildred Fisher, were at the meeting. They saw a brochure called *MCC Projects for Your Church and Family* which had just come off the MCC press. It spelled out about 38 material aid and cash projects which women could do. These two women went back home all inspired. With their mother, they made all the sewing projects in the brochure. Then they opened their home for other women to come and make things to contribute to the MCC program.

After their projects were advertised in their local churches, the sisters began to get invitations to present

material aid projects in other churches. They traveled
as far as Connecticut and California to give demonstrations. One summer, they loaded up their car with
Christmas bundles and many other kinds of finished
products. They came to Akron to visit the central offices
and Material Aid Center.

"Susie helped the whole relationships with the Apostolic Christian Church to grow," John Hostetler says.
"She went to their annual district meeting once and to
their churches for speaking engagements. She encouraged the Fisher sisters' efforts. Susie was able to
make the material aid story exciting."

Susie knew well how to build relationships within
the Mennonite Church, too. She would let the churches
know what MCC needed and the things would start
coming into the center. She also had the ability to get
along with other staff members. Anna Myers spoke
about the spirit of the team working in the center.
"Sometimes it would get frustrating," she said. "But if
anything did happen between workers, we usually
thrashed it out until we were working together again."

MCC Material Aid Center

The workers look back nostalgically to those early
days in the Ephrata Clothing Center in the old Ephrata
Mennonite Church. With the increase in giving of material goods, however, the quarters became too small.

In 1971, they moved to a new location. No longer did
the "knights of the road" visit them. The name changed
from MCC Clothing Center to MCC Material Aid Center,
indicating that they processed more than clothing. It
also housed the Self-Help Gift Shop, formerly located in
Edna Byler's home in Akron, which sold items made by
needy people.

But the network of giving did not change. When they

needed to take care of some unusual request, the people responded. One time MCC needed a big truck to haul little pigs to Georgia. Susie informed several churches and soon had a truck lined up.

Another time, Urbane Peachey, then Middle East director, requested baby clothing. Donations always included more diapers than kimonos or sacks. The request came in on Thursday and the shipment was to go the following Wednesday.

Susie knew it would take several thousand items and that they had to do it locally because of lack of time. She contacted the secretary of the women's coordinating committee of the Lancaster County sewing circles.

"It isn't just bad news that travels fast," Susie says. "Even those from farther out sent in the kimonos and sacks. They started coming in and coming in. It was just fantastic. And we got the needed bales. This didn't always happen, but you could see the hand of God at work. There's no other explanation."

More and more people became interested in the material aid work. Women would come to work a day at a time on a regular basis or give a week or two of steady work. Some came in from as far away as Ohio and Virginia to give two or three weeks of work. The Amish started giving more and volunteering to help at the center. Some came from long distances bringing a busload of 40 to 60 people.

"I remember one Amish woman that had a baby about every year," Susie says. "She would always bring the children along, never missing a regular workday. The babies would play happily all day. The Amish train their children well, and they always seemed to behave in the center." Anna Myers recalls how the Amish wanted their children to have work to do. She found buttons and safety pins from the mending for them to sort. The older ones helped with the clothing.

The all-day volunteers brought their own packed lunches for the noon meal. Anna fixed coffee for them, feeling Susie had so many other things to do. After lunch some of the groups took time to sing before going back to work.

An older conservative man once said, "I think this is a foretaste of heaven." He meant that all kinds of Mennonites worked together—Brethren in Christ, General Conference, Old Mennonite, conservative Mennonite, and Amish. People of other denominations worked at the center, too. As the man concluded, "We all work together in the name of Christ."

"We didn't talk about politics or religion," Susie says. "Oh, we did talk about what the Lord does, but it wasn't 'Why do you do this or that that way?' "

Shift to Development

As certain major emergencies subsided and MCC emphasized country development more, the need for used clothing decreased. The material aid staff had to find ways to help the people in the churches make the transition from giving material goods that were expensive to ship to giving money.

John Hostetler made a statement on "material aid in the 70s" to help people understand what was happening. He outlined how MCC had responded to war and famine in the 1920s, to rehabilitation of Europe in the 40s, and to the needs in other countries in the 50s.

Then he wrote, "We have learned that giving material aid supplies to people in developing countries is a wonderful way to show compassion and share our abundance, but it is not sufficient in showing them how to rise above despair and experience the whole life with dignity.

"The majority of MCC workers feel," Hostetler continued, "that it is a greater challenge to be involved with teaching people in developing countries how to help themselves rather than only sharing material aid supplies. During the 1970s we anticipate a leveling off with shipping supplies overseas while increasing the sending of people with development skills."

Point by point, he followed with what this would mean in people's giving. MCC would need homemade bedding, used clothing, used shoes, laundry soap, and homemade bandages in limited amounts. Christmas, layette, and leprosy bundles should level off. MCC would need, however, an increased amount of bar soap, health kits, school supplies, sewing kits, sheets, towels, and yard material to undergird the medical, educational, and development projects.

Because of increasing shipping costs and lower cost of products within overseas countries, the statement continued, MCC would buy as much as possible in developing countries. For this buying and for supporting the development projects, MCC called for giving more money.

This new direction meant a shift for those in the Material Aid Center. How would they help the people understand what was happening? "It seemed like all we had to do was relate to the people and tell them why this was happening," Susie Rutt says. "We would explain while we were sorting clothes just why a certain thing would not be sent." They also placed photos of overseas development work around the center.

Susie felt the Self-Help shop in the center also helped people to understand other people's need to help themselves. They could see items in the shop made by people who might otherwise need material aid if they did not have work.

Susie willingly went to women's groups to explain the new emphasis. Churches within a radius of several hundred miles learned of Susie's ability to translate material aid work into an enthusiastic report and asked her to speak at their churches. She spoke in churches in Pennsylvania, Maryland, Virginia, and New York. She appeared regularly on the program of the semiannual Lancaster County sewing circles' meeting that included 90 to 100 churches.

Before going to a church, Susie found information on any special requests that had come in to MCC to share with her audience. These requests came in the periodic reports each volunteer sent to MCC. Susie often showed slides which workers contributed.

She would sometimes feature one country, such as Haiti, to show the material aid work being done, especially if the special requests were for that country. At the time she showed slides of Haiti, the special requests were for lightweight clothing, hospital supplies, towels, sheets, and pillowcases, all of which were needed in the Haitian setting.

As other needs developed, she solicited not only for material goods, but also for money. When the new Material Aid Center was being built, she went to quite a few churches to raise funds for it. She also encouraged groups to invite returning MCC workers to their meetings so they could hear about the work from someone who had been on the site.

The center staff had to think about what to do with the many volunteers who came into the center to work as the material aid goods leveled off. Some three to four hundred volunteers came in each month. "If we would have cut down on volunteers," Susie says, "people would have lost interest and stopped giving."

They decided to emphasize quiltmaking. The

comforter and mending room now also became the quilting room. As interest in quilts made a come-back in the American culture, quilt sales rose. Many volunteers came in to practice the art of quiltmaking. One 90-year-old woman came regularly every week.

Woman's Day, a magazine sold widely in grocery stores and on newstands, featured an article on Pennsylvania Dutch quiltmaking. The writer, Marilyn Lithgow, came to Susie to talk about the quilts produced by Mennonite women. A photographer came down from New York City to take pictures. Later Mrs. Lithgow wrote a book called *Quiltmakers and Quiltmaking* in which she talked about her Mennonite background and the art of their quiltmaking. She refers to the MCC relief sales in the book and the sale of quilts at them.

After the article appeared, over 2,000 letters came in to MCC requesting quilts and quilt patterns. Sometimes people wanting to buy a quilt placed their orders directly with the center. Olive Weaver, a long-term worker in material aid, took a call once from Michigan. A woman wanted a specific quilt made. Olive knew the quiltmakers were especially busy. She asked the others what to do.

"Let's put a big price on it so she won't take it," someone said. "Tell her it will be $400." Olive quoted that price. Much to her surprise, the woman accepted it and eventually paid that price for the quilt they made.

They also had an order from Australia for a certain quilt. The person described by letter what she wanted and included the payment in advance.

Relief Sales

The rise of relief sales provided a convenient outlet for the sale of quilts. Buyers from all over the country came to purchase quilts at the various Mennonite relief sales in the United States and Canada. In 1976, Susie hit on the idea of contributing quilt patterns and directions for making the quilts to sell at $1.00 a piece. They sold 260 patterns.

The first MCC relief sale began in the 1940s and still operates biannually on a farm near Gap, Pennsylvania. It wasn't until 1957 that another began. The Zion Mennonite Church of Birdsboro, Pennsylvania, started a Tri-County Relief Sale that included Lancaster, Chester, and Berks counties.

From these first two sales others mushroomed around the Mennonite world in Canada and the United States, bringing in cash by the thousands of dollars. In 1976, a congregation in Hokkaido, Japan, held their first MCC Relief Sale, netting $3,000.

Relief Shops

Another phenomenon that also boosted the need for converting used and homemade goods to cash was the many new relief shops that sprang up first in Canada and then in the United States. The women of three churches in Altona, Manitoba, joined together in 1971 to start the first shops in their area.

MCC Canada promoted the idea. "How can a good heavy coat be turned into light filmy saris that people in India and Bangladesh need?" John Wieler, associate executive secretary of MCC Canada, asked. "One way is to turn it into cash. Recent experience shows that a good used coat may be sold for approximately $15 here in Canada. In Calcutta, MCC can purchase 15 new saris with this same amount of money. The question is, how does one sell good used clothing?" The answer was community thrift or relief shops.

He outlined how women had organized shops by set-

ting up a committee, getting volunteer help and donations, keeping rent and other costs low, and giving the
proceeds to MCC. The shops also carried MCC self-help
items, which reinforced the story of development as the
new way to go. By 1976, $300,000 had come to MCC
relief shops.

Now the spirit of the Material Aid Center was spreading out into the grass roots. Just as the people in the
early days of the Ephrata Clothing Center built up an
esprit de corps, the women working in the thrift shops
found one of the chief benefits to be the new relationships they were building, the sense of community
as Mennonites which they developed.

They were also relating to others in a way they had
not been able to before. They were communicating with
persons who came into the shops to buy and with
those who brought in items for sale. The shops ended
up doing as much for the women who worked in them
as for the faraway recipients of aid overseas.

Retirement

Susie watched the clothing program grow and take
new forms during her 25 years with MCC material aid.
She saw Christmas, leprosy, and layette bundles plus
sewing, quilt, school, and medical kits pass through to
people who needed them. Carefully keeping account of
what went out, Susie made records which showed an
increase from ten to twenty tons a month and supplies
going to thirty countries during her work years.

Feeling that she had served her term long enough as
center director, Susie decided to retire. At the 1974
MCC annual meeting in Hillsboro, Kansas, the MCC
board gave recognition to Susie Rutt for "much time
and energy contributed to the work of the Mennonite
Central Committee." John Hostetler noted that Mrs.

Rutt, during her 26 years in Ephrata, "has been one of the most effective persons in communicating the work of MCC to interested constituents."

He commented further, "With Susie there is no energy crisis. She has the attitude that there's always room for one more volunteer—young or old, conservative or liberal, rural or urban."

Susie retired from work at the center, but not from work. If you visit the Rutt home, the duplex where they have lived for so many years, you will probably see a quilt spread out on a frame in the dining room. Groups and individuals often ask Susie to make special quilts for them.

The Ephrata Historical Society and The Cloister, a historic site in Ephrata, had her do one with "fractur" print, a decorative type print from colonial days. She was also asked to do a memorial quilt for the University of Virginia.

A comment on a complicated, well-made design will probably lead Susie to say, "Yes, I designed it, but I'm not an artist." The original designs in her quiltmaking belie her modesty. She donates the quilts with reimbursement for the cost only.

Susie Rutt is a master artist now in quiltmaking, but during her lifetime she also mastered well the art of serving. It's still true that if you need something done, you can call on Susie.

8.
Christian
Neff (C. N.)
Hostetter, Jr.

By
E.
Morris
Sider

The year is 1960. MCC chairman C. N. Hostetter, Jr., is on a world tour. In Korea he records in his diary on September 29: "Went with Jake [Klassen] and an interpreter as we took a jeep load of food and clothes to a haven for the beggars and feeble minded. What a road! What needy people! What little of this world's goods some poor people have! I tried to take a few pictures."

Two days later he is with the MCC staff at a retreat. "After a Korean dinner in which I ate my first roasted grasshopper we had a worship fellowship and I spoke on Philippians 2, 'Joy in Service' and then slept Korean style on a heated floor with mat for mattress and another for cover." On October 11 he visits a school and sits with the Korean faculty around low tables. "After the dinner of Korean food we played games. I was penalized [for losing] by being asked to sing a song and I sang 'The More We Get Together!' A very fine spirit was felt throughout the evening."

Those selected passages reflect the spirit of one of the noted leaders of the Mennonite Central Committee. Here obviously is a leader with a concern for the needy of the world, one who finds a biblical joy in service, one with a sense of humor that makes him fit comfortably with those whom he seeks to serve.

Christian Neff Hostetter, Jr., was born into a Brethren in Christ home. He had roots, however, among the Mennonites. His mother, Ella Neff, came from a family whose Mennonite ancestry is probably as old as Anabaptism itself. The Hostetters may be traced back to Jacob Hostetter, a Swiss Mennonite who immigrated to the United States in 1712 and settled as a farmer in Lancaster County, Pennsylvania. By at least the 1840s, however, one of the Hostetter lines had become Brethren in Christ, since we know that Jacob Hostetter, the great grandson of the original Jacob, became a bishop in that church in 1843.

Bishop Jacob's grandson Christian (and C. N. Hostetter, Jr.'s father) also became a bishop and a noted leader in the denomination. A man of quiet dignity but great ability, he also served for five years as president of Messiah Bible School (now Messiah College), for many years as chairman of his denomination's Foreign Mission Board, as secretary of General Conference (the governing body of the church) from 1916 to 1927, and frequently as its moderator.

Christian Hostetter was also a man of firm convictions. When converted at the age of thirty, he substituted fruit and vegetable farming for the tobacco crop that Lancaster farmers, Brethren in Christ and Mennonites alike, considered necessary to pay off their debts and make a comfortable living. Similarly, he was so struck by the poverty he saw when he visited Africa and India in his role as missions board chairman that on his return to the United States he refused to eat candy for the remainder of his long life. And yet he was a man of great tolerance—he never, it appears, even as bishop condemned his brethren who continued to grow tobacco, nor did he discourage his children or others from enjoying their candy.

It was into this kind of home that C. N. Hostetter, Jr., was born in 1899. The inheritance of ability, the atmosphere of quiet conviction and dedication to service, and the wide tolerance of differing points of view clearly influenced the boy in his formative years at home.

An Early Sense of Call

His early life as a farm boy holds no surprises for us. From the diary which he began to keep at the age of fourteen, we read of him cleaning beehives, planting and picking potatoes, threshing grain, spreading manure, pruning and spraying fruit trees and helping to sell the harvest on the Lancaster city market, and raising pigeons for a little pocket money (although the careful ledger which he kept indicates that he made little profit from his enterprise). He faithfully accompanied his parents to religious services conducted in both meetinghouses (churches) and homes, and frequently took his Mennonite grandmother, who lived with them in her later years, to Mennonite church meetings in the area.

At the age of fourteen, he made his commitment to become a Christian. This occurred in a revival meeting conducted by his father in the local congregation. For several months previously he had been under conviction, but he wondered whether he could be saved. He was willing, however, to be used of God even if that were not possible; thus he knelt by the stovepipe running through his bedroom and prayed: "Lord, save me! And if you can't save me, I'll still help you all I can to get other people saved."[1] The next evening at the close of the service he simply stood at his seat (according to the custom then prevailing in the denomination) to declare his intention to follow Jesus.

Young as he was at his conversion, Hostetter now became an earnest Christian, his earnestness heightened by a premonition that life had some heavy loads for him to bear. His diary records a systematic reading of the Bible and praying, not only on Sundays but throughout the week as well. Once while tramping silo for a neighbor he memorized the entire Sermon on the Mount. He would sit for hours reading the *Evangelical Visitor* (the denominational paper) and the *General Conference Minutes.*[2]

In 1915 he enrolled at Messiah Bible School. There early in the winter he received what he called his sanctification experience (a filling of his life with the Holy Spirit); the event convinced him even more firmly that his life must be spent in the service of God and the church.

Thus he very diligently applied himself to his schoolwork, alternating his studies by walks in the country or swimming in the stream that runs through the campus. He took a leading part in prayer and missionary circles, and on Sunday afternoons frequently visited people in the community who were in spiritual or physical need. One of the Canadian students on his return home in the spring of 1916 reported that when he was about to leave, young Hostetter came to his room to pray for him, even though the two throughout the year had not been together much.[3]

After three years, Hostetter interrupted his schooling by remaining at home to help on the farm. He became increasingly active in the life of the local congregation and in the district. While at Messiah Bible School he had learned how to read music, and so he started a singing school. He was made superintendent of the

Sunday school at the mission at Lancaster city; the school soon became the largest in the denomination. He became leader of the newly formed Young People's Society in the local congregation. It is not surprising then that in 1920 his district should elect him to ministry, even though tradition at that time was against placing so young a man, and unmarried at that, in such a responsible position. Hostetter now took his turn preaching at the various points that made up the district.

Winning People to Christ

He returned to Messiah Bible School in the fall of 1920 and two years later graduated from the four-year theological course. That summer he and several other young men traveled around the countryside looking for a likely place to conduct evangelistic services. He and fellow-student Albert Engle decided on a rural location at Iron Springs near the mountains in southern Pennsylvania. There in the local schoolhouse the two young men, not long out of their teens, held a remarkable meeting among rough farmers and mountaineers, which resulted in the founding of a permanent congregation.

Hostetter returned home from that experience to marry Anna Lane, from whom he had taken typewriting and business courses at Messiah Bible School. Shortly afterward the young couple moved to Refton, one of the preaching points in the district which up to that time had been without a resident minister.

Several features marked Hostetter's ministry at Refton. He soon developed a large following of Mennonites who were attracted to his more evangelical style and content of preaching, as well as to the more regular services held by the Brethren in Christ. Hostetter, however, refused to capitalize on this situation; under his ministry few, if any, of the local Mennonites were taken into the congregation as members.

His ministry at Refton was also marked by the beginning of a Sunday school and eventually a vacation Bible school. The latter was the first of its kind in a wide area around Refton (perhaps in the entire country), and it seems clear that it was one of the first in the denomination. Hostetter made the school a cooperative effort, drawing teachers from Mennonite and other local congregations. The school grew both in size (it eventually had to be held in five buildings at the same time) and in fame: almost overnight Hostetter became an authority on vacation Bible schools, frequently writing and speaking on the subject, both within the denomination and in the wider Pennsylvania community.

Hostetter was also becoming known in the denomination as an evangelist. The year following the spectacular revival at Iron Springs, he conducted an even more remarkable one near Fordwich, Ontario, Canada. At that place, the Brethren in Christ church (then known as the Howick congregation) was a very small and dwindling body. What followed must have been a startling though pleasant surprise for the local brethren and sisters. Hostetter, still only twenty-four years of age, visited throughout the community, speaking with people of all denominations and sometimes helping the farmers with their work. Soon the tent, which served as an auditorium, was crowded, and even the preachers from some of the less evangelical churches were proclaiming the revival meeting the best thing they had seen for years.[4] Something of that same experience was frequently repeated in the years that followed, leading to Hostetter's reputation as one of the denomination's leading evangelists.

He was soon performing other activities for the church. It was a natural step to go from pastoring a small congregation and holding revival meetings to becoming a member of the Home Mission Board in 1924, a position he held until 1953, for most of those years as secretary. This new position gave him a share in the oversight of a number of small and often struggling congregations in Pennsylvania and such southern states as Kentucky, Tennessee, Virginia, and Florida. That he handled his charges with firmness yet with love and respect may be illustrated by the following account which he wrote to a fellow board member after returning from a weekend of council meeting and love feast services at one of the stations:

> *They gave me quite an emotional farewell on Sunday morning. The interesting part is that most of the people who expressed their appreciation publicly particularly emphasized the "spankings" that Brother Hostetter gave them. Tears flowed freely and the folks were generous in their praise. However, remembering how many times we had to speak in terms of very frank and pointed corrections, it was encouraging to note the responsive attitude from these folks....* [5]

Stereoscopes and Peanut Butter

Typical of Brethren in Christ polity in those years, Hostetter served in his pastorate without remuneration. For income, he turned first to selling stereoscope sets, working the area around Hagerstown and Gettysburg. He had some success, especially among Mennonites, but after six months he decided that to make a satisfactory living at the job he would be required to use sales techniques that would not complement an effective Christian witness.

So he left that work and for several years sold peanut butter for John Moseman, a Mennonite minister who operated a food produce business in the city of Lancaster. He remained with Moseman until 1928 when he began to sell calendars. This last work was more seasonal in nature and thus allowed Hostetter larger blocks of time for his congregational and denominational activities. Here again he refused to compromise principle for sales—before setting out on the road with his displays he discarded all the "girlie" calendars which the company had included in his packages. This did not seem to affect his sales much; in the early thirties, despite the economic depression, he was earning on commission some $3,000 a year. Then in 1934 came the call to Messiah Bible College to be its president at $800 a year.

No Task Too Large or Small

Over the years, Hostetter had kept in close touch with his alma mater. He returned almost annually to address the four-day Bible conferences held in January, to which major figures in the denomination were invited as speakers. In recent years he had usually taught in the winter session of the school. And in 1928 he had been elected president of the Alumni Association. Under his direction the Association raised funds to build the Alumni Auditorium, constructed in 1934. Because of his close association with the school, his stature in the denomination, and his proven ability in finances, Hostetter was a logical choice as college president. He remained in that position until 1960, thus holding the longest tenure in Messiah College history.

Because he lacked an academic degree, Hostetter spent his first summers in school after becoming president. He obtained first a ThB. degree from the Winona Lake School of Theology, and then an MA degree in college administration from the University of

Chicago (eventually he received honorary doctorate degrees from both Houghton College and Greenville College). At the same time he worked hard, perhaps too hard, at his administrative duties. He not only taught classes (usually two in the same semester) but also performed such activities as editing and proofreading the college bulletin, acting as marshall at graduation exercises, overseeing the business office, and at one time serving as dean of men—all activities that most college presidents would have delegated to others. He considered, however, that a small, struggling college could not afford a large staff, thus he was himself prepared to carry a heavier than normal load.

After the war years, Hostetter also worked hard to develop the college's physical plant. First came a dormitory in 1949 at a cost of $175,000 and later a library and a college-community church building. Typically, Hostetter personally did much of the fund raising for these buildings, in the process making for the first time many community contacts that continue to serve the college as a basis for financial support and good will.

In addition to developing the physical plant, Hostetter had several overriding concerns for the college. Perhaps above all he saw the college as the source from which the denomination in particular and the Christian church in general could draw their workers. He thus sought to inspire students with a vision for Christian service, particularly for service with the denomination and with the Mennonite Central Committee. "Some people remember themselves into oblivion," he frequently told his students, "while others in service forget themselves into immortality." Relatedly he was also concerned to keep the college close to its constituency. Thus dress and social codes continued to be conservative in nature, not so much because of Hostetter's personal convictions as for the effect social practices at the college would have on the denomination. He encouraged his faculty and the school's music groups to join him in an active ministry not only in the college but among the congregations as well.

Hostetter himself was part of the local ministry in the Grantham congregation, and in fact eventually became the bishop of the small, three-congregation district of which Grantham was the largest member. He carried for this work a pastor's heart. Thus when confessions had to be made (in earlier years, the church believed that public repentance should be followed by public confession), Hostetter would characteristically stand by the one confessing, sometimes with a supporting hand on the person's arm or shoulder. Similarly, on one occasion at a funeral when only two relatives of the deceased attended, Hostetter left his seat in the audience and went to the front of the auditorium to sit by them in a gesture of comfort and support.[6]

Seeking Unity and Peace

As Hostetter moved into his late forties and early fifties, the tempo of his life increased, partly because he began to move in wider circles. He was one of the Brethren in Christ leaders who helped to move the denomination toward contacts and fellowship with the larger Christian community. He served on the committee which studied and recommended affiliation with the National Association of Evangelicals (NAE) and the National Holiness Association (now the Christian Holiness Association), recommendations which General Conference accepted.

While active in both organizations, Hostetter was particularly so in NAE. He served two terms as the denomination's representative on NAE's Board of

Administration and was a member of its education commission. Most significantly, he spent well over a decade on the World Relief Commission (WRC), the relief arm of NAE, for nine years as its president.

Hostetter's association with NAE was not always a comfortable one, as much as he valued that organization's contribution to the denomination and to the Christian community as a whole. The most difficult moments were when militarism and the "God and country" theme raised their related heads.

Such a time came during the NAE annual convention in 1955 when General William K. Harrison presented what amounted to a case for Christians participating in war. Not only members of peace churches present but also such NAE leaders as George Ford, Stephen Pain of Houghton College, and the president, H. H. Savage, were dismayed, since this was a breach of the tacit rule which holds that members should associate on the basis of what unites, not divides, the NAE body. Hostetter was chosen to give a reply the following day.

Back in his hotel room, he spent several hours sounding out ideas for his address with his longtime Canadian friend, E. J. Swalm. By 4:00 a.m. the next day he was awake and in prayer. In the morning session he presented by all accounts a diplomatic yet masterful forty-minute defense of the peace position. The address appears to have been well received even by those who did not agree with his views, and was shortly afterward printed as an article in the August issue of *United Evangelical Action,* the official journal of NAE.[7]

Hostetter tried on several occasions to arrange for an exchange of ideas on war and peace within an NAE study conference format. He unsuccessfully pressured the Commission for Social Action to sponsor such a session at the same 1955 convention noted above. In a strongly worded letter to Carl F. H. Henry, the Commission's chairman, Hostetter pointed out that "the inclination of evangelicals, and particularly fundamentalists, is to take for granted that the Bible approves participation in war and classify all opposition to it as identified with the pacifism espoused by liberals. Our evangelical fellowship should be better informed."[8] These were prophetic words in light of events at the ensuing convention.

Following the convention, Hostetter again pressured Henry to arrange for a study session in the following year. Henry replied that although he did not approve of what had happened at the recent convention, he was weary of the matter. Besides, peoples' minds were made up on the subject and it was too difficult to get collegiate men to carry on an effective discussion.[9]

Hostetter was somewhat more successful with the Commission for Social Action in 1960. With the encouragement of Guy F. Hershberger (Mennonite scholar and peace advocate), he managed after some effort to persuade the Commission, now chaired by A. D. Zahniser, to sponsor a session on the Christian and war. The peace groups brought J. A. Toews from Winnipeg to present their position; V. Raymond Edman, President of Wheaton College, was asked to speak on the other side. A small group of Brethren in Christ and Mennonites attended the session. Three other men were present—the chairman, an old friend of Edman's from missionary days in China, and the man whom Edman sent to read his paper. In that situation, there could be little meaningful dialogue.[10]

A Leader of MCC

Outside of his own denomination, Hostetter's most significant work was done with the Mennonite Central

Committee. He associated easily with Mennonites, obviously owing at least in part to his family background and to his continuing interaction with them at Refton and elsewhere. What may be described as his first formal connection came in the Council of Mennonite and Affiliated Colleges, of which Messiah College was a member. According to his diary, he seems particularly to have enjoyed attending the foreign student conferences sponsored by the Council, and almost every year drove a carload of Messiah College foreign students to these annual events. In 1951 he conducted the Council's student tour of Europe.

He was also active as counselor and adviser in the Civilian Public Service camps during the war. Beginning in 1941, he made several tours of many of the camps, some as far away as Colorado, and visited those closer at home on an almost regular basis. This suggests his effectiveness as a counselor. "He could sooth the CPS fellows," one camp director has recalled. "These boys at that time thought they were going through a period of awfully bad luck. Some visitors would come to the camp and be shocked when they didn't find everything and everybody perfect. But C. N. [as many people called him] was not shocked when he found conditions less than ideal; he was immediately sympathetic, and the fellows could sense his sympathy."[11]

In 1945 Hostetter took the place of Orville B. Ulery on the Brethren in Christ Relief and Service Committee, and in 1948 became the denominational representative from that committee on the Mennonite Central Committee. In 1951 he was chosen as the additional member of the Executive Committee when MCC decided to strengthen the committee by expanding the number of its members by one. This new position soon increased his activity in MCC, including giving testimony in 1951 against the Universal Military Training Act, the first of several occasions in which he gave testimony before a congressional committee.

And then in 1953 he was elected chairman of MCC to succeed P. C. Hiebert. At first thought, this is somewhat surprising, considering that Hostetter was Brethren in Christ and not Mennonite, and that the group he represented was one of the small ones in MCC. But there were factors distinctly in his favor. It was important at that time to have the right "mix" in MCC official positions. The Old Mennonites already had two strong men on the Executive Committee in the persons of Orie O. Miller and Harold S. Bender. Similarly, a chairman selected from the General Conference Mennonites would have given that large group, in some estimates, a strong (perhaps too strong) position on the committee. And it was not appropriate to assume automatically that Hiebert's successor would come from his own group, the Mennonite Brethren, partly because Hiebert had held the chairmanship from the beginning of MCC. "In this predicament," Henry Fast has observed, "it appeared like a Spirit-guided compromise to nominate and elect Brother C. N. Hostetter of the Brethren in Christ to serve as chairman. But as a matter of fact, he had already so commended himself to the respect and love of the membership that I believe everybody was happy and grateful over his appointment to this honored and responsible position."[12]

There is in addition, however, an intriguing thesis that behind Hostetter's selection may be seen the skillful yet brotherly hand of Orie O. Miller. This view suggests that Miller knew P. C. Hiebert would soon be retiring and that he considered Hostetter to be a worthy successor. He thus had as one of his own objectives in increasing the size of the Executive Committee in 1951 the bringing in of Hostetter to the smaller, more active group, where he would more likely move to the chairmanship. This thesis is lent a small amount of credence by an entry in Hostetter's diary which reveals that at the meeting in which Hiebert announced his resignation (nearly a year before Hostetter's appointment) Miller approached Hostetter and asked whether he would consider accepting the chairmanship. Hostetter records that "I deferred and suggested that Orie become chairman. . . . To this Orie did not fully concur."[13]

Hostetter brought to his chairmanship of the Mennonite Central Committee several controlling interests. He had a genuine sympathy for needy people, as might be expected from one of his nature. He emphasized his social concerns particularly to his fellow Brethren in Christ and his NAE colleagues—both groups, because of their evangelical backgrounds, stressed the gospel ministry and were inclined to view social work as smacking too much of liberalism and standing in the way of saving souls. Thus in a presentation to the NAE convention in 1966, after showing that by precept and example Jesus taught his followers to feed the hungry and relieve the suffering, he insisted that twentieth-century Evangelicals make the same error as the Jerusalem church did when it separated evangelism and relief by neglecting the Grecian Jewish widows. "Hundreds of you," he continued, "must do something more for relief. . . . The church or congregation that does not have Christian relief in its budget is failing to do its duty. . . . [That church] is as much remiss as the church that does not support missions."[14]

On the other hand, within MCC circles Hostetter tended to emphasize the need for the gospel witness. This was undoubtedly owing to his well-founded understanding that in doing work of a social nature it is easy to be active for action's sake, and thus to minimize the spiritual foundation of MCC work. He must also have taken into account that there were those both within and without Mennonite circles who thought that MCC had already reached that state of inferior grace.

Thus in his leadership role in MCC Hostetter repeatedly reminded his colleagues of the need for the gospel to accompany and indeed to be the basis for their social work. It was somehow natural when at the 1966 annual meeting of MCC (Canada) he was asked what changes he saw over the years in MCC that he should single out for his reply the changes in MCC's efforts to witness. "Whereas we earlier separated relief and mission work rather sharply," he pointed out, "we now expect our volunteers to give an unapologetic Christian witness in all the relief and service work they do."[15] One reads into that statement a sense of personal accomplishment.

But this in a certain measure misrepresents Hostetter's overriding point of view, which was that Christian witness and Christian social concern must go hand in hand—in fact, must be part of the same package, to use a metaphor appropriate to MCC. Thus in a devotional address to the MCC annual meeting in 1963, he insisted that "we cannot compartmentalize man, but must recognize that his nature is a unit, a living personality. We must be aware of his total need." He followed that remark with a caution that social work should not be used to catch sinners in the gospel net:

> *Evangelism and relief work are difficult to combine, lest we reap a harvest of "rice Christians." To use relief or Christian social service as a "bait" for evangelism was not Christ's way and is unworthy of his followers. Jesus fed men because they were hungry. . . . Because of the difficulties man may conclude that evangelism and relief*

> must be totally separated. But the nature of man and the
> teaching of Scripture show that these are not only related;
> they are interrelated.[16]

It was in character that Hostetter should write to Executive Secretary William Snyder that there should be personnel doing MCC work and mission work at the same time; what better way to strengthen ties of mutuality between mission boards and MCC.[17] It was also in character that the reports which he wrote while traveling for MCC overseas should usually comment on missions, or missions potential, arising out of the work of MCC.

Such views complemented his conviction that relief work calls for flexibility and openness to change. To the supervisor of a young medical worker in Asia, he once wrote that the young man must take a realistic view of matters—he must remember that "most service in the Orient must be done *with* and *under* nationals and that in nearly every hospital he will find: (1) great limitations by lack of help; (2) inefficiency and slowness of administration; (3) practice of oriental situational ethics that seem questionable to a Westerner." But still he must attempt to serve.[18] To the director of WRC work in Vietnam, Hostetter once wrote, "I know of no work in the world that requires more flexibility that the ministry of Christian relief," and then went on to encourage him that the mark of a strong leader is one who is not afraid to bend for fear he will break.[19]

A Person Who Cared and Loved

In his own leadership roles, Hostetter was well known for bringing people together and for getting them to share a sense of brotherhood. His personality helped to achieve those ends. He was a warm man, intensely interested in people (including his grandchildren, to

Christian Neff (C.N.) Hostetter, Jr.

whom he liked to read and send presents, and with whom he enjoyed playing games). At the college he learned to call each student by name; one of the ways in which he accomplished this was to look up and down the rows of students at chapel time, trying to fix a name to each face and making a note to himself when he was unable to do so (leading some students to think that the president was taking attendance). He smiled much—a full facial expression that included a twinkle in the eyes. To this was added a finely toned sense of humor and a fund of jokes and stories (often Pennsylvania-Dutch in nature), which he frequently related at difficult or tense moments in a business meeting, and which helped to bring the group together again.

Hostetter was concerned that in a business meeting all voices should be heard. He would encourage less forward men to speak their views, and would attempt to arrive at a consensus. Although himself having special interests in the peace section of MCC (he served on the section as a member-at-large until 1964), as well as in relief and mental health, he appears not to have played an advocacy role in these and other concerns. He was careful also, as MCC chairman, not to move into the work of administrators, which surely helps to explain the respect with which he was held by personnel at MCC headquarters and abroad, and the freedom they felt to call on him for advice.[20]

A distinguishing feature of Hostetter's chairmanship of MCC, as well as his presidency of WRC, were the devotional meditations he gave before committee and annual meetings. These meditations were simple and practical, and clearly biblically based. When he was finished, the members had a sense that in the hours ahead they would be doing God's work.

He saw in these Bible studies a related purpose—that of bringing people together. An administrator who accompanied him on one of his trips abroad recalls that the first thing Hostetter would do when he met a group of MCC workers would be to reach for his Bible and say, "Let's have a Bible study" and the group immediately felt comfortable. When questioned about this practice, Hostetter said that people are best brought together around the Word.[21]

Travels to Help and to Heal

Hostetter made several trips abroad, usually traveling in the interests of both the Mennonite Central Committee and the World Relief Commission. His first major trip followed shortly after his resignation of the college presidency in 1960. In nine months of traveling he visited all of the areas in Asia where the two agencies carried on their work, as well as examining the MCC program in Jordan and Greece. Other trips followed: to Jamaica, Santo Domingo, and Haiti in 1962, to Algeria, Greece, and Jordan in 1963, a return trip to Vietnam (mainly to clear administrative problems for WRC) in 1966 and in the same year another one to Haiti (again primarily for WRC), and a tour of a large part of Africa in 1967.

He performed, perhaps above all, a pastoral function on these trips. Experiences on his African visit in 1967 illustrate the seriousness with which he took this part of his work. He had been in Burundi and had booked a flight out of that country to visit missionaries and relief workers elsewhere. The flight, however, was overbooked and Hostetter was one of six forced to remain behind. The next flight out was four days later. In order to keep his appointment with workers in Uganda, Hostetter made a 600-mile trip over rough and dangerous African roads. On another occasion while in Africa he persuaded some MCC relief workers to drive him in a jeep some 300 miles to visit a few Paxmen working in the hills.[22] Such activity was not easy for Hostetter (he was by then sixty-eight years of age); it is very probable that it led to a minor stroke sometime while he was still in Africa.

He was also the troubleshooter on these visits abroad. This was the major purpose for his 1966 trip to Vietnam. "It looks as though we shall have to turn to you personally," wrote one of the administrators of WRC, "to size up the situation on the field, or get your ever-willing organization MCC to do the job. . . . Believe me, we all appreciate what you are doing. . . . You are the only one on our committee who has the insight, experience, etc., required in this worldwide responsibility, so we have to lean on you continually."[23] He successfully handled a delicate situation to the apparent satisfaction of all involved. On Hostetter's return to the United States, one of the WRC leaders in Asia wrote to Wendell Rockey, the Executive Director, that "if Dr. Hostetter had not been there, none of this could have been possible.... Dr. Hostetter is a wonderful man of God and it was a very inspiring and profitable experience being with him."[24]

Although more the pastor than the executive on these trips, Hostetter wrote lengthy descriptions of what he saw and made recommendations for what he considered should be done. These, it appears, were composed with care and after consultation with the MCC staff whom he was visiting. One MCC administrator, then an overseas director, has observed that Hostetter did not go overseas with preconceived ideas and that when he wrote a recommendation it was not only Hostetter's but the workers' as well. Thus the people in the programs were not later caught by surprise. "We didn't complain, 'Why didn't he say that when he was here?' or 'Who told him that sort of thing?' No, it was 'Here we go! C. N. really heard us and he took it to the Executive Committee, and there it is, in black and white.' "[25]

Hostetter's concurrent roles as chairman of MCC and president of WRC were interesting and generally profitable. The profit was undoubtedly greatest for WRC. By the time Hostetter became president of that organization he had developed a considerable background in relief work by virtue of his association with MCC; WRC was able, as suggested above, to tap this background knowledge and through him to make contacts and develop programs which normally would have been unavailable to the Commission. Thus in 1954 Hostetter brought Wendell Rockey, newly appointed as executive director of WRC, to Akron where Rockey spent several days talking to MCC administrators and observing MCC methods of shipping, packaging, and publicity.[26] Similarly, Hostetter was a good bridge between the two bodies in obtaining workers for the WRC program and in arranging for WRC in some locations to work through MCC facilities.

But there was profit also for MCC in Hostetter's dual role. WRC was a source for some of MCC's supplies, particularly in Asia. There was also something of a psychological dimension to the relationship. Such groups as the Mennonite Brethren, the Evangelical Mennonite Brethren, and the Evangelical Mennonites tended to consider that MCC had too many ties with such ecumenical groups as the Church World Service and the World Council of Churches agencies. Hostetter's position on WRC provided MCC a link with the more evangelical church agencies and thus gave some assurance to the more conservative, evangelical wing of the Mennonite constituency that MCC relationships were not one-sided.[27]

Although Hostetter considered that he owed service to WRC in the interest of relief work in general, and while he was convinced that the Brethren in Christ had much to gain from their association with NAE, he was clear in his commitment, as well as his denomination's, to the work of MCC. To William Snyder he remarked on more than one occasion words to the following effect: "Now, William, you don't have to worry. The Brethren in Christ are working through MCC, and our money will go there. My role in the World Relief Commission is to help and encourage them in their vision of relief work."[28]

Following his resignation from the college presidency and after his return from his world trip in 1961, Hostetter taught at Messiah College for three years on a part-time basis. In 1963 he accepted a pastorate at the Brethren in Christ church in Palmyra, some thirty miles east of Grantham. His pastoral work clearly delighted him, perhaps because it reminded him of his first happy and successful pastorate at Refton. At about the same time he began service on the denomination's Publication Board. These and still other duties he carried along with his work on MCC and WRC, a heavy load for a man who already in 1959 had reached his sixtieth year. Through the years, Mrs. Hostetter had shared her husband's great interest in MCC; at Palmyra she continued that interest by collecting soap and quilt patches for relief projects.

In 1967 Hostetter began to restrict his activities, particularly his interchurch work. He never fully recovered from the mild stroke which he probably suffered during his African trip in that year. On his doctor's advice, he resigned his positions with both MCC and WRC, and shortly afterward the pastorate. In 1970 at Upland, California, he attended his last of many General Conferences. Before returning home he joined part of his family for a day in Disneyland where among other amusements he took a grandchild for a ride on the rollercoaster. Repeated strokes led to his moving to Messiah Home (now Messiah Village), where with his wife he resided until his death on June 29, 1980.

C. N. Hostetter, Jr., is a bright example of a talented and dedicated man giving his life to many causes and thus becoming a blessing to untold numbers of people throughout the world. His is not the tale of rags to riches but the story of grace spread abroad.

Notes

1. *Christian Living,* September 1969, p. 6.

2. Ernest J. Swalm, interview, March 21, 1978. All interviews are on tape and in the C. N. Hostetter, Jr., Papers, Brethren in Christ Archives, Messiah College, Grantham, Pennsylvania.

3. *Ibid.*

4. *Evangelical Visitor*, August 20, 1923, p. 2. A fuller account is given by Hostetter in his diary, July 13-August 8, 1923.

5. C. N. Hostetter, Jr., to Albert Engle, July 16, 1952. Home Mission Board Members Correspondence, File Folder, Hostetter Papers.

6. Virgie Kraybill, interview, November 9, 1978.

7. For two accounts of this event, see George Ford, taped letter, February 1979, and the Swalm interview.

8. C. N. Hostetter, Jr., to Carl F. H. Henry, December 14, 1954. National Association of Evangelicals, Correspondence. Hostetter Papers.

9. C. N. Hostetter Jr., to Carl F. H. Henry, May 2, 1955, and Henry to Hostetter, May 6, 1955, in *ibid.*

10. For a description of the meeting, see John Howard Yoder to E. Morris Sider, February 22, 1979. Hostetter Papers.

11. Harry Martens, interview, January 15, 1979.

12. For a detailed explanation, see Henry Fast to E. Morris Sider, March 6, 1979. Hostetter Papers.

13. Hostetter Diary, March 22, 1952.

14. "The Urgency of World Relief," in Relief NAE, File Folder. Hostetter Papers.

15. MCC (Canada), File Folder. Hostetter Papers.

16. *Gospel Herald*, April 16, 1963, pp. 317-318.

17. C. N. Hostetter, Jr., to William Snyder, March 10, 1955. MCC Correspondence/Hostetter, C. N./1958. Mennonite Archives, Goshen, Indiana.

18. C. N. Hostetter to Jacob Klassen, July 16, 1962. MCC Correspondence/Hostetter, C. N./1962. Mennonite Archives.

19. C. N. Hostetter, Jr., to Peter G. Wiwcharuck, August 20, 1966. Peter Wiwcharuck File. Hostetter Papers.

20. William Snyder, interview, February 1, 1979. Also Edgar Stoesz, interview, March 8, 1979.

21. Stoesz interview.

22. *Christian Living*, September 1969, p. 5.

23. Clay Mitchell to C. N. Hostetter, Jr., August 23, 1966. Mailing Lists, File Folder. Hostetter Papers.

24. Elmer Kilbourne to Wendell Rockey, October 20, 1966. Elmer Kilbourne, File Folder. Hostetter Papers.

25. Peter Dyck, interview, February 1, 1979.

26. Wendell Rockey to E. Morris Sider, February 24, 1979. Hostetter papers.

27. I owe this insight to Jacob Klassen, taped letter, March 1979.

28. William Snyder interview.

9. Cornelius Wall

By
Christine
Wiebe

Cornelius looked down at the photograph of the young woman. With her hair pulled back and her high-necked dress, she looked like many other girls in 1916. But to Cornelius she was special. His engagement with Agnes was still a secret—a pleasant secret to occasionally pull out with the photograph during the frantic work as a Red Cross worker with the Russian Army.

"Wall!" The head doctor stood in the door of the hospital room. Cornelius slipped the picture back into his pocket before turning around.

"Yes, sir?"

"I would like all of the medical corps to meet immediately in the yard."

"I'll be there," Cornelius said. As the doctor turned, Cornelius frowned. He already knew the purpose of the meeting.

"A blitz attack on the compound is expected from the Kurds," said the doctor to the gathered workers. "I want all men to gather arms from the wounded and fan out around the compound."

Cornelius hesitated as the group scattered to the sheds hidden in the mountainside to find rifles and grenades. What do I do now, he thought? Pick up a hand grenade and disobey my conscience? Or refuse to arm myself and disobey the captain's order?

"Wall, you stay with the wounded." The doctor's voice interrupted his thoughts. "But arm yourself with hand grenades."

Cornelius knew what he had to do. He hurried up the mountain to the shed in which he slept, knelt and prayed.

He had joined the medical corps instead of the army because he did not believe it was right to kill. To take up arms now would make that earlier decision meaningless. Although it was a serious offense, he knew he had to disobey and take the consequences.

When he hurried back through the compound of old shacks and buildings he saw the doctor had found a rifle and had stationed himself by a log in the yard. Cornelius stood in the door of the shed of wounded men and waited for the attack.

"Wall!" the doctor barked.

"Yes, sir." He stood erect without moving.

"Get your hand grenades, Wall. I want you to be ready."

Cornelius swallowed before answering. "I am not arming myself, sir. I prayed and realized it is against my conscience to arm myself."

The doctor cursed.

Cornelius took a slow, quiet breath and held it. But the doctor said nothing more. Evidently he did not plan to punish him.

Cornelius released his breath and turned to check on the room of wounded men behind him. The men lay quietly on the hay and straw which served as beds. The compound was silent; like statues, men with rifles waited behind trees and buildings. What would he do if the Kurds, an Armenian tribe in the hills, actually attacked? Cornelius wondered and waited.

When three stacatto shots tapped in the distance Cornelius could see the doctor stiffen and recheck his rifle.

"The scouts are back!" The shout emerged near the edge of the compound and echoed from man to man. In a few minutes the reporters appeared in the compound and Cornelius gathered with the other men to hear.

"We could not find the Kurds anywhere," they said. "There is no danger of attack."

Cornelius took a deep breath of thankfulness. Relieved smiles appeared on the faces around him. Gratefully he walked back to the room of wounded soldiers.

He thought once again of Agnes. She waited at home in Blumenort, one of the many villages in the Ukraine. Some day after the war was over they would get married. Cornelius knew his father would help them go to a Bible school in Germany. Perhaps then they would be missionaries.

It was spring now. That meant the young people of Blumenort would spend more time roaming the grove on the south side of the village, as he and Agnes had done before he left. Cornelius knew Agnes had little time for leisurely walks in the meadows now. As the eldest daughter she had added responsibilities in her parents' home, running much of the household.

And he had little time for thinking about Agnes. When World War I broke out between Russia and Germany in 1914 Cornelius had stopped teaching and joined the medical corps, a team of about 25 men who ran a field hospital on the Russian western front. The front extended from the top of Germany to the bottom of Austria-Hungary and around the border of Servia. The soldiers dug trenches behind tangled masses of barbed wire. When one side attacked, they bombed the enemy lines before scrambling over the wire into no-man's-land, a stretch of open ground pitted with shell craters. The number of deaths was appalling.

During lulls in the fighting, Cornelius worked night and day to gather the wounded. Crumbling cities and people marching inland with a few salvaged belongings provided a constant moving backdrop for their work as they moved with the fighting.

Wedding During War

As a teacher Cornelius was released from the army in 1917. He praised God and made his way home to family—and Agnes. Perhaps now they could get married and he could go to Bible school.

"Why do you get married now?" asked one friend. "This is such a dangerous time."

Cornelius and Agnes knew the friend was right. Besides the struggle with Germany for the past three years, Russia had internal problems. When the people of Petrograd rioted for food in March 1917 soldiers joined in and the riot became a revolution. The collapse of the Czarist regime in Russia unleashed a vicious pack of Red Army "soldiers" across the Ukraine.

How could Cornelius and Agnes plan the program, clothing, and food for a wedding while the Red Army advanced steadily, shooting and stealing? More than once local bandits had already swaggered into the Walls' home, leaving with any blanket or loaf of bread that caught their eye.

But Cornelius and Agnes also knew the time had come to get married. They talked to their parents and the proper arrangements were made. On Christmas Eve day the Heinrich Duecks invited the Johann Walls to their red brick house for late afternoon *Faspa*—coffee, zwiebach, lebkuchen and whatever else could be found.

Before the guests sat down at the table Heinrich Dueck made the announcement. "Tonight Cornelius and Agnes will sit at the head of the table. For they will be married on March 1."

"Congratulations, son and daughter," said Mr. Wall. As Cornelius and Agnes exchanged engagement rings more congratulations showered the couple. Much laughter and talking mingled with the bread, cheese, and jam that was passed around the family circle.

Although before the announcement the couple had not been seen together at any official gathering, tonight they could walk to the Christmas Eve program together.

Soldiers patrolled the streets while the wedding took place several months later. In past years wedding gifts would have included towels, and sheets, and table-cloths—new ones carefully embroidered by women of the village. But now all such things had been stolen.

"Here is a needle, Agnes," said one woman.

"And a spool of thread," offered another.

"Where did you get them?" Agnes asked. She knew the women did not have extra sewing materials to spare.

The women smiled as they said, "They are for you."

In better times Agnes had taken a seamstress course. Although now she did not have fine materials in abundance, she would still need the thread and needle to mend the little clothing they had.

"Thank you," she said to the friends who spared pans and furniture from their own bare kitchens and parlors to give the new couple a start.

"Leave the Ukraine," urged the German soldiers when their army occupied the Ukraine after the Russian Western Front broke up. An armistice had given Germany large amounts of Russia's land. "Go to Germany where it is safe," the soldiers said.

Although this was a chance to go to Bible school, the Walls did not feel the time was right. "Let's wait until things settle down," they agreed. They loaded their secondhand wedding gifts and some chicks into a boxcar and traveled to Tschongraw, a Ukrainian village, where Cornelius would teach in the village school.

When a Bible school opened in the same building as the teacherage Cornelius could hardly stand to continue teaching. He desperately wanted to attend Bible school. Although he was released from his teaching contract so he could attend the school, disappointment returned. After two years of occupation, Germany's hold on Russia broke and war resumed. Cornelius' dreams were elbowed aside by another call from the draft. In addition to the world war, Red Army soldiers, who had been temporarily held in check by the Germans, swarmed back over the Ukraine.

Bible school would have to come later—much later. Although he could not fulfill his dream, he did not have to go into the army either, as long as he was teaching.

While in Tschongraw a little girl had been born. Cornelius, Agnes, and baby Mary moved on to another teacherage in Baschlitscha, another village in the Ukraine.

Shedding of Blood

It was October in Baschlitscha. Cornelius was glad to have a copy of *Die Friedenstimme*, the German newspaper of his home community. He combed the paper, mentally recording the news Agnes would want to hear.

"*Blumenort destroyed by Red Army. Village Set on Fire.*"

What? He read the headline again, not wanting to believe the cold black letters. He forced himself to read on. The Red Army soldiers had come through the settlement and penned all the men to be found in a cellar.

Then they had thrown in a bomb.

Dazed, Cornelius read the list of those who were dead. A friend. Two neighbors. A man and his two sons. The list went on, the letters swimming on the flimsy newsprint.

"Johann Wall. Hans Wall. . . ."

His father and brother—dead. He read on to the end of the list, satisfied the other relatives had escaped the slaughter.

What to do now? He contacted his brother Jacob to go with him to Blumenort. They found that the village was now occupied by the White Army, an anti-communist force opposed to the Red Army.

"You may collect the things stolen from your house," a White Army soldier told Cornelius when he arrived in Blumenort to find his sister and sister-in-law who had survived.

Cornelius smiled wryly at the thought of having a few of their former comforts around them again. Would it be right to take back the stolen goods by force? Another family now ate from the dishes they once used. Cornelius and Jacob prayed about the matter. They realized taking back the stolen goods would only cause more hatred.

"No," they told the soldier. "Do not force anyone to give up our things."

"What?" The soldier could not understand what he heard. "You do not want your things back?"

"That is right. We have prayed about it and do not want anything back. The shedding of blood must stop."

But the shedding of blood continued. The Red Army swarmed across the Crimea, plundering all in their path. Although Cornelius could finally attend Bible school in Tschongraw, the tension in the country erased most of the joy of study.

One evening Agnes and Cornelius were shaking dirt out of the straw they had gathered in the fields for fuel. A laugh broke the evening quiet outside. They looked up, the shower of dirt from the last shakes settling by their feet.

The door swung open, and the room was filled with shouts, stomping, and more laughter. Cornelius knew it did no good to resist. He stood quietly beside Agnes and little Mary in her crib as the soldiers yanked open drawers and cupboards.

Cornelius noticed one soldier feeling the leather trousers hanging on a hook beside the door. The soldier smiled as he threw his find over his arm.

"Please don't take them. They are my only pair," pleaded Cornelius, stretching out his arm.

"Now, what is that?" The soldier's eyes flicked over the ring on Cornelius' hand.

"That is my wedding ring," said Cornelius, lowering his hand slowly.

"Take it off," the soldier ordered. "I want to see it."

Cornelius struggled to get it off, but his knuckles had swollen. He could not pull it off.

A sword flashed between them.

"Give me that ring." The soldier grinned. "Or else I will take it off for you."

"No—I will get it off." Cornelius wrenched the ring over his swollen knuckle and off his finger. "Here."

The soldier snatched the ring from Cornelius' outstretched hand. "There," he said, stroking the ring casually before slipping it on the little finger of his own hand. "That looks good."

"We Are Going to America"

The Wall's possessions were almost gone. With his father's death Cornelius' hope of financial support to finish Bible school had vanished. Their sickly cow no longer gave milk, despite Agnes' attempts to gather the bits of straw left behind farm wagons on the road. Another baby was on the way.

"We do not want you to go," said friends and relatives when they told them they wanted to go to America. "Things will get better soon. Stay here, continue your work, and trust in the Lord."

But things did not get better. After Arthur was born in September it took until the end of November for Agnes to get well. They could not get the food they needed to make her well. Finally in January she was well enough to travel. They headed for Batum, an open harbor from which they could contact Uncle Henry for help. They hoped Uncle Henry, who had already reached Canada, could send them some money.

They traveled by train first to Feodosia, a harbor on the Black Sea.

"Cornelius, look." Agnes' whisper made him sit up straight to get a better look at two-year-old Mary who had squirmed to the front of the boxcar. His brow wrinkled as an officer bent over her.

"Where are you going?" asked the man.

Little Mary smiled. "We are going to America," she said proudly.

The man smiled back, and then glanced around the car. He knew there were few legal methods of leaving the country. His job was to turn back those people who obviously did not have money for the long trip.

"Where are your parents?" he asked.

Mary squirmed around on the seat and pointed to Cornelius and Agnes. "At the back there. See?" Mary laughed. "They let me sit in the front."

"Yes, I see them," he said.

Cornelius and Agnes held their breath.

The officer chuckled and continued on his way, checking permits. By the time he reached Cornelius and Agnes they had prepared a piece of bread with a slab of bacon on it. They offered it to the man. He looked them over carefully.

Another poor couple, he thought, trying to get out of the country.

"Where are you going?" he asked.

"We are going to look for food."

A believable story. Many beggars rode the trains from village to village looking for something to take back to their families. Too bad their child had blurted out the truth. He could hardly let this couple move on.

But that little girl was a pretty child. She deserved a better chance than what Russia could offer now. There was almost no food to be found—even for officers. The man took the bread and bacon and moved on.

Ships and Lights

A gaping hole in the side of a huge steamship loomed above the restless crowd waiting to board at Feodosia. This was the only ship left that would leave for Batum, where the Walls could contact Uncle Henry. Cornelius herded together his family and the relatives who had come with them.

As the gangplank grated into place and the gate lifted, young and old pushed and fought their way to the opening. Cornelius kept his family near the back of the crowd. Slowly the stream of people hurrying up the plank came to their group.

Mother and Mary slipped into the stream. Arthur in his cradle had already been carried up. Now it was Cornelius' turn.

A grating sound made him look up. He stepped back just in time to miss a grate dropped in front of the gangplank. He stared in disbelief at his wife, children, and relatives on the boat.

"That's all. Move away," said a guard behind the gate.

"But I've got to get on," pleaded Cornelius. "My family is already on the boat."

"We can't handle any more," the guard said. "Get out of the way."

Cornelius watched sailors pull up the gangplank.

I've got to get on, he thought. Turning swiftly, he pushed his way through the small leftover crowd and dashed down the pier, stopping in front of the fat rope cables slung between ship and dock. Without thinking he climbed on the cables and carefully picked his way up their length over the water.

Once on ship he took a deep breath and looked back at the cable still swaying from his steps. At least he was on board. He squeezed his way through the crowd to his family so they could look for a small spot for themselves, their basket, and bundle of clothing.

The trip was difficult, as was the wait in Batum for a message from Uncle Henry. Agnes had malaria. Because there was not enough food, the baby did not survive and on a hot day in April they buried him in his cradle on the slope of a hill. Finally Uncle Henry's letter came, in late spring, promising the needed money. The Walls boarded a French freighter for the long trip to New York. The 22-day voyage was not pleasant because of the food. The beef had a strange rotten odor, making it almost impossible for Agnes to eat.

On November 30 the ship's crew told the passengers that at night the lights of New York would show up on the horizon. Cornelius and Agnes did not go to bed that night. They stood and watched as close to the front of the deck as they could.

"Let's pray, Agnes," said Cornelius.

They stood close together, their heads bowed.

"Our heavenly Father, we thank you for saving us from starvation in Russia. In the new land in which we will live, help us never to forget that once we were refugees. We want to leave the work which brings fame and wealth to others. We ourselves want to do the work which no one else can do, or no one wants to do. We want to accept only the assignments you provide. We commit ourselves and our future to you. Amen."

Welcome Home

Money from American relatives was passed on to them in New York. They left by train for Kansas in December of 1922. Farms, herds of cattle, and huge barns outside the train windows rushed past, but the famine and fear of Russia were still fresh in their minds. Was this wealth a dream? Or were they finally waking up?

"Hillsboro!" the conductor called.

Cornelius' stomach lurched as the train slowed to a stop. Outside the window he saw a small crowd of people gathered on the platform. Surely those people had not all come to meet them. Several men in the crowd took the Walls' big gunnysack of bedding and a basket with a few pieces of clothing that the conductor handed down.

The people surrounded them as they stepped out of the car. "Welcome to Hillsboro," an older man said, shaking Cornelius' hand.

"We have prayed for you and thought of you on your long journey," said a woman as she hugged Agnes.

The Walls were so overwhelmed by the welcome from the Bruderthal church they could hardly say anything. Several days later they were surprised again.

When they arrived at the house they would rent for

Cornelius and Agnes Wall

twelve dollars a month, they found the yard full of cars. The church people welcomed them into a home already furnished with beds, tables, chairs, a coal stove, flour, spices—everything they could imagine.

The Walls walked in awe through the rooms.

"Thank you," they said. "Thank you."

In the yard they had room for a garden of potatoes and other vegetables. Mary had a sandpile by an old oak tree. The Walls were thankful for the space and freedom of their home.

Back to School

Cornelius wanted to go to school, but he was embarrassed by the green army trousers and gray army shirt he owned. A professor at Tabor College, the school in Hillsboro, presented him with a hat and jacket that blended more easily into the 1923 fashions. Then he felt he could attend college.

Since his Russian education was not recognized in the United States he had to start over with high school courses. He did not feel comfortable with the students, who were much younger and laughed over jokes he did not understand.

Learning English was a struggle. The familiar German was too tempting to speak in the German community of Hillsboro. He painstakingly copied notes from the blackboard so he could memorize them at home.

After school he rushed home to work for Dr. Jacob Wiebe. He spent every spare hour after classes painting, cleaning, shoveling—whatever needed to be done—for 25 cents an hour.

Agnes helped by making things stretch farther than seemed possible. When Mary showed up in church one Sunday with a new dress, one woman was curious.

"Where did your get the new dress for Mary?" she asked.

"Oh, that's the piece of material you gave me," Agnes answered.

"But I only gave you a small piece." The woman eyed the garment more carefully. The seams were neat and straight, evident of Agnes' training in Russia. "Agnes," she said at last, "you can make a dress out of a handkerchief!"

Besides sewing, Agnes cooked and cleaned for the boarders who lived with them to provide more money. She made *borscht, zwiebach,* and other Russian Mennonite dishes. Space was tight, but everyone was considered part of the family.

In 1927 Cornelius began to teach at Zoar Academy in Inman, Kansas. His knees shook as he stood in front of his first American class. Cornelius was glad for the time he had had to observe students and teachers at Tabor College before becoming a teacher himself. He might have amused or angered the American students if he had come to class with a long black teacher's cloak and expected the students to rise when he entered, as classes did in Russia.

It Is Their Religion

The years that followed were hard on Agnes. After a bumpy drive to Chicago to find work during the summer of 1929 she suddenly became sick and was rushed to the hospital.

"She has lost a lot of blood," said one of the doctors after he examined her. "She cannot last more than ten minutes." He walked over to the window to join another doctor who was already staring at the grass below.

"Mother," Cornelius called to Agnes on her hospital bed. He shook her gently and she opened her eyes.

"I have to go," she said. "Please take care of my children."

When Cornelius brought Mary and little Agnes into the room, she kissed them and then Cornelius. As the girls quietly tiptoed out of the room, he felt Agnes' hand turn colder. The pulse beat was faint and slow. He did not want to believe what the doctor had said. He stood and watched her slow breathing.

"Daddy!" It was seven-year-old Mary, shouting as she ran back into the room. "Daddy, I know Mama will not die."

Cornelius smiled at his daughter. "How do you know, Musja?"

"The Lord Jesus just now came to me and told me Mama would not die. See—I am wiping off my tears because Mama will stay with us."

"Thank you, Musja," said Cornelius. As he put his

arm around her shoulders he felt a new peace, although there was no reason to believe Agnes would get well. They stood quietly beside the bed.

"How can these people take the situation so calmly?" asked a doctor who stood by the window.

"It is their religion," answered the other.

Just then another doctor strode into the room to Agnes' bed. He looked at her eyes briefly. "What are you doing for this woman?" he demanded.

"Nothing," replied the doctor who had examined her. "There's nothing we can do."

"How about operating?"

"It would do no good. She is dying."

The new doctor's voice was intense and low. "Look, this woman has a family," he said. "We've got to do something. Let's get her on the operating table immediately."

Within minutes nurses wheeled her away. She had lost much blood, but after several blood transfusions her pulse returned and she grew warmer. Although it took many months for her to recover completely, the Walls praised God that she had stayed with them.

Mennonite Central Committee

After six years of teaching at Zoar Academy and then at Hesston Academy in Hesston, Kansas, the Walls were ready for a change. In 1933 they moved to Henderson, Nebraska, where Cornelius was pastor of a country church for three years. Then he accepted an offer to teach Bible school in Mountain Lake, Minnesota.

The Walls lived in a tent while Cornelius attended summer school in Winona Lake, Indiana, in 1936. When two visiting professors from Princeton Theological Seminary visited their tent and learned that Cornelius wanted to go to school, they invited him to their school.

The warmth and encouragement of these two men drew him to Princeton, New Jersey, for four years of study.

Then the letter from Mennonite Central Committee came. "Will you and your wife go to Germany and provide spiritual leadership for the refugees coming from Russia?" asked Orie Miller, the executive secretary of Mennonite Central Committee. "You two can understand these World War II refugees best because you were once refugees yourselves."

Although Cornelius and Agnes were both past 50, they remembered their refugee days during the Russian revolution. They remembered the death of their son Arthur and the struggle to find food. They remembered the loss of their rings and clothing to bandits. They thought of the sickening ride across the Atlantic Ocean and their anxious thoughts as they waited at Ellis Island to be admitted to the United States.

They remembered their promise to God to do the work no one else wanted to do or could do. By this time both daughters were independent, so they had no responsibility to care for children.

"Yes, we will go to Europe," they told Orie Miller.

Gronau Refugee Camp

Heaps of rubble and partly destroyed walls rushed past the train windows as the Walls traveled to the Gronau refugee camp where they would work. Small children stretched their hands up to the windows for food when the train sighed to a stop at each station.

After picking up an old Volkswagen in Neustadt on the Haart, the Walls began the final part of their journey. They passed demolished bridges and deep bomb craters, more fresh scars of the recently ended war. Cornelius and Agnes knew such devastation left mental and spiritual scars as well. It was difficult for people to trust each other after seeing the cruelty of which they and their neighbors were capable. It was difficult to believe in a God who would allow such cruelty.

It was evening when Cornelius and Agnes arrived at the camp. Through the open balcony of their room they saw the camp half a block away where hundreds of refugee families lived side by side, with only blankets for partitions. They would be preparing now to sleep on straw ticks on the dusty cement. These people had been driven from their homes in Russia. In the panic of flight mothers, fathers, and children had been wrenched apart.

The Walls pondered these things as they unpacked their belongings, turned off the light, and settled down for the night. What can we tell people who must live with destruction day after day, they asked themselves? Then a rich chorus of voices rose in the evening air through the open balcony.

"Who is singing?" Agnes asked. Cornelius got up to look out.

"Come here, Agnes," he said. She followed him out on the balcony. Beneath them in the court yard stood a group of people singing to their fellow refugees.

Oh God, I want to be at peace,
At peace in the depths of my soul,
Not saying yes, not saying no,
Not straining up, not bending low,
No, quiet, quiet, quiet, still!
Yes, quiet, quiet, quiet, still.

Long after the sounds died away in the night air, the confidence of the singers echoed in the Walls' minds. Although the thought of people torn from their homeland and families had depressed them, now they knew there was no need for despair. If these refugees could sing in the midst of their problems, then the Walls could enter their work joyfully.

Praying and Listening

Because the refugees learned to love the Walls, Onkel and Tante (Uncle and Aunt) soon became their new names. Onkel Wall led Bible studies and spoke in worship services. Both Onkel and Tante Wall listened to many refugees tell their stories of flight from Russia. They prayed with the people.

"Tante Wall, I am shaking all over," said a young refugee mother.

"Why? What is the matter?"

"I have been called before the commission and I am so afraid."

Tante Wall took her hand and held it. She knew the examination would include a doctor's exam and questioning to make sure the woman could read and write. An okay from the commission meant immigration to Holland for the mother. Rejection would mean another six months of waiting while she tried to improve her health with meager food supplies.

"Tante Wall, will you pray with me?"

"Of course, Katrine," said Agnes. They bowed their heads and prayed that God would go with the woman and help her as she answered the examiner's questions. When she returned from the investigation her face was beaming.

"I got the okay!"

"Wonderful!" said Agnes.

Not all refugees returned from the commission smiling. A slow shuffle and sloping shoulders signaled the rejection of one young man who had struggled with tuberculosis for months.

"Why, Onkel Wall?" he asked. "Why must I sit here in

this filthy camp? If I were strong enough to work, I would, but there is no work to do. Even if I had money, I couldn't find food to buy. Why can't I get well?"

"I cannot answer your question," Cornelius said. "I wish I could."

"Then who can help me?"

Cornelius paused before answering. "When we left Russia in 1922, we also asked why."

"You mean you were once refugees also?"

"Yes, during the Russian Revolution we felt as you do now." The young man was quiet. "We didn't know why my father was killed. We didn't know why our little son died of starvation. We didn't know why Agnes was so sick or why bandits robbed us of most of our furniture and clothing."

"Then what did you do? Didn't you get angry at God?"

"We had to draw a line through all of the past," Cornelius continued, "and look to the future. Instead of asking Why? we had to start asking God what he wanted us to do in the present."

"Onkel Wall, I can listen to your advice," the young man said, "You speak from experience."

The House by the Side of the Road

The German and Swiss young people who learned to know the Walls during their refugee work enjoyed their friendship with Onkel and Tante Wall so much they asked them to return to Europe after a brief stay in Canada. "We have to spoil them first," Cornelius said when he first thought of starting a Bible school for the young people. Although the uprooting of war had brought disillusionment to many of the youth, some were searching for something solid on which to base their lives. Cornelius and Agnes "spoiled" them with

Bible studies and weekend retreats. Soon they were asking for more and more Bible studies.

So the Bible school began, with the help of Mennonite Central Committee and the European Mennonite churches, lasting for only a few months in the winter. Students stayed in the homes of church people and attended classes in the Basel MCC center.

As each school year passed, the length of the term and the number of students grew until they needed to look for a bigger place. Cornelius helped find the old Bienenberg hotel and restaurant which the school bought. Today Bienenberg Bible School is still found on the same lovely knoll overlooking the village of Liestal. While Cornelius was principal of the school many young people studied and shared with him in prayer meetings and Bible studies. Agnes worked long hours counseling the girls and organizing aid for the school for Mennonite women.

When retirement time came in 1958 their European friends urged the Walls to settle in Europe. But because they missed their family in America, they settled in Hillsboro, Kansas. Cornelius said he wanted "to live in my house by the side of the road and be a friend of man."

Although this wish came true—many people have felt his warm acceptance—Agnes' death in 1973 was a great loss for him, since they had lived and worked together for 55 years. But something she said encouraged him:

"When I am dying, do not disturb me or call me back. I am ready to go. Instead, keep on living. When your work is done the Lord will bring you home and I'll be there to greet you."

10.
Elfrieda
Dyck

By
Marion
Keeney
Preheim

Elfrieda gripped the wheel until her knuckles turned white as she followed the car ahead. She wondered why she had allowed herself to get into the driver's seat in the first place. Only recently had she learned how to drive, and then only on England's small country roads. Now she had to drive through the crowded London streets following a small car whose license plate she had memorized in case she momentarily lost sight of it.

It seemed years since her brother C. F. Klassen had telephoned her in the summer of 1941. "This is C. F.," he had said. "Our MCC workers in England have just requested two Canadian nurses. I'm to find them. It occurred to me that you might like this assignment." C. F., much older than Elfrieda, almost seemed like a stranger. He had done much in Russia and Canada for Mennonite immigrants and now he served as a member of the Mennonite Central Committee, a relief organization.

"What does that mean?" Elfrieda asked him.

"It's very much like mission work," he said.

Mission work was the furthest thing from Elfrieda's mind at that time. Shortly after nurses' training in Winnipeg, Canada, she had come to the Steinbach Hospital

Elfrieda Dyck

in Manitoba. After two years of work there she had no thought of leaving.

"The assignment is for a one-year term," C. F. continued to explain. "You would not be earning a salary. MCC pays your expenses, and you get $10.00 pocket money monthly. The work is in a war zone with air raids all the time, but I'd like you to think about taking the assignment so I can contact MCC Akron soon."

Elfrieda had found it difficult to think about work overseas. She knew so little. People in the churches had not served in such assignments. She couldn't discuss it with her family because they lived too far away. Then she thought of a nurse who had served overseas during World War I. They talked for hours one evening and prayed. The next day Elfrieda called C. F. and told him she would go.

England and Peter

By the summer of 1942, her passport and papers processed, Elfrieda was finally ready to go. She met the other nurse, Edna Hunsberger, at an MCC meeting in Chicago. They both went for orientation in Akron, Pennsylvania, MCC's central offices.

Ernest Bennett, assistant to the MCC executive secretary Orie Miller, drove them to New York City for their departure. He told them he did not know the ship's name or from where it would depart; the shipping company would contact them about details. Already Elfrieda had a hint of the difficulty of wartime travel and military regulations that would be so much a part of her future, more than she could imagine then— or even now as she left the city of London and headed through the English countryside for an unknown destination.

As she drove on, her mind wandered back again to

that time of departure in New York. The shipping company did call to give them the date, time, and pier, but they did not give the ship's name. The girls sent word to Akron and then took a long taxi ride to a pier in New Jersey. The $5.00 for the ride still seemed like a terrible price to pay for that taxi ride.

The nurses found they were going on a Greek ship in a military convoy of 30 ships. During the 17-day crossing they followed official instructions not to undress for the night and to carry lifejackets with them at all times.

When they finally reached London, they were met by John Coffman and Peter Dyck, the two MCC workers stationed in England. Peter seemed very young to Elfrieda. When the executives in Akron and her brother C. F. had talked about him, she thought he would be middle-aged. Elfrieda, 24, later learned that Peter was 26.

The next day John and Peter showed the nurses the MCC offices in London and a children's home south of London. Then they went to Birmingham in central England to see Woodlands, an old people's home, and to North Wales to what they called a "babies' home" named South Meadows. They had an MCC meeting, the four of them, to decide where each nurse would go. Edna went to the old people's home and Elfrieda to the babies' convalescent home. Both homes took in those who had been bombed out of their homes in the cities.

In 1943, a need developed for a home for older boys, some with police records and rough backgrounds. It was difficult to find male staff members because the army conscripted so many men. Peter opened a home for these boys near Manchester, renting a large English country home called Taxal Edge. He asked Elfrieda to come help with it.

Elfrieda reflected back on those days. She and Peter had tried in every way they could to make the place a home for the boys. They kept rabbits, guinea pigs, and hens for them. Peter had a large garden used as much for therapy for the city boys as for food.

Elfrieda's mother had died when she was 15 and her experience in cooking for her teenage brothers came in handy at the boys' home. The garden produced a lot of extra food, and gooseberries were plentiful. Elfrieda had never canned before, but she had read somewhere that one could bake for canning; she did all her processing in the oven.

Somewhere in the process of working together, Peter and Elfrieda discovered that they wanted to marry. They held the ceremony at Taxal Edge on October 14, 1944. Their term of service complete, they planned to return home that fall. However, MCC asked them to open relief work in Holland rather than return home. Elfrieda had no way of knowing what this next step would mean, but she and Peter were ready to serve.

To prepare for the possibility of relief work in Holland, they began working in a Dutch children's camp. The Dutch government had evacuated to London during the war, and the British had promised them that they could give Dutch children from liberated areas in Holland a period of recuperation. The camps lasted from three to five months. The Dutch staffed them with teachers, counselors, a few Dutch nurses, and a doctor.

The camp in which Peter and Elfrieda worked had 500 children and about 150 Dutch adults. Peter worked as a warden and she as a camp nurse. Three months later the war ended and they immediately made contact with the Dutch in London to get permission to go to Holland. Usually the army allowed only military personnel to go, but early in the summer of 1945 they gave the Dycks permission to enter Holland.

They packed an MCC station wagon full of clothing

and food. On top they put two motorbikes and a bicycle. The night before departure, Dutch headquarters called Peter. An official said, "Mrs. Dyck may go along, but only if she is the driver of the car." Apparently only military personnel with a certain function could go. Military women were not being sent in at that time, but they would allow Elfrieda to go if she functioned as a driver.

Elfrieda protested because she had only recently learned to drive. The busy London streets frightened her. How would she be able to keep her place in the convoy they said would be going? When she understood clearly that it was the only way she could go, she finally agreed to drive.

They were in number four car in a convoy of five. Only the leader had information about the route and destination. Both Peter and Elfrieda memorized the license plate of the car in front of them and followed it through the London streets and out into the countryside.

The next morning, after a night spent in army barracks, they found their five cars in the center of a convoy of huge army trucks stretching as far as they could see. They drove slowly south, much to Elfrieda's relief. The destination was Dover, England, and a "victory" ship on which they were to cross the English Channel. As Elfrieda watched how gingerly the vehicles had to drive up the narrow ramp, she put her foot down: She would not drive up that ramp. Peter drove the car up the gangway onto the ship.

They crossed the English Channel and landed at Ostend, Belgium. The Dycks drove north to Amsterdam, arriving at the only address MCC had given them—the Singel Church, the oldest Mennonite church in Holland. A caretaker told them where to find one of the church's pastors, Rev. Theo Hylkema.

The Work in Holland

Holland had just been liberated from Nazi occupation. Many people needed food and clothing. The Dutch Mennonites had anticipated the need for office space and had two rooms available for MCC in the historic Singel Church. Peter managed to procure warehouse space for the shipments of food and clothing which came not too long after the Dycks' arrival.

The shipment included a lot of lard in big tins and donated meats, fruits, and vegetables in glass jars. Not too many jars broke during the voyage, but Peter cabled back that MCC should can in tin cans. This suggestion began the MCC canning operation.

He also asked for more workers. Elma Esau, the first to arrive, helped Peter run the distributions. Peter began traveling to contact social agencies and churches in different areas to reach the most needy.

By the time more large shipments arrived there were 14 more workers who served in distribution centers all over Holland. In each place they contacted the nearest Mennonite church, often using the church building and members in the distributions. Most often the aid went to non-Mennonites because the thrifty Dutch Mennonites were only a small percentage of the population.

MCCers usually stayed about a week in each place, leaving Amsterdam on Monday and staying through Friday. Some churches asked them to hold a service at the end of the week; Peter would give a talk and others sang or took part in the service in some way. Word of the services spread and it became a pattern that the local people would ask the MCCers to give a program after each week of food and clothing distribution.

Eventually they found a house in Amsterdam to serve as the MCC center. The unit met together on Sunday nights. When Dutch friends heard about it and asked to come, they decided anyone who could speak English could come. The first guest was a young man who later served as pastor at Witmarsum and Pingjum, Menno Simon's churches. The next Sunday more came and many more joined as time went on. Many times discussions went on until late at night; Elfrieda served tea and cookies, a treat during post-wartime scarcity.

The unit lived in crowded conditions. Food was not plentiful during this period in Holland. Sometimes Elfrieda, who served as unit matron, could carry home all the week's rations rather than use a car because the amount she could purchase was so little.

But the work continued to grow until the MCCers, with the help of Dutch Mennonites, had distributed something to one out of ten Dutchmen.

The Refugees

One day Hylkema came to the MCC house in great excitement. "Read this and tell me who you think the people in this story are," he said. He had a newspaper clipping about 33 refugees from Russia who had come across the Dutch border. The article said they spoke a strange language that sounded like Dutch and claimed their ancestors were Dutch. The University of Utrecht had sent some professors of language to listen to their dialect, the article stated. These people pronounced the word for horse *pead*. In Dutch *paard* is horse. The clipping gave other examples.

"That's Plattdeutsch," Elfrieda said. "They must be Mennonites." Elfrieda knew the language well. Born during the Russian revolution, March 10, 1917, she lived in Russia until she was seven. Her father died in 1924; her mother took the family to Canada in 1925. Even in Winnipeg, Canada, they retained their Russian

Mennonite customs and traditions.

When Peter came home and saw the article, he became excited, too. He and Hylkema drove down to meet the people. When they talked to them in Plattdeutsch, they amazed the refugees who thought no one in Holland would understand them. The refugees told them that thousands of Mennonite refugees were fleeing Russia. Some Mennonites had fled from Russia with the retreating German army in 1943 and were in Germany. Peter, who was also an immigrant to Canada from Russia, wondered how he could help his people. They told him the Dutch government planned to send them back to Germany because they were in Holland illegally.

Peter talked to officials and finally they agreed to allow Mennonite refugees to cross the Dutch border. They issued a "Menno" pass in three languages: Dutch, German, and English. When refugees came to the border, officials called in someone from MCC to identify those who claimed to be Mennonites. Not able to keep up with the work and these identifications, Peter located a Dutch priest living nearby who knew Mennonites in Holland. Officials allowed him to specify who could get a Menno pass.

About 430 refugees trickled into Holland in this way. In the meantime the Russian government learned about the procedure and put pressure on the Dutch government to stop it.

MCC had promised the Dutch government to house, feed, and clothe the refugees and eventually move them out of the country. They had one camp of about 150. The rest the Dutch Mennonites took into their homes, mostly in northern farming communities. The MCCers wondered where they would send them and began thinking of Canada.

Then word came from Germany that some U.S. army officials had discovered a group of Mennonite refugees in the American sector of Berlin. (Berlin and Germany were then divided by the allies into four sectors: the American, British, Russian, and French.) This group said they were Mennonites of Dutch origin, but had lived in Russia for 150 years. They claimed the American Mennonites would help them if they could contact them.

The only American Mennonite in Germany at that time was Robert Kreider, who was the MCC representative for CRALOG, the Council of Relief Agencies Licensed for Operation in Germany. The American military personnel contacted him. He suggested they contact Peter Dyck in Amsterdam.

A man named Colonel Stinson, head of the U.S. army's refugee section in Berlin, called Peter. "Of course I would like to come and take care of those people," Peter said, "but I can't get into Germany." The army only allowed military men in at that time, and Peter knew this.

"Okay," Stinson said, "I'll cut you an order," the military way of saying "issue an order."

To Germany

Peter left in a small car packed full of tins of chicken, dehydrated potatoes, and some flour. The Mennonite refugees did not have refugee status because they were illegally in the city, and they were not German citizens, so they had no ration cards with which to buy food. When Peter got to Berlin, the people could hardly believe what was happening. Here was one who not only brought them food, but also spoke their language. He must be one of them.

To get food, the Mennonite men had been crawling

out at night and going back into the Russian zone. Peter tried to think of a way to find more food. He saw some Dutch ambulances in the streets of Berlin, and learned that they were taking sick Dutchmen, who had been used as forced labor in Germany, back to Holland. The Red Cross ambulances were coming back into Germany. He asked if they would fill them up with food from the MCC warehouse for the Mennonite refugees in Berlin.

Peter called Elfrieda from Berlin on a military line. "Each Sunday two Red Cross ambulances leave for Germany," he said. "You are to send food supplies with them. Get the right stuff, the most nourishing staples you have. We may lose it at the border, but we must take the risk."

"We accompanied those ambulances with prayer," Elfrieda says. "Both got there on Monday. Even though border officials inspected all other vehicles, they did not check the ambulances. We told the drivers not to put up a fight if the inspectors threatened to take the food. MCCers continued to fill these two ambulances each week. During all the months they helped us, the inspectors never once asked about the contents."

The 150 Mennonites in Berlin had been living in a bombed-out building, and never came out in the daylight because they had no right to live there. The army personnel discovered them when they saw smoke from a cooking fire coming out of the site. After Peter began working with them, he asked Stinson's refugee division if they could give the group better housing, since the military routinely requisitioned housing for its purposes. They gave the refugees a row house of three dwellings.

Later, as refugees continued to arrive, they increased the number of houses to twelve. The army provided bunk beds, straw ticks for mattresses, blankets, and fuel. All food and other supplies came from MCC.

Then Peter began to hear about other refugees who needed help. He started traveling, which made it impossible for him to take care of everything for the Berlin group. He went to Stinson and said, "I can't take care of these refugees by myself. I need my wife who is in Holland here to help me."

"Dyck, hold it," the colonel said. "I have a wife in France. I can't even bring my own wife here."

"This is different," Peter said. "I want my wife to come as a worker. I can't leave these people without someone to look after them while I do my other work. She isn't coming as my wife."

Stinson agreed to "cut an order" for Elfrieda. She received a call from his office three weeks after Peter had left for Berlin. "How do I get to Berlin?" she asked Stinson's secretary.

"Mrs. Dyck," the secretary said, "that's up to you."

Elfrieda wondered what to do. How she wished Peter were there to decide for her, but he wasn't. She knew overland travel was difficult and decided to try KLM, the Dutch airlines. "I need to get to Berlin," she told the clerk at the airline desk. "I have a job there."

"We have one flight this afternoon and one at 1:00 a.m., but everything is booked," she said.

"That's too bad," Elfrieda said, but just stood there.

The clerk turned back to her. "Are you British?" she asked.

In her slight British accent Elfrieda said, "I've been working there three years." She got out her American traveler's checks and held them in her hand, knowing the value of the American dollar.

"Are you going to pay with American traveler's checks?" the clerk asked.

"Yes," Elfrieda said.

"Let me check to see if that flight is really full," the clerk said. Somehow it was no longer full. "How much is that?" Elfrieda said, quickly putting her signature on the traveler's check. In no time at all she had her air ticket.

"I'll never forget the reaction of the MCC unit," Elfrieda says. "They could hardly believe what I told them."

The next surprised person was Colonel Stinson. Peter was taking his meals at the officers' mess. He took Elfrieda along with him the morning after she arrived, the day after Stinson cut the order for her to come. "This is my wife," Peter said.

Stinson jumped up. "Are you here already?" he said. "I can't believe it."

He didn't ask where she would stay and she moved in with Peter. Peter was living alone in a large house owned by a lawyer, one requisitioned by the military. Several days later Elfrieda had to go to the military housing office to fill out some papers. "Where are you staying?" the officer asked. She explained.

"You can't stay there," the shocked officer said. "That's bachelor quarters. You have to go to women's quarters." He gave her addresses of several houses. He told her no American women had arrived yet, and she could pick what she wanted. "I only need one room," she told the owner of one house. "You can have the rest." The owners were living in the attic with two small children because of army orders.

"We can't move down," the woman said. "I want to keep my job of cleaning the house. Maybe eventually I'll get my own house back."

So Peter and Elfrieda lived in big houses four blocks apart, wishing they could just have two rooms together.

No one ever moved in with either of them the whole time they lived in separate houses. Much of the time Peter was gathering up refugees in the various zones. When he was in Berlin, they would phone each other to say good night. Thus Elfrieda was lodged in Berlin.

Camp Life

Camp life developed as the numbers increased. The refugees held regular worship services in a bombed-out school building to which people brought their own chairs, boxes, and benches. Refugees skilled in teaching taught the children and youth. Elfrieda ran a clinic staffed with a refugee doctor and nurses. For operating the camp Elfrieda had an administrative assistant, a secretary, and other office staff from among the refugees. Refugee women organized for large-scale cooking under Elfrieda's guidance.

As the camp took shape and order, those in the American refugee section noticed how well it was run. Stinson would send officials to the camp to see how the Mennonites did it.

For Christmas 1947, Elfrieda, Peter, and the refugees busied themselves with a program. They invited Stinson and some of his department heads. Some of the military men had tears in their eyes as they watched the refugees celebrating Christ's birth.

After the large gathering, Peter and Elfrieda returned to their apartment. (The army had finally allowed them to stay in the same house.) Some of the refugees were waiting there to show them the spare room they had fixed up. The room had a small Christmas tree; under it were gifts that they had made. The youth, under the guidance of their teacher, had made a thick scrapbook as a calendar for the New Year with a voluminous amount of artistic drawings. One woman had cut many blue flowers from a dress she owned to applique on a tablecloth.

As the camp grew, Stinson told the Dycks they had to make plans to transfer the Mennonites out of Berlin. Because of the investigations done by C. F. Klassen, they knew Paraguay would accept the refugees.

Finding a Way

Ships were scarce in the post-war period. They approached the Dutch who said no at first, but the queen happened to hear about it. "If it's for the Mennonites," she said, "we must help them." They secured the *Volendam*, located at Rotterdam. Thus they had the U.S. army's permission to leave, a country ready to receive them, and a ship. But how could they get permission to take Russian citizens through the Russian zone? The Russians were shipping Russian citizens who had fled the country back to Russia.

One evening the American military called Peter and Elfrieda into the allied headquarters which housed all those who controlled the zones. When they announced themselves at the entrance, an American soldier escorted them to a room where a high-ranking military man was sitting. Guards closed the doors and stood outside.

"We have decided to assist you in getting the Mennonite refugees out of Berlin," the man said. "The army will come Monday and take you out through the Russian zone. Your job is to get the people ready without telling them when they are to go. You are not to talk to anyone else about the exact time. I don't know how you will do that, but that is your job."

Now they had 1,100 people to get ready without letting them know when they would leave. They also planned to take 1,000 from a camp in Munich,

Germany, and over 300 from the refugees that had crossed into Holland.

The Dycks held meetings with the people in the Berlin camp, explaining that they should get ready to leave. They said any who wanted to could wait in West Germany for a chance to go to Canada. Most decided to go to Paraguay.

The office staff helped to prepare the travel documents. People did their packing. Peter went to Bremerhaven, the port from which the *Volendam* would leave, to make shipping arrangements. He came back on Sunday to see if the people were ready to go; he and Elfrieda walked from room to room in all the housing. Everyone was ready.

They were still working on travel documents at 10:00 that night when the phone rang. "It's all off," Colonel Stinson said.

Peter just couldn't believe it. "We've had permission all the way from the top of the refugee division of the army," he said.

"That's true," Stinson said, "but General Clay, the supreme commander of the U.S. forces in Europe, heard of it. Because of some conference coming up with the Russians, he feels we can't do anything like this now. He says, 'Do not move the Mennonites.'"

Meeting with General Clay

That same night Peter wrote a letter to General Clay. It was not a long letter. He wrote about the plight of the Mennonites and concluded it by saying, "In the history of the Mennonites there have been times when their fate was determined by one person. We are looking to you, General Clay, at this time to help our people leave Berlin."

The next day Stinson called Peter to his office. "I've

been up all night trying to solve this problem," he said. As he talked it became clear that Clay held the key to the refugees' fate.

"I guess Clay is the one to whom I must go," Peter said.

"I'm a lieutenant colonel," Stinson said. "I have never had an appointment with Clay. And you, a civilian, are going to see the general?"

That morning Peter went to the general's office, taking his letter with him. At the office the secretary told Peter to fill out forms requesting an appointment.

"How long will it take to see him after I fill out the forms?" Peter asked.

"About three weeks," the secretary said.

"I'm sorry, I don't have that much time," Peter said. "Is General Clay in his office now?" he asked.

"Yes," the secretary said.

"Does he have to come through this door?" Peter asked.

"Yes."

"I hope you don't mind if I wait," Peter said.

As Peter waited, the secretary became more and more uncomfortable. She finally took his letter in to General Clay. Soon the secretary's phone rang and she was told to send Dyck in.

The general spent almost an hour talking with Peter, trying to be of help. "Even if we get them in a train and put guards on the train, there will probably be shooting," he said. "The ones who will be hurt will be your people. Do you want that on your conscience?"

Peter asked if he could fly them out. At that time the Americans as well as others had assigned airways, but they needed permission to fly through other zones. "You must know that without Russian permission shooting will occur," Clay said. "Let's leave it up to Washington. If they say move the Mennonites, we'll move the Mennonites."

Peter telephoned MCC Akron, his first transatlantic call. He asked them to put in a good word in Washington for the refugees. MCC sent someone to Washington, D.C., but the answer Clay got back from the State Department was, "Do not move the Mennonites without Russian permission." In the meantime, MCC had also notified Mennonite churches in the United States and Canada. Many, many people prayed for the refugees in Berlin.

A Time of Uncertainty

That Monday night Peter and Elfrieda called all the refugees together at the school. They told the people, "We have a ship. We have a country. We have the travel documents. But we have just gotten word that the Berlin people cannot go through the Russian zone." As Peter stood there trying to explain the situation, he wept. In the silence that followed one refugee after another stood up to say something.

"I have spent ten years in Siberia," one said. "I know what it is like. Don't feel bad. You have tried. It must be God's will for us not to go." Others got up to comfort Peter and Elfrieda.

Peter left Berlin to help the other refugees go, and Elfrieda stayed in Berlin to resume camp life. She had, for example, stopped coal supplies because she thought they were leaving. Sometime during the next day Colonel Stinson called her to American headquarters. "Just in case there would be a turn of events, how much time will you need to get ready?" he asked.

"Give me one hour to get all the people together," she said. "They won't mind leaving all their things behind if they can go."

The following day she was in her apartment when a refugee who was her administrative assistant called and asked if they could have a prayer meeting that evening. "By all means let's do," Elfrieda said. She told him she might be late because she expected a visitor that evening.

When Elfrieda got to the camp that evening, the meeting was already over. She went into one of the houses. There she met old Mr. Sawatzky setting his suitcase into the hallway. When she asked him why he was doing that, he said, "We've just prayed for a miracle. I have never done that before in my life. When I got back to my room, I couldn't just go to bed. I had to be ready in case the Lord is going to answer our prayer and perform a miracle." As she went from room to room Elfrieda noticed other people collecting their things.

The Lord Is Going to Do a Miracle

The next morning was Thursday, the day the ship was to leave from Bremerhaven. Before time to leave her apartment that morning, she got a call from Stinson. "Mrs. Dyck," he said. "I've heard by the grapevine that General Clay is going to see his Russian counterpart today. In case you hear anything from him, let know. Don't go to the camp today. Stay in your apartment near the phone."

Nothing happened until 3:30. Then General Clay's secretary called asking for Peter. "Peter is in Bremerhaven," Elfrieda said. "Could you give me a message?"

"We will call Peter Dyck in Bremerhaven," the secretary said. "If we cannot contact him, we will call you back." Click, down went the receiver. The boat was to leave at 4:00.

At 5:45 the telephone rang. "This is Colonel Stinson's

office," someone said. "Would you please report immediately to the American headquarters?" Click, the person hung up.

Ice sheeted the streets. By now Elfrieda felt secure enough in her driving to go speedily through the slick city streets. She got to the offices just at closing time. As she came into the building, she heard the refugee section secretary saying, "Colonel Stinson has given orders that we are not to accept any calls in this office unless it is about the Mennonites."

The secretary ushered Elfrieda into Stinson's office. Heads of various military departments—food, transportation, medical services—ringed the room. Elfrieda was the only woman in the room and one chair remained empty. "That chair is for you," Stinson said, "unless you don't want to take the time to sit down."

"It depends on what news you have for me," Elfrieda said.

"All I know is we are moving your people tonight," he said. "You told me you needed only one hour to get them ready. Now I'm giving you one and a half hours. The plan is for us to send trucks to your houses and pick up people and baggage, take them to a railroad siding, put them on freight cars, and transport them to Bremerhaven. Your job," he continued, "is to inform your people and make sure they understand they are not to speak about this on the streets. Have them outside the houses with their baggage ready for the trucks to pick them up at 8:00 tonight. You must also have work crews ready to load the baggage on the trucks and unload it at the station. We will be sending only a driver with each truck."

Elfrieda never did sit down. As she was leaving the building, they called her back for a telephone call from Bremerhaven. It was her brother C. F. Klassen. "Isn't it wonderful that you're going?" he said. "Peter has already left for Berlin to help you."

"Since when have you known?" Elfrieda asked.

"Since 4:00 this afternoon," he said.

"Cornelius, I have just heard about it two minutes ago," she said. "I have to go now. The people don't even know about it yet. Also, I think we'll have a baby on the way because I have a woman in labor. Good-bye." Click, she put the phone down.

As Elfrieda drove closer to the refugees' houses, she saw that all the buildings were dark and realized the electricity was off. This happened periodically for reasons they never discovered. It was 6:30 and already dark. This meant the people would have to get ready by 8:00 without light.

The first house at which she stopped was one with a seating capacity of 300 in the dining room; people from other houses came to eat here. Because of the blackout they had stubs of candles lit on the tables. "Good evening," Elfrieda said. An expectant silence fell on the people.

"The Lord is going to do a miracle," she said. "I've just heard we're going to leave Berlin. Would you all finish your meal as quickly as possible, clear away the dirty dishes, and go back to your houses and rooms? As you walk through the streets do not speak. Please go silently. Pack your belongings and be outside your doors at 8:00 tonight."

She went from one house to another until people in all twelve houses knew. As she made the rounds she met refugees in the streets. They spoke not a word, but some would reach out and clasp her hand in passing. She wondered why no traffic was on the streets and she could see no others besides the Mennonite refugees. Later she learned that the American army had blocked off that whole section in preparation for the refugees' exodus.

At 8:00 she was at the camp office and met with colonels and majors from the refugee division. She had told Stinson earlier in the day that one of the refugee women was in the city hospital in labor, so now he sent an ambulance accompanied by his German secretary with orders to release her from the hospital.

The woman was already in the delivery room with the doctors masked. They practically threw the secretary out, but he showed them the written order and insisted she had to come right then. The woman thought for sure the Russians had her now. The shock stopped the labor pains. It wasn't until much later that she had the baby.

Another ambulance came to take the sick in the camp to the train. Then ten-ton trucks began to arrive. As Elfrieda sent her first crew out to the initial truck, they came running back, eyes wide with fear.

"Mrs. Dyck, Mrs. Dyck," they exclaimed, "that is a black man in the truck." The driver, an American black, had grinned down at them from high up in the truck's cab. The Russian Mennonites had never seen a black man before. In this tense situation it frightened them even more than it might have otherwise.

"That's all right," Elfrieda said to the refugees. "We have a lot of black people in North America." She went up to the truck.

"I just looked at them and they all ran," the driver said.

"They have never seen a black before," she said. "Now that I've explained, they are ready to go."

"Come on in here," the driver called. "Let's get going." By this time everyone was laughing at grown men being so shocked.

The evacuation went smoothly, but Elfrieda had very little time to pack her own things. From her apartment she got the people's travel documents, put a few things in a small suitcase, and took a box of flashlights she thought might be useful on the trip. As she left the house she only talked briefly with the lady of the house. "I am leaving," she said. "My husband is coming later tonight."

Stinson and Elfrieda made one last visit to the housing to make sure no one had been left behind. They walked through all the houses. They didn't find anyone there, but both noticed that the women had left everything neat and orderly, and had even washed the floors right before they left. When Stinson remarked about it, Elfrieda said, "That's our Mennonites."

While they did the camp inspection, Bob Kreider helped with the loading at the station, even to seeing that each boxcar had one of the flashlights. Arriving back at the station, Elfrieda wondered what to do about Peter's coming. Bob agreed to call the border, tell the guard to be on the lookout for a Peter Dyck, and relay the message, "The train is gone." Bob left and made the call.

Peter came with his brother C. J., who was driving the car. C. J., an MCC material aid worker in Northern Germany, had come to Bremerhaven to help with the embarkation. When they got to the border, a sleepy guard told them, "The train is gone." They questioned him to see if he knew any other details and soon realized he did not.

They decided to go to Berlin anyhow. They went to the Dyck apartment and the woman of the house said, "Your wife went out of the house with one suitcase, said she was leaving, and that you would be coming soon." They questioned her and realized she had no more information than that. C. J. and Peter were hungry. Although the woman had never done anything more than clean the house, Peter asked her to heat up a can of chicken he gave her. C. J. went to sleep for a while so he could drive back to Bremerhaven as they had planned.

Peter was straightening up the apartment when the telephone rang. It was Bob Kreider. At 1:30 he had decided to call the apartment just in case Peter had arrived there. "Peter," he said. "Elfrieda is still in Berlin. The train is about ready to leave."

Peter woke C. J. up. As they were dashing out, the woman came in, not only with the hot chicken but a whole meal. They had to tell her they had no time to eat it. They never saw her again to explain what happened that night.

When Peter arrived at the station, Stinson threw his arms around him. "They're leaving," he said. "They're leaving. It's the last of the Mennonites." The boxcars were all locked so Peter had to jump on the passenger car which was the only car he could possibly get into. It happened to be the one in which Elfrieda was with the refugee hospital cases. Just as he got on, the train took off. It was 2:00 a.m.

As the train pulled out, Stinson turned to Bob Kreider and said, "Good. There go the Mennonites. I hope I never see another one!"

Through the Russian Zone

The first thing Peter asked when he got on the train was whether they had written permission to go through the Russian zone. Elfrieda said she only had travel documents to go to Paraguay. Colonel Stinson had told them to leave. Two army officers were in the next train compartment. They never saw them and never knew whether they had documents or not.

By daybreak they expected to be out through the Russian zone, which would now be East Germany. But that is not the way it went. The train moved slowly. Since there was only one train track, they often had to go onto a siding to let other trains pass.

They traveled all day Friday through the Russian zone. Late Friday afternoon they came to the British border. Before they crossed into the British zone they had to stop on the Russian side; the Russians inspected all trains. They watched as inspectors walked down to inspect other trains and wondered if now this would be it. The refugees in the boxcars could not see what was going on, but the sick and their attendants in the passenger car watched fearfully.

Peter went to the British engineer. "Do we have to wait here?" he asked.

"When the light is red, I must wait," he said.

Peter gave him some food, hoping this would encourage him to go across. They could see the inspectors coming down to their train when all of a sudden the light turned green and the train pulled out.

As it pulled out into the British zone, Peter jumped from the passenger car. He ran to the first boxcar and threw open the door. "We're out," he called in to the people. "You're free now."

He went to the next car and said the same thing. The people began to sing. "Now thank we all our God," they sang, "with hearts and hands and voices...." As he continued to open boxcar doors and give his message, the rest took up the song until all had joined in singing the hymn.

They had some more hours to travel to Bremerhaven where the ship was waiting for them. It was bitterly cold. In one boxcar, straw caught fire en route and they had to throw their stove out of the car. These suffered the most. By the time the train arrived in Bremerhaven, one baby had pneumonia and one old woman had died.

On to Paraguay

The *Volendam* received them on board with a cup of hot cocoa for each person. Soon 1,000 from Berlin were settled in their cabins and 100 decided to stay in West Germany in hopes of joining relatives in Canada later. With those from Holland and Munich, Germany, the total number of refugees on board the *Volendam* when it sailed that February 7, 1947, was 2,305.

The trip took 21 days and the boat had only a skeleton crew. Elfrieda and Peter organized the refugees on board ship to do the rest of the work. They did various chores such as cleaning, sewing, and staffing the ship's hospital; the ship had a doctor, but the refugees did all the nursing.

Five women gave birth to babies on board ship, including the woman who had been in labor in the Berlin hospital. Five persons died on board ship. They arrived in Paraguay with the same number with which they had started, 2,305.

The young men were organized into guard duty shifts; they watched after the safety of the children, and at night looked out for any emergency. Those skilled in teaching held classes for the 600 children. They had no paper, pencils, or books, but they kept the children occupied.

They had one whole week of MCC clothing distribution. Not being able to get MCC clothing into Berlin, they had bales loaded on to the ship before it left Rotterdam, Holland. They laid things out on deck and called people by categories to get what they needed. In all they distributed 35,000 articles to men, women, expectant mothers, youth, and children. The crew watched the process in amazement, never having seen anything like it before.

The refugees had church services, Bible studies, and a Bible course taught by one of the ministers. A choir practiced and sang at services.

Just before landing in Argentina, officials notified them of a revolution in Paraguay. This meant they could not go up the Paraguay River to the Mennonite colonies. They had to set up a camp in the Buenos Aires port area. The Argentine military gave them 75 army tents. A high fence surrounded them with guards on duty because the refugees only had transit visas for Argentina. For three and a half months they lived and slept in tents.

Eating took place across the street at an immigration hall which held 1,000 people. Three times a day in two shifts they crossed the street with police escort. Elfrieda planned the meals, bought the food, and organized the work. Refugee women cooked the meals. Boys peeled potatoes, as many as ten sacks (600 pounds) a day, and the girls served the meals.

From the start, teachers held classes out in the open area. Religious services continued, including a baptismal service. An American pastor visited the camp and gave a message.

Sports equipment bought in the city helped provide activities for some of the youth. Those who were cobblers asked to have tools; they began repairing people's shoes. When some carpenters saw this, they asked for hammers, saws, and wood; they made bases for sandals, and women sewed linen strips on for sandal tops.

Elfrieda wondered just how long they would have to stay in the camp. Living in such cramped space was difficult in itself, but the heavy rains that came made it even harder. In heavy downpours, the refugees had to take the luggage they kept under their folding cots and put it on the cots. When the revolution ended, they were able to send the refugees into Paraguay. They needed to set up another camp near Asunción, however, to organize groups going to different parts of Paraguay.

New Assignments

Elfrieda and Peter spent a month visiting the Mennonite colonies which were already in Paraguay and Brazil. Then the MCCers located there took over the work with the refugees and the Dycks flew back to the States in July 1947. They thought this would end their MCC sevice. But MCC asked them to go through the Mennonite churches in the United States and Canada to tell the refugee story. On their own, the Dycks had filmed events along the way. They put the film together and started out.

People traveled miles to hear about the refugees, and Canadian Mennonites had a special interest because they had so many relatives among the refugees. Elfrieda kept some statistics: The total number who came out to the meetings was over 100,000; the offerings totaled $65,000; and some also sent contributions directly to MCC.

While they were traveling, MCC contacted them about going back into refugee work. By November 1947 they were on their way back to the work. Peter went to a refugee camp at Gronau, Germany, near the Dutch border where MCC did most of the refugee transport processing. MCC put Elfrieda in charge of a refugee camp in Backnang, Germany. She lived in Stuttgart, but she was not to be there for long.

The MCC office was getting another transport ready for departure in 1948, and this time they asked Elfrieda to escort the transport by herself. The *General Stuart*

Heintzelman, an American army boat chartered by the International Refugee Organization, left Germany on February 25, 1948, with 860 passengers. They followed a routine similar to the first transport, which included a week of MCC clothing distribution. The trip took 16 days. No revolution stopped them this time and the refugees went to the colonies immediately.

Elfrieda was to wait in Paraguay for Peter, who was to come on another refugee ship. She received no cable and no ship arrived. Finally she decided to go back to Europe on the ship rather than flying since it would be free of charge.

When they were on their way, the ship's captain said, "You know, Mrs. Dyck, we are no longer under the International Refugee Organization. I'm under army orders now. We may have to go to Panama or Australia." At 10:00 that evening he got orders to go to Panama.

As soon as the ship docked, Elfrieda cabled MCC Germany. The ship was loading army officers and their families for a trip back to the States. When they were getting ready to go, the captain said to Elfrieda, "We saw how you managed the refugees on the trip to South America. Would you help get these families settled in their cabins?" She did as the captain asked her.

Arriving in New Orleans, Elfrieda received word to fly to Newark, New Jersey, and on to Europe. When she got off the plane, Elma Esau of MCC Akron was waiting for her. "We can't waste any time," Elma said.

Elfrieda wondered what the rush was. "Don't you know?" Elma asked. "You're supposed to escort the next ship to Paraguay in seven days." Elfrieda calculated: She would have five days sailing on the *Queen Mary* and two days to get ready for the next transport.

When she got to England, she phoned from the ship to get a flight to Amsterdam immediately. Peter met her at the airport. He said she would not be leaving in two days because the ship chartered by the IRO was being repaired.

The Charlton Monarch

The ship, *The Charlton Monarch*, was an old oil tanker which a Greek shipping company had converted into a passenger ship. The captain delayed the departure again and again, but finally said it was ready. Elfrieda took a work crew of 120 refugee men on board to get ready for the departure the next day, a standard procedure for each trip. But the ship did not go the next day; it took nine more days to work on repairs.

After her first interview with the captain and his officers, Elfrieda had an uneasy feeling about the trip. She sensed a lack of cooperation between the officers and captain and expressed this to MCCers working on the transport. Nevertheless they went ahead with plans for receiving the passengers, who arrived on schedule the next day.

The accommodations also bothered Elfrieda. Space, always limited, seemed much more so on this ship. The kitchen particularly did not look clean. After the women were on board she told them to take out all dry rations for children under two and prepare the food themselves. The people had a hard time eating when they saw the dirty aprons, towels, and clothing of the chief cook and his assistants.

They left from Bremerhaven for South America. They only got as far as Holland, two days journey, when engine trouble developed. The officers came to Elfrieda and said they were leaving the ship. They had no intention of going all the way to South America with this captain. The captain had to wire to England for new officers and wait until they arrived.

Late one afternoon, while they were waiting, someone said two men on land were waving at the ship. Elfrieda recognized Peter and C. F. and motioned them to come on board. They got a man with a small boat to row them to the ship. They had been in Rotterdam that day and, much to their alarm, heard that the ship was in port. The captain reassured them that the ship would leave the following day.

The next day the new officers arrived and the ship once more was on its way. The rest of the crew began talking about leaving as soon as they reached England. Elfrieda asked the captain, "Will we stop in England?"

"No," he said. "The crew is threatening to leave. We're not docking. We'll have a boat bring in supplies." He dropped anchor far out in the water and supplies came by boat. The crew grew upset and angry. Something mysteriously went wrong with the engines and the ship was delayed for 24 hours.

As they headed south towards Cape Verde Islands, the engine stopped ten times in the eight days. The refrigeration also went out of order. It did not take long until the people could smell the rotting food all over the boat. The crew did not clean out the rotten food, so the refugees finally took care of it. The people ate mostly potatoes, bread, and some vegetables.

The *Charlton Monarch* stopped at the Cape Verde Islands to take on fuel. The captain and first officers said they would try to find meat and fresh supplies. They asked other ships lying in the harbor to sell them some and tried on shore also. They came back with only 185 pounds of meat, which would not feed the 900 passengers and crew on board for more than one or two meals.

While docked at Cape Verde many people became ill; they had stomach aches, vomiting, cramps, and high fevers up to 104 degrees. It affected approximately 500 of the passengers. Elfrieda approached the ship's doctor. He said, "It's only the air."

"I think it has something to do with the food," Elfrieda said. "Not one of our children under two whose mothers prepare their food is sick." The doctor still did little to help. Some had such severe cramps, even grown men and women, that they fainted in the ship's hallways. The refugee nursing staff put them on tea and dry bread diets. No one died, but many lost a lot of weight. The refugees began to call the ship the *Charlatan Monarch*. (A charlatan is one who pretends to have more knowledge or skill than he really has.)

After leaving the islands the engines started giving problems again. Two boilers burst because of the crew's negligence. The ship was without electricity, which affected the water pump. Refugees had to carry water up in buckets from the hold. They could not flush toilets or do laundry; the only water used was for cooking and drinking.

As they kept going south into warmer and warmer climate, they had more problems. Not only the water, but also the ship's soap supply ran short. The bed linens could not be washed and a bad odor prevailed on board ship. The sun brought out more oil saturating this old oil tanker's decks. Even though the refugees scrubbed and scrubbed, it kept surfacing.

Adrift at Sea

Finally, the engines went dead completely and the ship drifted for two days and nights. Elfrieda pleaded with the captain to send an SOS. He said the chief engineer had to sign a statement that he could not get the engines repaired, but he would not sign. He was trying to get the crew to work.

Elfrieda had a meeting with her people each day because she had promised she would always keep them informed. "All during those days on the ship I had wonderful cooperation from the refugees," she says. "Keeping them current on what was happening seemed to help."

The people continued with their church services twice on Sunday, weekday evening devotions, prayer meetings, Bible classes, and youth meetings. They wrote and edited a weekly newspaper.

"I discovered a ship that is drifting can give you a feeling of being terribly alone out on the water," Elfrieda recalls. "Especially the nights were difficult. I usually spent them going around from cabin to cabin talking to people, especially the older women."

It was hot both from the outside weather and from the engine room; the heat permeated the cabins. At night the wind rose and made the waves higher. Portholes had to be kept closed because of the high waves, making the poorly ventilated cabins suffocatingly hot. The ship tossed from side to side. Anything that was loose slid across the floors. Because the electrical system had given out, only dim night-lights lit the hallways and the cabins remained unlighted. The ship's hospital delivered a set of twins and two other babies during this voyage, all by flashlight.

During the day the ship had sharks all around it because of the garbage thrown overboard. The people entertained themselves by watching them poke their heads up out of the water. The crew fished for baby sharks. At night the drunken crew made the passengers fearful. The captain seemed to have no influence on the crew. When Elfrieda knocked on his door, he would ask who it was and open for her. She could see a club and pistol inside his cabin near the door.

"What are those for?" she once asked him.

"That's in case some of the fellows from down below come up," he said.

The ship lay drifting a second night. Elfrieda thought about things past and present. How could she and Peter have known when they extended their MCC service what all would happen? They could never have predicted during their car journey in England to cross the channel what would lie ahead. By train, ship, and plane much adventure and trial had come their way. They had come to know separation and people suffering. The people, the work, these Elfrieda could not lose sight of. Plus she had the feeling that a purposeful God was at work even if the ship would drift.

After another night of drifting, Elfrieda went to the deck at 6:00 a.m. to see what could be done. She saw that the chief engineer was up and talked with him for a while. He agreed to sign the statement saying the crew could not repair the engine.

Finally a Port

Later on that day the captain told Elfrieda they had sent an SOS, but he had little hope of anyone answering it because the emergency radio system reached only 50 miles. Elfrieda knew the handicap because she had wanted to send a message to MCC of their whereabouts, but could not. Nevertheless, an answer came from a coastal vessel that night. Elfrieda let the passengers stay up past the 10:00 deck clearing to watch the lights of the little ship come closer and closer.

The waves were rocking too high for the boat to come up close. It dropped anchor and stayed near them through the night. In the morning the boat towed them into Recife, Brazil. Arriving after dark, Elfrieda expected they would have a quiet night. As soon as they docked, however, the major part of the crew immediately deserted the ship to go on land.

Elfrieda was in her cabin when she heard people passing her porthole talking about a hole in the ship. She went to one of the officers. "A valve is broken," he said. Since the crewmen responsible for repairs were on shore the officer had called the Recife fire company to come, pump out the water, and repair the valve. They came and did the work.

"We were thankful this had not happened out on the water," Elfrieda says. "We often had prayer meetings on these transport voyages. We prayed more because of the circumstances."

The next morning she took a taxi to the post office in Recife and sent cables to the International Relief Organization in Geneva and MCC in Akron and Germany. All this time they had been trying to find out where the ship was. The longest transport so far had taken three weeks. This ship had not been heard from in six weeks.

The shipping company flew in their supervising engineer. When he came on board, Elfrieda went with him throughout the ship to show him the conditions. He said the crew would get the ship fixed up in no time and they would be on their way to Buenos Aires, Argentina. Later he called Elfrieda to a meeting in the captain's office. "Be patient and all will be well," he said.

"I don't believe all will be well," Elfrieda said. "I told the captain at the beginning of the journey I would be open and straightforward with him at all times. I have already cabled the IRO and MCC headquarters about our whereabouts and difficulties. I want you to know I will do everything in my power to get our people to Paraguay without having to continue on this ship."

"Mrs. Dyck," he said, "you don't know how difficult it is to get shipping."

"I do know what the problems are," she replied. "If you can repair this ship, the best to you. I just want you to know I'm working on other means of transport."

A few days later Mr. Wood, a representative from IRO stationed in Rio de Janeiro, Brazil, came to see them. He first went to the captain and chief engineer to hear their story. They assured him within a week the ship would be on its way south again.

Then he sat down with Elfrieda. After her account he said, "I'm amazed. Usually it's the passengers who make the difficulties. Here your people are walking around as calm as if it had been any other trip." Elfrieda told him the reason for that was their faith and how they had prayed. Before he left the ship he promised he would be back within a week. If they were not on their way by then, he would see that they got to Paraguay some other way.

The crew was really working under the direction of the engineer the shipping company flew in. Toward the week's end they were ready for a trial run. They got the engines running, but when they had gone out into the water a short distance everything went dead. They had to be towed back into port.

Are We Really Going to Fly?

Seven days after his first visit, Mr. Wood came back. When he walked up the gangplank, he waved to Elfrieda and said, "I'll see you in a few minutes." He went straight to the captain and engineer. "You are not on your way," he said. "You did not get the ship repaired. I will have to find another way to get the passengers to Paraguay."

He came to Elfrieda's office and told her he planned to send two airplanes in each night. "Have groups ready," he said. "Each person may have 40 pounds of luggage. There will be off schedule flights to take them. I suggest you send your sick, aged, and crippled with the first planeloads."

He had arranged for three planes to come that night. As soon as he left, Elfrieda had a meeting with the people. She explained that three groups of approximately 50 people could go that night. MCC had been trying to keep families together. Now, she told them, she was asking them to send the sick and crippled men and women, the aged, and mothers with very young children on ahead. She gave them time right in the meeting to discuss it. They all decided to let them go.

She quickly had her office crew make up a list. After midnight they put the people on buses to ride to the airport. The bus Elfrieda rode on had quite a few old people. One after another they would ask, "Frau Dyck, werden wir wirklich durch die Luft fliegen?" ("Mrs. Dyck, are we really going to fly through the air?") Elfrieda reassured them that they would be safe and comfortable. They could sleep all night and wake up to find MCC workers meeting them in Paraguay.

As Elfrieda looked around the bus, she suddenly remembered that the immigration officials had told her only those who could walk onto the plane could go. She had a middle-aged man with a high fever and an old woman paralyzed on one side.

As they came closer to the airport, she said to the bus driver, "Could you just drive around the terminal building and get up close to the airplane?" He looked at her in surprise. "Why no," he said. "We always leave our passengers off at the airport building."

Elfrieda explained about the sick and aged. "Just try," she said. "If you're stopped, okay. You can go back and let us off in front. Otherwise drive right up close to the plane." To her surprise he pulled up to the steps leading into the plane.

The next surprise, however, was that officials flanked each side of the lighted steps. She didn't know that the story of their predicament on the seas and news of the departure that night had been in the newspapers. She quickly turned to the sick man, "Do you think you could pull all your strength together and walk up those stairs? We'll get you a seat as soon as we can." He thought he could. She had taken two young men along to help carry the hand luggage for the older people. "Just take Mrs. Klassen, hold her a few inches off the ground, and walk her up the steps," she instructed them.

They got the first planeload settled by 2:00 a.m., but they had no idea when the next plane would arrive. They waited several hours. Elfrieda got back to the ship at 5:00 a.m.

She slept a few hours while the refugee office staff prepared the list for the next group and got their baggage ready. They went to the airport and again Elfrieda got back to the boat at 5:00 in the morning.

The captain and chief engineer realized that she meant business in getting the people other means of transport. Annoyed at losing the charter, they said they were pulling out into the water "because it was too expensive to stay in port." The expense was not the stay in port, but the loss of transporting the refugees south.

Elfrieda decided to get the baggage off the boat before they pulled out. The IRO transferred it to another ship in port. Just after the baggage left, the ship pulled out. They could see the land, but it was quite a distance by boat. Now how would they get the people to shore? They arranged for a small boat to pick them up. Everyone had to go down a rope ladder and jump from a small platform at the bottom to the little boat. The first officer gave them only one sailor to help.

That night the waves rose high around the small boat. The sailor took his position on the small platform below. Elfrieda sent the people down the ladder. Sometimes the boat would be on a wave high above the platform, other times far below. The sailor had to push the people into the boat at just the right moment, when it was level with the platform. Sometimes they landed on all fours, but he got them all safely into the boat.

They followed this procedure every night, grateful that the sick, aged, and very young had gone earlier. Early each morning Elfrieda had to locate a boat for getting back to the ship. It took seventeen planeloads and one week for the whole process. The last plane had only seventeen passengers consisting of Elfrieda and her refugee office crew. They flew during the day in a small cargo plane lined with benches along the wall. Small quarter-sized slots ventilated the plane.

The refugees went on from Rio to Asunción. Elfrieda had a cable from the IRO in Geneva for her to remain in Rio. Their representative met her there and took her to a good hotel. "We want you to have a five-day rest in Rio after the ordeal you went through," he explained. Elfrieda protested because of the expense. She explained that as an MCCer she did not feel right in doing that. She told about the refugee camps, the transports, and the resettlement work and how church money financed it all. The man still insisted she needed some rest and said it would be at IRO expense. Besides, he explained, she could go back on a plane delivering refugees to Venezuela. This would save MCC the cost of a return air ticket.

After her stay in Rio, Elfrieda flew to Venezuela and waited a number of days for the refugee plane to come.

Then they took off with the next stop to be Puerto Rico; from Puerto Rico the plane went on to Hartford, Connecticut, where it was to load something for the airlift into Berlin which began that summer of 1948. The plane needed a few repairs which delayed them several days there.

Elfrieda called Bill Snyder in Akron. "Elfrieda, where are you?" he asked. "We've all been wondering." She hadn't cabled in Brazil or Venezuela because she did not know in either place when she would be leaving or arriving.

When she entered the plane she saw what it was airlifting to Berlin: a huge airplane motor which filled the plane from side to side. Workers had moved the seats to fit it in. Elfrieda took some seats to form a bed for sleeping during the flight.

After one stop in Gander, Newfoundland, they flew on toward Ireland. In the morning she looked out the window and noticed that one propeller had stopped. Later in the morning she saw another propeller slow down and stop on the other side. As they landed Elfrieda saw fire engines, ambulances, and other equipment coming out to meet them. At the airline desk the agent said. "My, we're glad you got down. The pilot was flying trans-Atlantic for the first time."

At the desk they told Elfrieda to rest in airport accommodations used for flight crews and to report back at midnight. When she did, no one was at the desk. She knocked on an office door and a stewardess came out. "Oh, no," she said, "we're not flying until morning." Elfrieda asked to see the captain.

"This is an off-scheduled flight," he said. "We will fly in the morning."

Elfrieda didn't realize she was crying, but the tears came streaming down her face. The direct flight from

Rio to Frankfurt would have taken 28 hours; it had been sixteen days now since she left the refugee ship hoping to go straight home. She told the captain her story. After hearing her tale, he ordered, "Call the crew together and get this lady some tea and toast. We're going on to Frankfurt tonight." In an hour they left.

Peter had expected her days before. She had had no way of notifying him since leaving Hartford. When he checked the airport they said they had never heard of the airline on which she was flying. When she arrived, she called Peter and sat down to wait some more.

When at last Peter and Elfrieda were reunited and left the airport, they traveled north, reflecting on all that had happened. They went to Gronau where all MCC processing of refugees took place and where Peter now worked. During the next few months of that 1948 summer, C. F. Klassen sent Elfrieda traveling in Northern Germany to visit refugees in the British zone and to obtain information for immigration purposes.

In October 1948, Peter and she escorted the fourth transport using the first ship on which they had transported refugees, the *Volendam*, with 1,700 passengers this time. They arrived in 21 days and transferred the refugees for the trip up the Paraguay River.

Peter and Elfrieda visited all the refugee places in Paraguay to see what they had accomplished in those months. Some had already built their houses out of mud bricks they made themselves. Even though doors and windows might not be in place, they were living in them.

Continuing to Serve

In 1949, Peter and Elfrieda finally returned to the States. Peter went back to Goshen College and

Seminary. On July 27, 1950, their daughter Ruth Elizabeth was born. Elfrieda gave herself full time to the job of mothering. In August of 1950, they went to the Eden Mennonite Church in Moundridge, Kansas, where Peter served as pastor. They spent seven years in Moundridge. There, September 14, 1954, Rebecca Ann was born.

In 1957, MCC asked Peter to be the MCC European director, which later included North Africa. Elfrieda did not have a particular assignment as an MCC worker. However, soon after they were settled in Europe, a letter came asking someone to buy articles for a parcel a refugee immigrant in Canada wanted to send to a relative in Russia. They found a way to send it through a Swiss organization. The parcel sending mushroomed into a full-fledged program that lasted ten years. Doreen Harms handled all the finances and paper work. Elfrieda bought the articles and packaged them.

In 1967, the Dycks returned to the States where Peter consented to be the European and North Africa MCC director with responsibilities also in East-West and constituency relationships. The next year, Elfrieda started working full time and later part time at the Fairmont Rest Home for the aged and infirm.

In the fall of 1974 Elfrieda accompanied Peter to Canada where Peter received an honorary doctor's degree from the University of Waterloo. At that same time, Conrad Grebel College held a banquet honoring Elfrieda for her life of service to people in need. At that banquet, Frank Epp, then president of Conrad Grebel, explained why they were holding the banquet for Elfrieda. In part he stated, "You provided a model for women who seek major responsibility in the twentieth century.... In a world eroding from lack of soul, you have made service luminous and attractive. Christian pilgrim and refugee, Canadian nurse, twentieth-century woman, healer of tragic division and Good Samaritan, for this life we honor you at Conrad Grebel College tonight."

Elfrieda retired from her nursing home duties in May 1976. She enjoys visiting and doing things for her daughters. She also wants to accompany Peter on some trips. One can be sure she will continue to serve others, for where there is an Elfrieda Dyck there is a way to serve.

11.
C. A.
DeFehr

By
Clara K.
Dyck

Cornelius DeFehr was born in the Ukraine on October 6, 1881, at a time when Russia was already seething with the discontent which was to explode into open rebellion and civil war almost 40 years later (1917-1929). His ancestors had lived at Heubuden, in Prussia, since the last half of the sixteenth century and he could trace his family tree back to Holland. In 1788-89 Cornelius' great grandfather, along with many other families, emigrated from Prussia to the Ukraine in Southern Russia in search of economic and religious freedom. Here his family farmed until 1904.

Setting Life's Pattern

"We have with us this year two Mennonite youths whom I want to introduce to you," the principal told his class the first day Cornelius and his brother Abram attended Banteschevo school, where Cornelius was to receive all his education except the first three years. "While they are of German ancestry," the principal continued, "they too are Russian citizens.... One thing, however, the Mennonites lack. They are not as hospitable to strangers as they should be." Perhaps this remark helped shape his life into the many areas of outgoing service with which Cornelius became so intimately involved.

During the winter Cornelius and Abram boarded at this 200-student school, but in spring and fall they walked the five kilometers back and forth. This began an emphasis on physical fitness that remained with Cornelius all his life. Little did he know then that even at age ninety he would be swimming regularly each week at the YMCA in Winnipeg, Canada!

Cornelius DeFehr recalls his early spiritual experience in his book, *Memories of My Life.* Minister Jakob Reimer was holding a Bible course in a neighboring village. On the final evening Cornelius observed that all the older folk had gone to the service but the young people had not. When urged to come along he said, "No, I must stay here to conduct a service for the youth."

He asked the boys to quickly round up the youths. The twelve who came all "decided to follow the Lord," Cornelius writes, "and I was one of them." So, at age 19, he started to walk with God and was baptized in the Mennonite Brethren Church.

It was during this time also that Cornelius met Elizabeth Dyck, both singing in the church choir. "Meine [my] Liese," he fondly called her with whom he would live together for sixty-nine happy years. They were married on November 13, 1903. Cornelius was twenty-two years old, Liese eighteen.

Until after their first son was born the young couple lived and worked on the farm with his parents. Then they moved to Millerovo in the province of the world-famous Don Cossack choirs where, as Cornelius records, "I was later to achieve great material gain and where I was also to experience total loss."

Here a childhood dream was fulfilled when Cornelius became general director and partner with his father-in-law and brother-in-law of a business firm they called "Implement Factory, Martens, DeFehr, and Dyck." Other assets compensated for their initial lack of capital resources, such as good health, courage, perseverance, ability to cope with hard work and long hours, skill to turn wood and metal into marketable products, worthy goal, and a God who blessed their ventures.

Though they had a modest beginning, after five years their factory employed 50 workers, and by World War I more than 100, of which about 70 percent were Russian. Gradually, too, output increased from manufacture of agricultural machinery like drills and mowers to threshing machines and hydraulic oil presses for processing flax and sunflower seeds.

War and Revolution

During World War I Mennonite men were exempted from military duty and allowed to perform an alternative service in either forestry or medical units. Cornelius DeFehr was excused in order to process the large 1914 orders of Russia's Ministry of Defense.

Russia's German-speaking citizens felt increasingly discriminated against during the war because they were looked upon as potential collaborators with the enemy. The Mennonites of the Ukraine suffered particularly in these years, for they lived right where the battle lines went to and fro.

The Red forces retreated for a time, and when they returned Cornelius lay unconscious, a victim of the typhus epidemic which haunted nearly every home. "Oh, how can I find a way to flee with my sick husband?" Liese cried in desperation. Then their faithful factory doctor had a scheme. "We will carry him into my Pullman car," he answered. And so they did.

Hidden behind the DeFehr factory along with the Pullman were eight freight cars. During this 30-below zero night 10 families took their most prized belongings and secretly boarded these freight cars. Just before dawn, December 7, 1919, factory locomotives hooked up the cars with the military train, and away they went.

Their flight to the Mennonite settlements of the Kuban took several weeks. Often when their boxcars were unhooked and shunted away to wait on a side-track, they feared it would be a permanent stop. "Hush, hush," mothers breathed softly whenever a baby cried. "Oh please, God, close the ears of the Red guards. Please, please, don't let them discover us!"

The DeFehrs remained in the Kuban five and one-half years, and even then they could not return home. They had many frightening experiences. One night a friend came to them on horseback. "Cornelius," he whispered, "your name is on the list. And Abram's, too. You're to be arrested and exiled to the coal mines in the Ural mountains."

It was a time when the corn stood high in the fields, so the brothers hid amid the tall stalks while they planned their escape. Their brother-in-law, who was employed in the regional administrative office, drew up the necessary documents, stamped them with the of-ficial seal, and arranged for their wives to bring wagons to the fields in the darkness of the following night. They fled together with their families.

As the Red army gained control in Russia they began redistributing the land they had confiscated. Because the DeFehrs were now refugees and owned nothing but a little house, they, their brother, and parents each received six acres. They had been living on the sale of rolls of factory belts brought along on their flight. Their money had become worthless. But now they had land and seeded it with wheat. "Let's open a small business in the village," Cornelius suggested to Johann Derksen, another small farmer. They began by shipping boxes of flour to the Baptists in Moscow in exchange for yard goods. Soon it was a whole carload of flour each time. Eventually they even built an oil refinery.

In 1917 the Communist government began seizing the property of private owners and organizing collective farms where everyone was to work together. But the government was inexperienced and inefficient. Thousands of sacks of confiscated grain were dumped on open fields where rain, mice, and winter storms quickly rotted it. So, too, the animals and chickens that had been slaughtered. Mass starvation followed.

Millions of men, women, and children died of hunger and of the typhus epidemic which now swept through Russia. Their undernourished condition made them easy prey to other diseases as well. Then marauding hordes, of which Nestor Machno was the most dreaded leader, ruthlessly ravaged the Mennonite villages of the Ukraine, killing, raping, looting, burning down farmsteads and whole villages. Even if they had had the means to begin anew, the people could not do so, because their courage had been buried with their many dead loved ones.

Ready to Help Others

In 1922 rumors flew across the ocean. "Mennonites in North America are preparing to bring us food," they said. Then Cornelius, or C. A. DeFehr, as he came to be known, was asked to go to Moscow to meet Alvin J. Miller, director of American Relief in Russia. It was a fact. Help had come.

Along with others, C. A. distributed a whole carload of flour and foodstuffs among starving villagers of the surrounding areas. Yet this was only the beginning. This relief, which saved the lives of thousands, grew into that international agency now known as the MCC.

The Mennonite privilege of military exemption which had been theirs under the Tzars meant little to the communists. Every young man who refused to take arms had to appear before a judge. Some communist judges knew the Bible very well. The one most feared had been a priest. Consequently, the youths asked permission for someone to help them in court.

C. A. DeFehr was asked to fill this role in the Kuban. He noticed that judges intended to confuse the youths and convince them that their argument was false, and that, in doing so, they often unintentionally gave opportunity for genuine Christian witness.

As God Warned Joseph . . .

In the effort to fulfill its slogan: "The old we destroy in order to build something new," the communist government had destroyed almost every means of making a living. In 1923 Lenin realized that this must bring on further problems for his government, so he proclaimed a new economic policy (NEP) which allowed more freedom and private initiative.

Factory owners were permitted to return to their factories. So C. A. went to the nearby city of Rostov to arrange for their return home. As God warned Joseph 3600 years earlier, so he now warned C. A., for in a newspaper in Rostov he read a hate-filled article reporting that some valuables had been found in their implement factory.

C. A. gained still greater insight into Russia's economic and political prospects at the General Conference of Mennonite Congregations which had its last session in Moscow in January 1925. "The future looks black for the Mennonites of Russia. We must leave our beloved homeland," he told Liese sadly when he came home. "But is emigration really the only solution,

Cornelius?" she asked in tears. "Is that what God told you in Moscow?" "Yes, my dear. God is showing us that we must move on. Like our ancestors before us. It is the only solution."

Later C. A. wrote in his *Memories* that many of the delegates he had learned to know at this conference died in exile or prison. "Only a few succeeded in leaving Russia," he wrote, "and I and my loved ones were among those fortunate few."

A New Start in Canada

Bishop David Toews with the Canadian Mennonite Board of Colonization in Canada, and B. B. Janz in Russia, helped to make the DeFehr emigration to Canada possible. It was hard for C. A. to leave, for he loved the Russian people and his homeland, but the loss of his possessions did not trouble him greatly. He looked into the future with hope and optimism.

Trachoma, an infectious eye disease, forbade entry into Canada for many people. It seemed it would be so for C. A. DeFehr as well. After many treatments a doctor finally diagnosed his problem as being simply an inflammation. How relieved they all were that now they could go. They landed in Quebec on September 11, 1925, and immediately boarded the train to Plum Coulee, Manitoba, where Liese's father had bought a farm in the village of Gnadenthal.

C. A. sensed that it was a good time to begin a new business in Canada, for crops were excellent, wheat prices high, and the post-war depression subsiding. "Let's set a new goal," he told his three sons. "You finish school, and I'll try to start a business. With God's blessing we should be able to enlarge by the time you're ready to join me. That is, if you then think you would like to." And all the boys agreed.

"How wonderfully our Lord has led," their mother reminded them, "that we live only 16 miles away from the Mennonite Collegiate Institute at Gretna. And that here you can not only learn the English language, but German and religion as well."

C. A. bought a half-ton Model T Ford truck, loaded it with cream separators and other hardware, and called on German and Russian-speaking businessmen. While in Hamburg, Germany, en route to Canada, he had discussed business prospects with his friend Herman Schuet who had supplied his wares in Russia. Mr. Schuet had promised to give credit on all orders until C. A. would be well established in Canada. This he did.

In the spring of 1926 the DeFehrs moved to Winnipeg where C. A. opened an implement firm. This quickly expanded to larger headquarters located near Winnipeg's downtown business section, with a railway line behind it for speedy shipping. Here his sons joined him one by one.

Depression and War

The economic results of the 1929 financial crash were felt the world over. On the Canadian prairies a long period of drought (1929-37) followed. Many people were forced to leave their farms and live on government welfare. This had a devastating effect on the DeFehr business and sales shrank drastically.

Then came the war of 1939-45. Again the influence of anti-German propaganda became obvious. "If it were not for our great God who always strengthens us and gives new hope, where would we be?" C. A. and Liese often told each other. After the war sales jumped, doubled, tripled, nine-folded. Now the DeFehrs not only imported from Germany, but from Sweden and the United States also.

Involved in Church Work

C. A. DeFehr had become more and more involved in church work. He had begun what turned out to be a twenty-five-year term as treasurer for Mennonite Brethren Missions; was a member of Mary-Martha Home for Girls, and of Gideons International.

Since education was his main interest, he served as member of the board of directors of M.C.I., the high school his sons had attended, collected financial support for this school, and became co-responsible for the building of a new school, 1945-47. C. A. had always regretted the break in fellowship which resulted in formation of the Mennonite Brethren Church in Russia, so he now appreciated the opportunity of building bridges between the two conferences, for this school served both. "For him the dividing line between Mennonite Brethren and General Conference was always bridgeable, even in the 30s when differences were at their worst," declares C. A.'s son William of Winnipeg.

Later he also became active as treasurer of the Canadian Mennonite Brethren Conference, served on the board of directors of the M. B. Bible College, and as chairman of Christian Press, Ltd.

Relief and Immigration

The involvement with relief and immigration which had begun for C. A. during the famine in Russia continued. In 1945 he was elected to the Canadian Board of Colonization which had been instrumental in bringing him and his family to Canada. And in 1947 he became a member of MCC, the primary Mennonite agency for resettlement. At the same time the MCC asked him to undertake the first of four trips to Paraguay to assist in resettling some of the more than 12,000 Russian and Prussian Mennonites left homeless in the refugee camps of Europe after World War II. Now it seemed that God had planned C. A.'s interest in people, and his twenty-year involvement in church and conference as a special preparation for this new assignment.

The refugees would all have preferred to come to Canada, but the doors of immigration were still closed there. They had suffered intensely under the Russians, however, and wanted to move as far away from them just as quickly as possible, for Russia still looked upon them as her citizens.

On the DeFehr's final day of orientation in Akron, Pennsylvania, a telegram arrived in which Peter J. Dyck reported from Berlin that the American occupation forces had refused to allow the 928 refugees from that city to travel through the Russian zone to the waiting ship *Volendam* at Bremerhaven. The dramatic miracle that carried them through is described by Barbara Smucker in *Henry's Red Sea* (Herald Press), and in other books.

So it happened that, on February 1, 1947, the same day the DeFehrs left North America on their first trip to South America, the good ship *Volendam* also embarked on her first of two voyages carrying Mennonite refugees to South America. The *Volendam* was to dock with her 2,303 passengers at Buenos Aires, Argentina, and from here these were to be taken to Asunción, the capital of Paraguay, in smaller groups.

Meanwhile C. A. DeFehr had to arrange landed immigrant status for the refugees. He also had to find accommodations that could be used until all immigrants had been taken inland. This was a gigantic task, especially since the Argentinian government did not wish them to stop over on its soil at all.

Tired and weary, he asked Liese one night, "Did you

know that the Holland America Line has warned us that we, the Mennonites, must pay $13,000 for every day the ship is delayed in harbor?" "Yes," she replied. "But where is this huge sum to come from? Would all those people have to return to the refugee camps of Europe if we can't raise it?" "That's just it. Back on the doorsteps of Russia, which they fear so much."

The DeFehrs hurried from one government agency to another, with the help of Argentine Mennonite missionaries, trying to find housing, as the *Volendam* steamed nearer and nearer. They almost despaired. Yet they prayed and trudged on. And God's timing is always right. On almost the very last day before the *Volendam* was to arrive their prayers were answered. Word came: "Permission to stop-over is granted."

Now the military authorities moved with great haste. Early in the morning of February 20 a long line of trucks drove to an open area near the harbor where soldiers set up 70 tents. C. A. was also informed that the refugees might use the kitchen and dining rooms of an adjoining immigrant hotel. Is it any wonder C. A. wrote, "That provision was a miracle before our eyes and we were grateful to God from the depth of our hearts."

The next problem: where to find enough mattresses and kitchenware for so many people. And how to have the food delivered daily....

And then February 22, the *Volendam* actually sailed into Buenos Aires harbor. Imagine the excitement of the 2,303 refugees as they took their first look at the continent that would be their new home. Were they joyful? Were they afraid?

Thanksgiving

The following day, Sunday, showed how they really felt, in spite of all the other emotions that might arise from time to time. They held an evening thanksgiving celebration on board ship. How much these refugees had to thank God for. That Peter and Elfrieda Dyck had come from Canada and found them when they were stumbling about Europe, homeless, hungry, many separated from their families through war and flight from Russia. For protection as they passed through the Red Sea of the Russian zone, and on the ocean. For making the Argentinian government willing to have them stay there temporarily.

Peter J. Dyck led the service, and two choirs sang. Then C. A. DeFehr spoke: "The Mennonites of North America, together with Mennonites of the Paraguayan colonies, are prepared to take care of you," he said. "And all this is being done through the MCC which was organized to help your parents when they were starving in Russia twenty-five years ago."

The next day they disembarked. Think how long it would take and how far the line of 2,303 people would stretch. Of course, some were babies carried by their parents. Some would try to run off fast. Others, grandmothers and grandfathers, the old, tired, and weak ones needed strong arms to support them as they walked down the gangplank.

There was much to do to take care of everyone. C. A. assigned Peter and Elfrieda Dyck to be in charge of the camp and organize everything. First they arranged two special tents: one for a hospital, the other for an office. Each person and family had to have a sleeping spot in one of the tents. Work groups were assigned to take care of needs in the camp, to peel potatoes, cook meals, wash dishes, etc.

This large group was composed of people of many trades and professions. Soon they were all busy—five shoemakers measured, cut, and sewed leather together to make and repair shoes. Teachers and children sat on the green grass between tents and held school. Later, when the first ones had left for Paraguay, they used nine tents as classrooms. "Everyone was working for everybody and everybody for one," writes C. A. No one was paid for work done, neither doctor, teacher, shoemaker, cook, or anyone else.

Meanwhile in camp Gerhard Warkentin preached. Under communist rule the Mennonites had starved for want of spiritual guidance, especially the young people. So they were most grateful now. Many shared tragic experiences and heartaches of their years behind the iron curtain. On Sunday, April 13, everyone rejoiced when thirty-six persons were baptized by Peter Dyck and J. Plennert.

Upon the ship's arrival C. A. DeFehr and Peter Dyck had immediately begun making arrangements to transport this large group to Paraguay. But one overwhelming obstacle faced them. Paraguay was in the midst of a revolution. George K. Epp, now of Winnipeg, was one of this first group. He tells how "scared stiff" most of them were. "Even if they had been permitted immediate entry," he declares, "most would have refused, for we remember too well the terrors of war we had just gone through in Europe. And the dangers of being caught between two firing armies."

But a group of 300 persons immediately went to Friesland, before the revolution spread that far. The others were to wait until the revolution was over. But it dragged on and on until it became impossible to continue this expensive existence any longer.

During this waiting time MCC, through C. A. DeFehr, called for six of the young refugees to go to Friesland and build a bridge across the Tapiraquai (Ant Eater) River and cut a road through the jungle so that the settlers and their belongings could be brought in from the port of Rosario.

George Epp was one of the six. "The revolution was still on," he recalls. "And when Rosario was occupied, we were held prisoner for a time. During dry seasons the river could be crossed on foot or by car, but this was a season of torrential rains and it had swollen to a depth of 10 feet, with a strong current. The Paraguayans had wanted to build a bridge here for the past twenty years, so they showed their appreciation by providing food and felling the huge trees which were so hard that sparks spattered with every stroke of the axe." What a surprise when the bridge stood ready in less than three weeks.

Paraguayan Mennonites live on either side of the Paraguay River. West of the river, in the swampy, subtropical thorny bushland of the Chaco are the colonies Fernheim and Menno. East of the river on its tributary, the Tapiraquay, on heavy but much more valuable jungleland, lies Friesland. It is near these three that the post-World War II immigrants would establish two new colonies: Neuland in the Chaco, and Volendam in the jungle.

Finally, on March 9, 1,202 refugees had been started on their way to the Chaco. They were preparing another group to leave when word came: "The revolution is on again. Communications with the Chaco are cut off." So they quickly decided to take the rest of the immigrants to Asunción.

"You have our permission to house your people at the Agricultural School at San Lorenzo, near the city," a government agent told them. Yet here, too, the army's uprising against the goverment hindered disembarkation from ship. This also ended at last.

Some time later C. A. heard about the trip of the

1,202 persons into the Chaco. After traveling up the Paraguay River to Puerto Casado by riverboat, then taking a narrow gage railway to End Station 145, trucks and horse-drawn wagons had taken them the last 60 miles. For the latter, all luggage was loaded first, then the people climbed on top. Often branches of trees lashed the faces of these high perchers and snatched away their kerchiefs. So those on the first part of the convoy would call loudly, "Achtung! Achtung!" (Take care! Take care!) as soon as they felt the first smarting swipes. Louder still was the lament, "They're eating me up." "They're eating me alive. I'll never see Fernheim." These were mosquitoes, but even worse were the tiniest Pulverinos, a fly that passes through the finest net and has an extremely painful sting.

When the last twenty-five had left the camp at Buenos Aires in the beginning of June, and C. A. was able to close the camp after four difficult months, he thought of God's leading with Moses and the children of Israel in the desert: "Thank you, God! Thank you!" he prayed. "Daily you cared for us. Daily you gave shelter from the burning sun and the downpours of rain. And daily you provided all the food we needed for those many people. Amen! Amen!"

The Search for Land

May 27 the search for land began when C. A., two of the immigrant men, a representative from Friesland colony, a purchasing agent, and a landowner, flew inland. C. A. was well-known among Mennonites as a successful Christian businessman and these Paraguayan agents also quickly recognized his leadership qualities, his ability to determine suitability of land and circumstances, and to finalize such huge business transactions.

By truck they drove as far as they could through virgin forest and across wild open prairies until they reached a tributary of the Parana River. From here they rode horseback along narrow jungle paths and through pathless dense forests. Deeper and deeper into the jungle.

They found very fertile red soil, heavy with valuable lumber that would quickly pay for the land to be cleared for homesteads. Fresh springs bubbled in abundance. Fruit and vegetables grew readily. There was a hospital nearby. The river teemed with fish up to 400 pounders. Floods were unknown, yet the river would easily generate hydroelectric plants. No locusts came here. It was only two days distance from Encarnacion, a major import-export center. Truly, this site seemed to more than say "yes" to the questionnaire that the prospective settlers had sent along as guide.

"No," said C. A. DeFehr. "No. It is not for us. Our people would not be able to cope with it. The timber is heavier than water and so it can't be floated down the river to the mills for sawing and sale. And there are no roads through the jungle."

In June C. A. and his surveyors again searched for land, closer to Rosario this time, on the banks of the Paraguay River. Mennonites from nearby Friesland came to get them for a thanksgiving service. C. A. saw how the wagon wheels sank deeply into the sand or else bumped over holes and ridges left after heavy rains. It took a whole day to travel the 50 Km. He quips about this in his *Memories.* "When the wagon leaned to one side the driver would have to stick out his leg to provide some counterbalance and to prevent the wagon from overturning."

The difficult search finally ended when they found excellent fertile jungle land north of Rosario. It included areas of woods with valuable timber, pastures, and low-lands. Also other assets, such as many fences, a dairy yard with buildings, a sawmill, cut lumber, and 750 head of wild ranch oxen, horses, and cows. Also large vessels could come all the way up to this site on the Paraguay River when it was high. They marked off 13,000 Hectar (about 32,000 acres), enough for 400 to 421 families. The price was to be 25 guaranis per Ha., which amounted to a total of approximately $260,000.

C. A. immediately wired Akron and MCC agreed to buy the land and to supply the new settlers with the most necessary items for their beginning on land and in the kitchen.

While most of the immigrants destined for this dense but fertile jungleland received the news enthusias-tically, some of those assigned to the Chaco bushland were afraid. "We have heard of the extreme hardships of the first pioneers in that 'Green Hell,' " they said. "Of the drought, duststorms, and locusts. And we want no part of it. Those settlers came from Russia in 1930 and their life is still primitive and hard. We want to stay here in Argentina. In the city." And 135 of them did stay.

C. A. understood but, though neither he nor MCC forced anyone to go to the Chaco against his will, they realized the hazards of leaving part of the group behind. Also, because of the continuing revolution over 1,000, that is, half of the immigrants remained at the San Loranzo Agricultural School under the leadership of the Ernest Harders. Perhaps it wasn't exactly the "land of milk and honey," but many mandarin trees grew on these grounds and the immigrants ate their fill.

The homesteaders of the new site were confident, hopeful, and eager to start building their homes at once. Before they could do so though there was much excru-ciating work ahead, especially so for widows and other women. For first of all they had to conquer the jungle. But before they could conquer the jungle and break the land they dug two wells for each village and built ovens and cookstoves of mud with two round holes in the top for cooking; then they had to tame wild oxen and horses to pull the heavy trees from the forest, and wild cows before they could have milk. And a cow wouldn't let down her milk unless first primed by her calf. This done, one could sit down with a pail, while the cow kept her eyes glued on her calf.

After that it didn't take long till they were cutting streets through the jungle, clearing land for building houses, and planting fruit trees and vegetables on every cleared spot of ground. Seven hundred persons settled in 11 villages on these 13,000 hectares north of Friesland. This colony became known as Volendam, named after the ship which had brought these brave immigrants to South America, and which itself had been named after a village in Holland where some of the first Mennonites came from.

George Epp summarizes C. A. DeFehr's role in Paraguay as follows: "He was a very sharp, clever businessman. The kind of man people listen to. And he used that gift to help his people. He not only helped us organize our colony and start a sawmill, but became involved in every phase of settling, both in Volendam and in the Chaco. He gave us his expertise and he must have been a tremendous resource person for MCC. And everywhere Liese went with him. Every spare minute he had, they went from tent to tent, from house to house, visiting people, encouraging, supporting, comforting, advising."

"And she was humble," adds Aggie Klassen of Winnipeg, who was one of these refugees to the Chaco. "One never thought of her as a rich lady." George Epp agrees: "They were real deacons and they didn't mind roughing it, coming from their prosperous Canadian environment. And they not only distributed money sent from Canada and the United States, but also much of their own. At that time $1.00 made you a king. There must be many who remember the $5.00, $10.00, $15.00 the DeFehrs distributed among them out of their own pocket when nobody had a penny."

The DeFehrs had promised MCC five months. They stayed eleven. At a farewell service at the sawmill the new Mennonite settlers told them, "Es geht gut!" (We are getting along okay). They were happy in their new homes and grateful they could live in peace and quiet, far from the land of their persecutors. Much remained to be done, but the Lord God had blessed his servants and given wisdom to build the foundation of a new Mennonite settlement.

"Our Heart Is in the South"

On February 16, 1948, C. A. and Liese arrived in Asunción once more. This time to help receive and settle refugee groups soon to arrive on the ships *Heintzelmann, Charlton Monarch,* and *Volendam.*

They saw at once why the Lord had led them back, for the faith of the former group had meanwhile been severely tested and the people longed for counsel and support in their almost insurmountable obstacles. Three plagues had swooped down upon both Volendam and the Chaco: ants, drought, and locusts (grasshoppers).

Menno Klassen who had been sent to the Chaco by MCC to establish an Experimental Farm (1946-49) explains: "Fighting grasshoppers and ants sapped the people's energy. And it was up to 118° F. in the shade. The people worked so hard. Yet ants took over, eating seedling crops. Long rows of white armies cut chunks of plants and carried them to their high hills till the fields were bare." When they seeded again, drought moved in. C. A. records: seventy-five percent of the fruit trees dried up. Even staple foods like kafir, beans and mandioca refused to bear. Prices of the few remaining products skyrocketed, some multiplying more than 100 percent. Horses and oxen were so starved and weak that they were unable to go for food. Gas for trucks was lacking.

Menno continues: "When in October the rains came at last and the fields stood fresh and green, grasshoppers moved in continuously from the hinterland. Farmers fought young hoppers with flamethrowers similar to blowtorches. Mature ones swooshed in like huge rustling gray or red (two varieties) clouds that blotted out the sun. They were three and a half inches long and a little mosquito bite was nothing in comparison to the pain of these landing on your face and clutching your skin.

"People would grab tin cans or plates, jump on their horses, and try to frighten them away clapping their tins while racing around the cloud." George Epp, too, remembers: "The moment children in school heard the swooshing cloud they would scream, 'Grasshoppers,' and race home, grab anything that made a noise, and join the chase. The grasshoppers devoured the whole promising crop in a few hours. Then the people stood and cried." The grasshoppers fell into the wells by the thousands, making the water unusable. "And yet," Menno declares, "in spite of these unbelievable trials and hardships, how thankful the people were!"

"Why do you try your people so," C. A. cried. "Lord, why? Wasn't Russia enough?" He appealed to Akron for assistance, but all MCC funds were needed to settle the new arrivals. MCC was entirely responsible for these since the older colonies, too, had been devastated by the plagues.

The *Heintzelmann* group arrived in Puerto Casado

on February 25, 1948. The DeFehrs were on their way to greet them, traveling in an autovia, a small, fast diesel-motored car which runs on railroad tracks and is usually used only for military dignitaries. Others had become dependent upon earlier groups, so that some had to be almost pushed on to their own land, like baby birds out of their nests. But after C. A. had helped them all make a new start they were happy for it. The 1948 arrivals on the ship *Volendam* built three more villages at the 1947 Volendam site. Some from the other two ships joined relatives, while the majority created a new settlement of 25 villages and 2,500 persons on land C. A. had found near Fernheim and Menno in the Chaco. "Let's call it Neuland," someone suggested, "for God has indeed given us a new land." "Yes, yes," everyone echoed. "Neuland it shall be." And so it is.

In Neuland 140 single women and seven widows founded "Das Frauendorf" (village of women). The oldest male was 15 years. Although Fernheim men assisted generously with muscle power, life for these was still indescribably hard. Breaking land, oxen, cattle, building houses, chasing plagues is not part of woman's birthright.

Aside from meeting ships, arranging for homesteads, transportation, and food there always seemed to be unforeseen problems. So, for example, C. A. spent much time locating the lost baggage of the *Charlton Monarch* immigrants. Also the 751 persons who wished to stay in Uruguay needed attention. Another problem: eight families of mixed marriage asked to have their own village. There were also those who had lost most of all: their faith.

When the DeFehrs returned home after nine months they felt that "A good part of our heart was now in the south and we wanted to return." Their son William underscores this: "They returned to Canada, but lived the rest of their lives in Paraguay. Their affinity for these refugees harked back to their own struggle to get out of Russia." "And mother knew the names and special problems of all those women and their children in "Das Frauendorf," William's wife, Erna, exclaims. "She kept track of them all!"

An Economic Evaluation

C. A. notes that it is inconceivable for one who has not seen the Chaco and jungle before the Mennonites came to realize the immense strides made in conquering this bush and jungle land. And yet, economic conditions remained precarious. It was recognized that an import-export trade would bolster the economy. Consequently, in 1952, C. A. DeFehr and six other businessmen and medical doctors from Canada and USA made an exploratory trip, visiting all the Paraguayan colonies to see how they could be helped.

Upon their return to North America these men founded the Mennonite Economic Development Association (MEDA), a company of shareholders interested in sponsoring new projects and expansion. Profits are still continuously reinvested and this help now extends into other areas of the world.

In 1948 C. A. had noted that the sawmills of Fernheim and Menno could not cut sufficient wood for building houses for the new settlers and for profitable sale and oil presses, so he rented three small power saws. He pursued this insight upon his return home, appealing widely and vigorously for funds to buy steam engines for Paraguay. Four of those huge black belching monsters, the kind used earlier for threshing on the Canadian prairies, were finally unloaded at the Asunción harbor. An enthusiastic C. A. DeFehr was in the midst

C. A. DeFehr

of the welcoming crowd, "pulling the ropes and being involved in every stage because he was so eager to get these engines safely to the colonies," reports George Epp who was there.

In 1957 MCC sent C. A. DeFehr to Paraguay for the fourth time, this time to evaluate past, present, and future activity there. Liese happily accompanied him. The Board of General Welfare and Public Relations and the Mennonite Missions Board assigned the DeFehrs to visit Mission stations and settlers in Uruguay, Brazil, and Colombia as well.

In Paraguay C. A. was impressed with a new highway and better roads where there had previously been only Indian trails. The experimental farm was beneficial in providing seeds, grasses, vegetables, fruit trees that thrived in that climate and soil. MCC was connecting the colonies by installing telephones. MCC had also helped build a mental hospital in Filadelfia. Trade was flourishing and buses traveled to Asunción daily.

Neuland now had a high school and dormitories, teacher training, a 30-bed hospital including Indian patients, old folks home, a store and developing industry, an oil mill with a large warehouse, creamery and cheese factory, a brick-shingle and roof-tile plant, a cattle ranch, the cooperative enterprise was expanding, and assistance was available for disabled and needy women.

Volendam and Friesland, too, were prospering in similar ways, except that the constant emigration drained away much desirable power. In regard to the future, C. A. reported that "the most important factors to me appeared to be the completion of the Trans-Chaco roadway, the prospects of finding oil in the Chaco, and a stabilized currency such as the country had enjoyed in recent years."

Seeing Mission Fields Around the World

Upon returning from his fourth trip to Paraguay in 1957, C. A. DeFehr, along with two others, made a trip around the world on behalf of the Mennonite Board of Foreign Missions. C. A. observed closely. He was grateful to meet missionaries and hear firsthand reports of their problems and successes. Returning home, they stopped to attend the Mennonite World Conference at Karlsruhe, West Germany.

At Home

C. A. knew that when he was away his sons efficiently carried on business at the DeFehr firm. And God blessed their work abundantly. In 1950, the twenty-fifth year of its operation, his three sons and one son-in-law became equal partners and shareholders of the company, relieving their father of much responsibility. In 1963 he sold the company to those four whose growing families, too, were becoming increasingly involved.

In 1963 the DeFehr's celebrated their diamond wedding anniversary in the midst of a large circle of family and friends. Gradually their health began to fail. Liese died in 1972, and C. A. in 1979.

William DeFehr pays tribute to his parents with the comment that "there was something unusual about them. They had an absolute passion for the work of the Lord, no matter how hard it was. Honest Christianity is very practical. My father was." Some years earlier C. A. himself had said, "Paraguay changed my life," and we know that he changed the lives of many in Paraguay, lives he and Liese had adopted as their own.

12
Jacob J. Thiessen

By
Esther
Patkau

"You can't expect much from this child," the midwife said, as she held up the wrinkle-faced, crying baby. "You'll be fortunate if he becomes a teacher." But this child who was prophesied to become "only a teacher," instructed thousands, and the influence of his life invigorated not only the local community where he lived, but also spread to Mennonite settlements in Europe and North and South America. J. J. Thiessen was more than a teacher. He was a proclaimer of the Word, a counselor, a leader of the Mennonite people, an initiator of a college, a shepherd of a congregation, and a friend of hundreds.

Jacob John Thiessen was born in August 31, 1893, in the village of Klippenfeld that his grandparents had helped establish thirty years earlier in the Molotschna settlement in South Russia. Work on the parental farm was plentiful. Grainfields were cultivated with horse-drawn equipment. The sheep herd and the hungry silk-worms helped to supplement the farm income, and the garden that stretched back of the house needed many hands to keep it flourishing. His parents, Johann J. and Margareta Neufeld Thiessen, welcomed each child as an eventual help in the work of the farm. As the third oldest of eleven children, Jacob often helped his mother in the kitchen, bringing in wood and straw to keep the big brick stove in the middle of the room heated. Here mother cooked all the meals and in wintertime baked all the bread. In spring he assisted in bringing in countless branches of fresh mulberry leaves to feed the ravenous silkworms on their racks, and later in picking off the cocoons to be taken to the spinning factory.

His parents earnestly tried to raise their children in the nurture and admonition of the Lord. He loved his mother, a quiet, sensitive, and deeply religious woman who worked hard to cook and sew for her family, but also found time to gather the children around her to sing and pray with them. Indelibly impressed on his tender memory was the sight of his mother responding to need in the midst of her work. When a neighbor came to ask for help she would take off her big apron, wash her hands, brush back her hair, and give of her time and counsel as best she could.

Interest in Education

By the time Jacob finished the six years of elementary studies in the village school, his father realized that his son's interests lay with books rather than in farm work, and he quietly arranged for lodging and study in the high school located in the larger village of Gnadenfeld. Though it meant breaking some of the close ties of home Jacob was delighted with this development and set himself the goal of becoming a teacher. He applied himself to his studies and his efforts were rewarded by the approval and recognition of his teachers.

As a young boy of fourteen he attended an evangelistic service and was deeply moved by the message. That evening, alone under the stars of the night, he wept bitterly and made a commitment of himself to the

Lord which he never regretted and to which he remained faithful throughout his life.

Following the difficult final high school exams in Gnadenfeld, he accompanied a friend on an excursion to the port town of Berdjansk, a place about which the local farmers who took their grain there, told interesting stories. Before departure his father warned them about pickpockets, but his companion who had traveled by train before paid no heed to the admonition. Once aboard the train he stretched out on the seat and promptly dozed off. Jacob enjoyed pranks and determined to teach his friend a lesson. Very cautiously he pulled the two gold coins out of his sleeping friend's vest pocket and hid them. As they neared their destination, his friend awoke and began a frantic search for his money. Only as they pulled into the station did Jacob admit the trick, warning his friend to be more careful.

Two years of pedagogical study in Halbstadt and several weeks of intense preparatory studies preceded the final qualifying exams for the teaching certificate. Of the more than twenty registered to write, Jacob was one of the successful six to obtain the prized teaching diploma. At age nineteen he began his first teaching assignment in the two-room school in Tiegenhagen, and soon was affectionately being referred to as "Teacher Thiessen." His thorough, conscientious lesson preparations, his punctuality, his firm discipline, his openness with students in the classroom and participation with them on the playground, as well as his friendliness with young and old quickly won him the love and respect of the community.

Alternative Service

A brief three years later his teaching career was interrupted by conscription, but rather than train for military assignments, he, with other Mennonite men, volunteered to work in government road-building projects in the forests of the Crimea. Since there was no road access to the site, the men had to carry their equipment and provisions on their backs the last seven miles. Living quarters were primitive. Sixty men lived in one barrack with walls of plaited twigs and a roof of boards covered with hay, that permitted the moisture to drip inside long after the rain had ceased outside. Thirty beds, with twenty eight inch wide hay-filled mattresses spread on the hard ground, lined either side, and a crude wooden table in the center served as dining hall for the meals prepared by two members of the group.

Without machines, road building was difficult. All the digging and packing had to be done by hand. Jacob worked together with Jacob H. Janzen, a teacher ten years his senior who found the work difficult. Thiessen offered to do Janzen's share of digging if the latter would entertain him with experiences from his travels abroad. What might have been a tedious job became instead an education in practical theology and literature and resulted in an accumulation of a wealth of knowledge and insight into understanding people.

Work hours were long and tiring. Evenings were brightened with daily devotional services, prayer, and singing. Since there was no church in the vicinity the men gathered for weekly Sunday worship. There were two ordained ministers in the group but Jacob was often called on also to lead in singing and to offer prayer or to counsel with the lonely and homesick.

Permission to visit families at home was not easily granted, but when homesickness became too strong, the men risked the anger of their overseer and slipped away to walk the thirty miles to the nearest train station for a trip home. For a period of time Jacob worked side by side with Jacob Epp, but he did not notice that Epp's twin brother, Henry, had found his way to the camp and took his brother's place for a month which his brother spent at home. Only when the brother returned was the joke discovered. Even the supervisor laughed at the incident instead of getting angry.

A change of government in 1917 released all teachers from alternative service to resume their teaching, and Jacob returned to his position at Tiegenhagen in June. On September 16, 1917, he married Katherine Kornelsen, and two days later they moved into the teacherage in Tiegenhagen to begin a long life together.

The months that followed the close of World War I were sad and difficult. The Russian soldiers returned defeated, disillusioned, and unemployed. The rich harvest of 1919 would have been adequate to feed the population, but the bands of bandits that roamed through the Mennonite villages directed their violent assaults especially against property holders. They plundered, destroyed, and burnt according to their whim. Lack of food brought malnutrition and starvation. Beatings, rape, and murders were common. Epidemics of typhoid and typhus swept the country. Fear gripped the hearts of the people. Jacob too was severely beaten and had to spend several days in the Muntau hospital, but he considered it a privilege to suffer together with his fellow Mennonite people.

Mail service was disrupted. Communication by word of mouth was not always reliable. Relatives were concerned for the welfare of other family members living in other villages. Jacob had received no word from his parents for some time and was anxious to see them, but he had no means of transportation, no money, and no warm clothing. It was January 1921. After prayer for guidance he borrowed a horse and sleigh from one

friend, a fur coat from another, and started on his trip.
At noon he stopped at a friend's house to feed and rest
his horse. By midafternoon snow began to fall and soon
developed into a snowstorm with strong winds. Darkness came and he still hadn't reached his destination.
His horse was tired. With the wind from the back, he
tried standing in the sleigh and opened his coat to
catch the wind as in sails to aid his plodding horse.
Then he led the horse until he too was tired. Nowhere
was a light or a sign visible to give an indication of
where he was. Realizing he was lost he stopped his
horse and was going to prepare to spend the night in
the field. Then he felt a heavy hand on his shoulder that
caused him to make a half turn, and there he saw a light.
Within minutes he was in his friend's home where he
could spend the night, and safely continue his journey
the following day. He was convinced that the Lord had
given him protection and guidance.

Emigration Begins

The difficulties in Russia did not decrease. Relief
came from North American churches to alleviate some
of the need for food and clothing. Through the efforts of
Bishop David Toews in Canada, the possibility of emigration opened up. The first emigrants left Russia in
June of 1923 and many others followed. Jacob was
interested in the welfare of the Mennonite people and
participated in the congresses where reconstruction of
the villages was discussed, but he was also sympathetic
with those who desired to emigrate. As a respected
teacher and leader in the community scores of people
came to him for counsel. And then he was asked to
assist three transports of emigrants in their departure
preparation in 1924.

This was neither simple nor easy. Special exit

permits in place of individual passports were needed for group departures. The list of emigrants had to be approved by the Kharkov office, then the families were subjected to medical examination by Canadian doctors. Those who passed were issued departure certificates which had to be taken to the passport department in Moscow for final processing. Once the visas had been issued, departure was by train to the border where final exit formalities were cleared.

Jacob took the list of about 1250 names and the necessary certificates to Moscow where he made immediate contact with the official translator of the Russian Canadian American Passenger Agency, and then made his way to the passport office. The angry official did not grant immediate permission. Only after hours of anxious waiting and fervent prayer to God were the necessary visas granted the following day. To avoid the numerous delays and unnecessary harassment that the transports of 1923 had encountered, he checked at the transportation commission office and requested protection. The female clerk who was authorized to deal with the request, reflected momentarily, "Mennonites! Where have I heard that name before?" and then recalled her association with Mennonites who had worked in the Red Cross during the war. In less than an hour she had prepared the necessary papers and had notified the railway stations from Lichtenau, the point of departure, to Moscow, ordering no delays in the passage of this transport.

Word spread quickly through the villages and final preparations were made. On June 23 the area around the station was crowded. Bells pealed out the departure hour. Jacob, as the leader who was to accompany the train of fifty cars to the border, watched the emotions of joy and sorrow in the crowd as the train pulled out of the station. "Till we meet in eternity," someone called from the moving train. There was sadness at leaving family members and friends behind whom they would never see again, but there was joy at the prospect of going to a land where there would be opportunity to establish a new home. As the sea of faces gradually faded into the distance, Jacob thought of what might come; he could only foresee a dark future for those remaining. As the train pulled into the darkness, someone began singing softly, "If thou but suffer God to guide thee ... " (Wer nur den lieben Gott laesst walten), and Jacob with the others joined in in encouraging one another with the singing of other hymns. God was guiding these refugees. What would happen to the others?

The train rattled through the night at top speed. No stops. No delays. When the train came to a rest stop at one station, the agent came to Jacob and asked. "Who are you? Where are you going?" Calmly he answered, "These people are emigrants and are traveling to Canada." Shocked, the agent countered, "For three years I have been beating against a stone wall requesting an exit permit, and all has been in vain. And here, these people, 1250 of them, are leaving in a transport." It was a miracle that God was performing before the eyes of the world, and Jacob acknowledged that it was the hand of God. He helped clear the final formalities at the border, then waved farewell from the station platform as the emigrants crossed the border. His work in Russia was not yet finished. That summer he accompanied two more groups to the border and was glad that he could serve his people in this way.

Through this work and the many trips to offices in Moscow he became acquainted with many foreign officials who visited Russia. Among them was Vincent Massey, who later became Governor General of Canada, and his wife. They invited him to come to Canada to teach in Mennonite schools. That friendship was renewed in Saskatoon in 1932.

In the mass emigration most of the families from Tiegenhagen had left and the student numbers had dwindled, but the village of Fischau needed a teacher. When he returned from his third trip to the border, the villagers from Fischau came to move his possessions to their community, and for two years he taught their children. But restrictions on teaching religion became more stringent and the future looked dark. Jacob came to the realization that his future work was not to be in Russia. Application for the necessary papers was made, their possessions sold, a brief trip made by rented car to say farewell to parents and brothers and sisters who were remaining, then a farewell service in the Fischau community, and on October 28, 1926, Jacob, his wife, Katherine, and their two daughters, Hedwig and Katherine, were on the transport train with four hundred and sixty others leaving Lichtenau for the last time. Their dog accompanied them to the train station and for weeks waited there for their return, until one day he was found dead along the railroad tracks.

A month later they arrived in Canada. They made their first home with friends, the Bernhard Wiens family, in Waterloo, Ontario. Everything was different. Jobs were few and the unemployed many. Lack of knowledge of the English language was a barrier to teaching. For weeks Jacob searched for a job, but couldn't find any. One day he walked from place to place, asking in twenty-five different shops, but all turned him away. He returned home discouraged. Surely God knew he needed to find work to provide for his family. When would God answer his prayers?

A few days later he went into the countryside to look

for work. It was raining, so he stopped at a service station to warm up. A friendly man approached him, "Are
you one of those newly arrived immigrants? You know,
a man of your age and build shouldn't sit around. You
should work!" "Yes," Jacob replied, "that's why I am
here. I'm looking for work." He told how he had searched
for work for many days without avail. "Come to my office in two days, and I will give you work," the man said.
Jacob went home rejoicing.

The two days passed very slowly, but when the appointed day came, Jacob went to the office. He arrived a
bit early and the clerk at the desk informed him that the
man was not there yet. "Return to this office in fifteen
minutes," she told him. He went out and walked the
streets. Fifteen minutes seemed like a very long time,
and he returned. Again the girl said, "He is not here."
Jacob began to doubt: did the man really mean he
would give him work? A few minutes later the person
for whom he was waiting came, and offered him employment at the Goodrich Tire Company. Through this
experience he learned to sympathize with the unemployed and his faith in God was strengthened.

Not long after this Bishop David Toews of Rosthern
invited him to work with the Canadian Mennonite
Board of Colonization with offices in Rosthern. It wasn't
easy for him to make the decision to leave, for he
considered the finding of this work a definite leading of
the Lord. But friends encouraged him to accept the
Toews' offer, and he did. From the day of his arrival in
Rosthern on March 4, 1927, he was never again without
work, and he praised God for his wonderful leading.

Paying the Travel Debt

Jacob's first assignment was to visit the immigrants
that were delinquent in the payments on their trans-

portation debt. Most of the immigrants that came to Canada in the years 1923 to 1926 had come on credit terms under an arrangement made with the Canadian Pacific Railway and had promised to relay that fare when they found work in Canada. Many were anxious to settle this debt and made payment for the fare a priority; others through sickness or other setbacks were unable to pay immediately, but a third group did not sense any obligation to the Board.

In his visits he encountered various attitudes and responses, yet with faithfulness he continued in this unpleasant task. For twenty years he and others worked hard as collectors until finally, in November 1946, the day came when he could tell the ill Bishop David Toews, whom he had succeeded as chairman of the Board, "The debt is liquidated. I have sent the final payment to the Canadian Pacific Railway."

At first Toews was skeptical, but when Jacob began to praise the Lord that finally the debt was cleared, Toews too joined him in singing, "Now thank we all our God" and with tears of joy praised God. His promise on behalf of the brotherhood had been kept. Almost two million dollars had been collected and paid. Thiessen then called on the congregations to hold a praise and thanksgiving service to God for his victory.

On one of his trips to collect money in the Peace River district of Northern Alberta Jacob became painfully aware of his inability to use English. Though the German-English dictionary was his constant companion, progress was slow. Would the day come when his children would be able to converse fluently in English, and he not be able to understand them? He could not picture himself living in a country and carrying out his responsibilities without the knowledge of English. On his return to Rosthern, he enrolled as a student in the German English Academy in order to learn the English language.

Dark Days and Spiritual Growth

But the problems of time and money weighed heavily on him. With the birth of their third daughter, Helen, family expenses had increased. Katherine was weak and could not leave home to find employment. As secretary and member of the Canadian Mennonite Board of Colonization, Jacob was receiving a remuneration of 25 dollars a month. After prayer and serious deliberation they decided to take in four boarders to supplement their income. Part of the school expenses were paid with borrowed money, part from his meager earnings. Jacob went to work with determination. He spent the day at school studying and evenings at the typewriter with office work. For two years this was his schedule, but the hours of intense work and tension began to have their effect.

Christmas was dismal in 1928. Katherine was in the hospital for the birth of their son, Walter, Jacob had the flu but also had to take care of the children and the household. The boarders, instead of returning to their homes for the holidays, stayed with them, also sick with the flu.

A year later Katherine became seriously ill and was hospitalized for several months. Worry, fear, and concern almost overwhelmed him, but he became quiet before God, and received new strength from reading the Word. Later he wrote:

> *These circumstances weighed heavily on us. Yet I am*
> *thankful for the experiences and the moderate results in*
> *Rosthern. Without this introduction it would have been*
> *impossible for us to take on the mission and*

*congregational work in Saskatoon. Without it we
probably would not have had the contact with youth nor
been able to satisfactorily do the many faceted work.*

Even the dark days were growing experiences and he
could thank God for them.

A Home for Girls Away from Home

But God had more work for Jacob Thiessen. The immigrants, especially girls looking for employment, were
moving to Saskatoon. On Sunday they gathered for worship service with guest ministers, but they were in need
of a regular counselor. Already in Rosthern, Jacob had
occasionally taken speaking assignments which Bishop
Toews because of his many trips and heavy work with
the Board could not fulfill. Every weekend from July 23,
1930, till the end of the year, Jacob went to Saskatoon
by train to hold meetings with the employed girls on
Thursday nights, do visitation work in hospitals and
homes on Friday and Saturday, and hold services on
Sunday. The rest of the time he continued in his work
with the Board.

But there was more to be done than a commuting
worker could do, and so the Home Mission Board hired
Jacob as a full-time worker for Saskatoon with a salary
of 60 dollars a month. He moved to the city with his
family in January 1931.

Their residence immediately also became the Girls'
Home, where from 60 to 100 girls who lived as domestic
help in the homes of their employers, came to spend
their one free day a week. For twenty-five years the
Thiessens were houseparents for over five hundred
girls who appreciated this "home-away-from-home" atmosphere of warmth and love. Many of them came in
the afternoon to browse through the periodicals, to read
or to play piano in the Thiessen's living room, and

stayed for the six o'clock supper that Katherine prepared. After an hour of Bible study and discussion some of the girls left for choir practice while the rest stayed till around ten in the evening, their hands busy with knitting, crocheting, embroidery, or other needlework, fashioning articles that later would be sold at a mission sale with proceeds given for relief, mission, or other needy projects. While their hands worked, Jacob would share news from the local church or from their home congregations. Sometimes he lectured to them on Mennonite history, telling them of the hardships their forefathers and mothers had endured for the faith, or the girls read prose and poetry. The girls laughed as they shared their mutual humorous or embarrassing experiences. Laughter, singing, and congenial conversation cheered and warmed all who came. As the girls left one by one, the houseparents were at the door to bid them a farewell with an encouraging word and a handshake. Each one knew that she was being prayed for and that she was an appreciated individual. Jacob's heart had room to love them all and he treated them like members of the family.

A Friend of the Poor

Guests and visitors for meals in the Thiessen home were many. J. J., as he also came to be called, took time to listen to each one's story and to give counsel where he could. Nor were those who came with requests for money or a handout turned away. One gentleman came often, and punctuated his conversation with so many Scripture words that the children named him "God-bless-you." One day after "God-bless-you" had been there again and had liberally handed out his compliments about "You are the best minister in town," having received his requested money, the oldest daughter told her father, "Dad, he's probably feathering his mattress with your money. He doesn't really need it." But her father replied, "Child, if he asks for it and doesn't need it, he has a problem. But if he asks for it and needs it, and I don't give it to him, I'll be answerable for it." That's the way J. J. was—always ready to help the needy.

On Sundays the Thiessen family walked from Third Avenue across the Broadway Bridge to Victoria School, about two miles. After the morning Sunday school classes they walked home for lunch. In the afternoon, J. J. and some Sunday school teachers took the noisy streetcar to the Pleasant Hill district where they held a worship service at three o'clock and then Sunday school in the mission hall. They returned home for "vaspa" of home baked zwieback, and then walked to Victoria School for the worship service or Christian Endeavor program.

During the week J. J. visited the sick in the hospital or in the sanatorium, or did house visitation. He listened to many sad stories, prayed with people, and tried to encourage them to trust God and live honest lives before him. Many of them were very poor, and just giving a word of advice or encouragement was not sufficient.

One day a father of a large family came to him and asked for a loan of three dollars. They needed groceries; he had no work and no money. "I will pay it back," he promised. J. J.'s salary had not been paid, and he had only three dollars left in his wallet. What should he do? If he told the man that was all he had, the man probably wouldn't believe him, and might even suspect his honesty. Though he needed the money himself, Thiessen thought the man might be in greater need, so he handed him the three dollars and said, "Friend, I will not loan them to you, but I give them to you." He didn't expect to ever see this man again. Several weeks passed, and J. J. had almost forgotten about the money. But answering a knock on his office door one day, he met the man with the three dollars in his hand. "I have come to give you back your money," he said, "and to thank you for helping me. Now I have found work and can buy groceries again. I took these three dollars from my first paycheck." J. J. was grateful for this man's honesty, and they remained friends until the man died several years later.

Building Christ's Church

The congregation in Saskatoon grew and under his leadership organized as a church in 1932. He was giving himself wholeheartedly into the ministry of preaching, visitation, and teaching, and had visions of the growth of the congregation, but the blessings were to be accompanied by trials. On a Sunday evening during the service he suddenly was overcome by dizziness, but managed to finish the message. That evening he prayed to God, "The church needs a leader, and they have asked me to help them. Are you going to take me away from them so soon? Let me live at least five more years to serve this church." He couldn't go to sleep immediately, but then he thought he heard a voice telling him to go to the doctor in the morning and request a blood transfusion. The diagnosis was pernicious anemia, and the doctor was willing to administer the transfusion. But where would the blood come from? Concerned, yet trusting God, J. J. left the doctor's office and on the street met a student friend, who volunteered to donate blood. And the blood types matched! Later when more transfusions were needed other members of the congregations willingly donated to help their leader. God answered his prayer and gave him not only five, but forty-five years in the service of the congregation.

The facilities of the classrooms at Victoria School were inadequate for the growing congregation. With encouragement from J. J. funds were pledged, contributed, and together with a loan from the Home Mission Board a church building with a seating capacity of two hundred and fifty was ready for use in October 1936. All, even the young, had participated to make this their church. At the dedication service, a little boy pressed twenty-five cents into J. J.'s hand, with the words, "Now one part of this church belongs to me." The united effort had made it possible for them to obtain their own building. It was spacious but gradually it became too small. Sunday school classes were meeting in the hall and under the stairs. People were being turned away for lack of space. Again a united effort was made, and in 1956 a second much larger building was erected on a different site.

Even before the new building was finished, the old building was sold to the Mayfair Mennonite Church and moved to another location to relieve their congestion. As the city of Saskatoon expanded, more Mennonite families moved to the city and J. J. with others had reached out to them with spiritual counsel and Bible study. What was started as mission work in homes in the Mayfair district of Saskatoon developed into an organized independent congregation. God had given the increase.

The Sunday school classes begun in the Pleasant Hill district in 1928 were supplemented with worship services, home visitation, and Bible study sessions in the homes. Though progress was slow, the patient, faithful ministry of J. J. and others saw the mission grow to another organized independent congregation with its own building and leader.

The new building for First Mennonite Church was spacious at first too, but with Thiessen's relentless search for "stray sheep" among the Mennonite people, his capable shepherding of the flock, and the blessing of God, the church again filled to overcrowding. Membership reached the five hundred mark in the spring of 1964. Search was made for a building site in the Nutana area, a building erected, and in 1965 seventy-six members transferred their membership from First Mennonite Church to become charter members of the new Nutana Park Mennonite Church. It was another united effort to build the kingdom of God.

Visiting Refugees

Many of the immigrants that came from Russia in the 1920s had left family members and relatives behind, and letters brought word of their continued suffering and needs. At First Mennonite Church, as also in other congregations, special efforts were made to raise funds to be sent to alleviate these needs. Music fests, choir programs, and drama presentations drew large numbers and the proceeds went for relief. J. J. shared news items that filtered through to him, led the congregation in prayers, and kept the church informed of the needs.

After World War II, many of the displaced Russian Mennonites were living in refugee camps in Europe. As successor to David Toews as chairman of the Canadian Mennonite Board of Colonization in 1946, he set himself and the Board two goals: first, to end the transportation debt, and second, to work with the government and the Canadian Pacific Railway to rescue hundreds of these refugees out of western Europe and seek to bring them to Canada. In 1948, as a member of the MCC Executive Committee, he visited the camps in

Paderborn, Muehlenberg, Fallingbostel, Gronau, Backnang, and Ludwigsberg in Germany, and in Oxboel and Aalborg, Denmark. Arrangements were made for him to hold worship services, speak with individuals, interview officials at the International Refugee Organization and Canadian immigration offices in Germany and Geneva. On his return to Canada, he reported extensively on efforts of the Mennonite Central Committee in its work with the refugees and encouraged congregations not to grow weary in praying and giving. By the end of 1949, 6,005 refugees had come to Canada and that number continued to grow until by the end of 1961, it reached 12,052. Through the efforts of MCC a large contingent of those who did not receive permission to enter Canada were subsequently relocated in Paraguay, South America.

In 1950, as chairman and representative of the Conference of Mennonites in Canada, J. J., together with Katherine, made a trip to South America to visit the Mennonite settlements in Brazil, Uruguay, Paraguay, and Argentina, and the mission station in Colombia. Thinking of the Bible story of Joseph looking for his brothers, he claimed this trip was a "search for his brothers" of the Mennonite faith. For three months they traveled, speaking to people and listening to their stories of hardship. To become better acquainted with their problems of economic, religious, and social life, arrangements had been made for him to meet with village officials, Mennonite Central Committee representatives, farmers, and church leaders. He made tours of industries and experiment stations. He visited in farm homes. He participated in Bible study conventions, attended conferences with ministers, deacons, teachers, and women's mission societies, preached in congregational worship services, attended prayer meetings, spoke at mission festivals and at weddings. He attended youth gatherings, visited hospitals, senior citizen homes, and schools.

When they came to Rosario, Paraguay, one midnight, the only hotel in that town did not give them a room to spend the rest of the night. The driver of the truck with whom they had come took them to a driveway. They spread their "ponchos" (travel blankets) on the grass, ate their lunch of boiled eggs and "schnetke," and then went to bed under the starry sky. J. J. put his briefcase under his head for a pillow, and in a few minutes was sound asleep, but not for long. He was unaccustomed to the grassy bed, and kept turning from side to side, from left to right. "How good it is that God has given us two sides," he said, and was off to sleep again. A few minutes later he sat up, looked for his Canadian winter gloves in the travel bag, slipped them on, and with his hat on his head was off to slumber land again. In the morning he told Katherine, "I am a nonresistant Mennonite, so I had to put on my gloves that I wouldn't kill these torture spirits of Paraguay." He was talking about the mosquitoes that had buzzed and stung all night. "And," he continued, "how good that I brought my old hat. I could keep it on even in my sleep to protect my head against them." Katherine hadn't slept at all, but Jacob said, "This is the best night of my life." Even in very unpleasant times he could find something to be thankful for and to laugh about.

Returning to Canada from this extensive and exhausting trip, he immediately picked up his regular tasks, and added to his already full load an itineration schedule that included congregations scattered from Ontario to British Columbia. In long informative reports he encouraged the Canadian churches not to give up in their assistance and financial aid to the brethren in South America. Some thought the colonies would never survive. "We have sent so much, and they keep asking for more." But J. J. replied, "We must help them now, and then they will become strong. They need machinery. They need buildings for factories. If MCC can't help them more now, then we should be willing to send them $50,000 or even $100,000." He told them about people in El Ombu, Uruguay, meeting in a sheep barn for their church services, about the Volendam houses where whole families lived in two rooms with dirt floors, and he spoke of the children who couldn't get an education. When the churches heard these reports, they were willing to again give to their brothers and sisters in South America.

Letters from ministers, teachers, doctors, colony officials, young people, organization leaders, and other individuals began to pour into his office with reports of success and failure and with requests for counsel and material aid. With assistance from Saskatchewan and British Columbia Relief committees about $5000 was spent to purchase refrigerators and medical instruments for the hospitals in Neuland, Volendam, Friesland, and Fernheim. Hymnbooks, Bibles, commentaries, concordances, catechisms, and other theological books were sent to the churches. Funds were sent to aid in construction and maintenance of church buildings, schools, hospitals, and senior citizen homes. Money was sent to buy wheelchairs for crippled patients. J. J. had seen the need and had been able to present it to the congregations in Canada.

A Love for People

J. J. loved people. To meet new people, get acquainted, and make new friends was a joy to him. One day he wrote in his notes:

*I love people since they are as different as the flowers in
the field. You can become disappointed in people, even if
outwardly they are nice and beautiful and strong, but
inside have perhaps been neglected. I appreciated
having friends, but finding more and more makes me
richer and I simply put them into my heart, and leave
them there with the thousands accumulated during the
course of the years I have been associating with people.
Perhaps some one will say, "Be careful! You might get an
enlarged heart." And I will say, "Perhaps I have it." . . .
The main thing is that the love of God wins out in the end.
But I am compelled as long as I am in the service of the
Master to sow love and to see life from the brighter side.*

He traveled by bus, train, or plane to the many
conferences and meetings. When he made stopovers in
larger cities like Chicago, Minneapolis, Toronto, or
Edmonton, he telephoned his friends. If he didn't know
anyone in the city, he looked through the telephone directory for Mennonite sounding names, called them,
and had interesting conversations with them. Often he
knew their parents or grandparents. After conversing
for a while, he usually closed the call with prayer.

In Lima, Peru, he had several hours to wait for his
connecting flight, so he again picked up the telephone
directory and soon found the name, "Alberto Thiessen."
"Could this be a relative?" he wondered. J. J. did not
speak Spanish, so he asked the clerk at the Braniff Airlines counter to help him make the call. The girl looked
up at him, laughed, and said, "I know that man." In a
few minutes she guided him into the manager's office of
the airlines and introduced him to Alberto Thiessen.
Soon they were in animated conversation in English.
Alberto had never heard of another person with his
family name, and was interested in finding out about
his relatives. His parents had died many years before
and he could not ask them. Jacob did not find a relative
but they had a long talk about the church and God.

Founding a School

J. J. loved the church and he loved young people. He knew that they were the future leaders of the church. He asked them what they were doing and what they were planning for the future. He knew that many of them would seek a good education for their profession, but he knew that they should also have theological training. If young people were to help build the church, they would need to prepare for that too. There were Bible schools in Canada, but no higher Mennonite theological training schools where young people could prepare to become ministers and missionaries. Together with others he prayed, planned, proposed ideas, and finally in 1947 the Canadian Mennonite Bible College opened its doors in Winnipeg. It was a vision that became a reality through the joint efforts of many persons, and J. J. thanked God for all those who were willing to help establish the college, to give so buildings could be acquired, faculty hired, and the library equipped. He was grateful for all the students who came to the school.

For twenty-five years he worked as chairman of the College Board and made many trips to Winnipeg for business transactions, to confer with faculty, and to fellowship with the students. After he gave up his chairmanship, he was given an honorary life membership on the Board, and he continued to attend the Board meetings. He called the annual trip to the commencement service in spring his "pilgrimage to Mecca." "It is not that I go to worship somebody in Tuxedo," he said, "but the hundreds of times when I have been in the college I have had deep feelings, and sometimes the needs of the school, sometimes the experience with the school, and sometimes the observance of the school has brought me to my knees and in very close relationship to my Lord. To me, as also to many others, the college was a special answer to a crying need in our churches in those days, and that's why we who know about the time have a right to meditate on the past, help to plan, and to pray for the future. This is what we do. May God bless our school in the future as he has done in the past."

He always met many friends at the college and reflected on the history of the school. He talked about the beginning of classes in the basement of Bethel Mission Church, then moving to a beautiful residence on Wellington Crescent, and a few years later purchasing property in the Tuxedo district and erecting buildings. The developments had cost much prayer and money. Then he added,

> *In retrospect, I see the many friends and co-workers who help to build up the college and who were so faithful in doing their share. Now the many responsibilities rest with another generation, and I praise the Lord for the spirit and the integrity and the tenacity with which this generation is continuing the work that was begun several decades ago. If we think of the many ministers and church workers who are active in our churches, schools, and mission fields, who received their start in CMBC, then we have reason to praise God for this wonderful school of ours.*

Graceful Retirement

For many years he was the minister, then the elder of the First Mennonite Church in Saskatoon, but when he reached age seventy, he thought the Lord might call him home suddenly, and he wanted to leave the congregation in the hands of a good leader who would continue the work in the name of Christ. In the fall of 1963, a younger pastor, Edward Enns, came to help in the ministry, and on January 1, 1964, J. J. ordained Edward as pastor. J. J. was asked to continue as elder

Delmar Studios

Jacob J. Thiessen

emeritus, which meant he would still continue in an active role in the work of the congregation. For eight years they "walked" together in the work at First Mennonite, and when Edward left for another church, Henry A. Wiens became the pastor and J. J. continued as elder emeritus. If he could not visit sick friends in the hospital, he telephoned them there. He visited other people by telephone too and prayed with them over the phone. Those more distant he visited in letters and encouraged them to grow in their trust in God.

Year after year he attended conferences: Canadian conference, General Conference, World Conference, Mennonite Central Committee meetings, and many others. In the summer of 1977 he attended the sessions of the Conference of Mennonites in Canada for the fiftieth time and listened to all the reports with great interest. Conferences were important to the congregations to help them work together on projects that they could not do as small groups. He wrote:

In my estimation the Conference of Mennonites in Canada has fulfilled a very important role in unifying our congregations and promoting interest in missions, education, and service. Participating in the Canadian Mennonite Board of Colonization, later Canadian Mennonite Relief and Immigration Council, our conference congregations have taken a very active part in alleviating human suffering and in bringing to Canada 30,000 of our Mennonite people.

In the last decade, as a result of change in the world and society, new problems and new concerns have rightly occupied the minds of our people. The different conference boards are instrumental in guiding the conference to meet these problems and to deal with them "for the perfecting of the saints, for the work of the ministry, for the edifying of the body of Christ."

August 25, 1977, was a beautiful summer day. In the morning, J. J. went with his son to the Air Canada ticket office to purchase a ticket for Winnipeg for the weekend. He was going to attend the ground breaking service for the Heritage Center to be built on the CMBC campus to house the archives and library. Coming home from purchasing his ticket he suffered a stroke, and a few hours later God called him from this life. Could he have spoken the last minutes of his life, he probably would have reiterated the words of the Apostle Paul, as he had done so often: "I have fought the good fight, I have finished the race, I have kept the faith. Henceforth there is laid up for me the crown of righteousness, which the Lord, the righteous judge, will award to me on that Day, and not only to me but also to all who have loved his appearing" (2 Timothy 4:7-8).

At his funeral a few days later many friends shared in thanking and praising God for the gift of his life and the influence it had been to bring blessing and joy into their lives. He was a man called of God to give leadership in the Mennonite Church during a period of upheaval and difficulty, and he remained faithful to his calling.

13.
John and Clara Schmidt

By
Maynard
Shelly

John and Clara Schmidt had found the good life in Mountain Lake. But they couldn't make it last.

John had brought his family to this cozy Minnesota community at the end of 1947. They had had three satisfying years here while John practiced medicine with Dr. Peter J. Pankratz.

"We really thought we had our life made," says Clara, "with a good partner, who had built an extra room for John. We had a hospital, a parochial school for the children, and an extra large backyard with trees planted. We had a nice house bought, and a car; and it was all debt free!"

Yet, John and Clara had the uneasy feeling that they weren't in the right place. Looking back on those years, John now says, "The best place in the world is the worst place in the world to be if that isn't where God wants you."

Paraguay was calling them back. Together, John and Clara had spent three rugged years in that poor South American country after John had worked for over a year as the only doctor in the Mennonite colonies in a wilderness called the Chaco.

Orie Miller begged them to return to Paraguay to take up a new work for the Mennonites and the Paraguayans. As executive secretary of the Mennonite Central Committee, Orie had taken John to Paraguay in 1941 and started him out as MCC's first worker in South America.

Now, plans had been made to build a hospital to treat the country's most serious health problem—leprosy. But no one could be found to take over the leadership of this work. Orie remembered John and Clara as persons who had once worked in Paraguay and had done good jobs. They seemed to be just the folks he needed.

John and Clara put off Orie's request by suggesting that he look for somebody else.

"But if you're the ones that are called," said Orie, "there isn't going to be anyone else."

The People He Couldn't Forget

As a boy in the Alexanderwohl Mennonite congregation in Goessel, Kansas, John Rempel Schmidt often heard Elder Peter H. Unruh tell about distributing food to Mennonites and others during the famine in Russia in 1922. Unruh had been one of the first five workers to go to Russia for the Mennonite Central Committee to help "our brothers in the faith."

At the close of many of his sermons, Elder Unruh would say, "Now we'll take a collection for the poor Russians."

John went on to university and to medical school. He had just started his residency in medicine in Baltimore in 1939 when he received a letter from Henry A. Fast, a member of the MCC executive committee, who had just visited the Mennonite colonies in Paraguay and wanted John to go and help these refugees from the Soviet Union.

At once, John knew that these were his brothers in Paraguay who were calling him. "I well realized that I could have been a barefoot boy behind a walking plow in Paraguay," he says, "if I had been among the fortunate ones not killed in Russia, or if my grandparents had not decided to leave for the United States when they did."

But he couldn't interrupt the plans that he had made for his medical training. He did tell Fast that he would consider the call in two years if the need continued.

"I was really moved by that letter," says John. "It was something I couldn't just forget."

In fact, John started dreaming about Paraguay. He wrote to Dr. Rudolph Unruh, a former missionary doctor, who was then practicing medicine in Halstead, Kansas. "I asked him whether he wouldn't want to go to Paraguay. He would be the surgeon and I would be the medical man. We would make a team." Unruh wasn't ready for such an assignment, but he remembered John Schmidt.

But John had dreams about more than Paraguay. "All my life, I had an interest for the opposite sex, even in grade school. I still recall the girl friends I had. In high school, things became rather serious, and I had to get hold of myself, especially when I started into university.

"I said to myself, 'Profession or marriage, but not both.'"

With the end of his medical training in sight, John saw himself being freed from his self-imposed vow. But now in Baltimore, he found no girl that suited him. So, he wrote to his brother Herb to be on the lookout for a good girl for him.

Herbert R. Schmidt, MD, Bethel Clinic, Newton, Kansas, had always been John's best big brother. When

John went to the one-room country school near Canton in McPherson County, Kansas, as a first grader, Herb was in eighth grade. But they both ate out of the same lunch bucket at noon.

Herb went on to the University of Kansas to study medicine. John followed to study chemical engineering and to tease Herb about the bones he studied and hung in the room they shared.

"Who knows," said Herb, "some day you may want to work with them too."

John scoffed and said, "That would be the last thing that I would ever do." And he thought he really meant it.

But when John found himself bogged down in the mathematics and calculus required of engineering students, he decided to take a course in biology to see whether something else might be more to his liking. It was. "I felt then that I would rather work with people than with figures," says John. Following Herb's leading, John switched to medicine.

And, when it came to finding a girl for John, Herb did have an idea where to look.

What Does the Lord Want with Me?

Clara Ann Regier was a student nurse at Bethel Deaconess Hospital in Newton. Herb took special notice of her when he learned that she had been chief clerk of the agriculture office at the county courthouse, a job that helped her earn her way through college.

And Clara noticed that she was being noticed. Herb had a reputation for not being able to remember a nurse's name. But when he saw Clara down the hall, he would call, "Miss Regier!"

Clara would say to herself, "Good night! What is this?" It took some time until she discovered the meaning of Herb's interest.

But Herb had judged her well. She had qualities that set her apart. Having finished grade school, Clara seemed destined to become the family housekeeper for her mother who was ill from time to time. High school seemed out of the question, for parents in the Mennonite community east of Newton at the time felt that girls really didn't need that much education.

Aunt Katie Andres saw things differently. She encouraged Clara to take correspondence courses even while working at home. "You need to go to school," she told Clara. And the next year, Clara did enter high school, completed her work in three years, and graduated with her class.

Clara had been baptized in the First Mennonite Church of Newton by Pastor J. E. Entz. It was the regular baptismal class and she was seventeen. Two years later, she attended a special gathering of the Garden Township Church, northwest of Newton. "They had this joyous type of camp meeting. After the meeting, there was a call for those who wanted to commit themselves to full-time service for the Lord. And I was moved to go forward in this strange church."

Some years later, Clara's mother reminded her of the meetings at Garden Township. "You came home," she said, "singing a new song that we didn't know: 'I'll Go Where You Want Me to Go, Dear Lord.' "

But for many years, Clara would wonder. "I would often ask, 'What does the Lord want with me?' I'd always felt that he had honored this decision."

But in 1933, Clara saw little more in her future than caring for her mother and housekeeping for her family. Then, Uncle Peter Andres asked her to work in the agriculture allotment office in Newton. "It was to be just for a week, otherwise my parents would never have let me to go work in an office."

The week stretched out into a month and then into a year, and then into eight years. After several years of working in town, Clara ventured to enroll in Bethel College while still holding her job part-time and living at home.

Since school teaching held little attraction for her, Clara did not know what she would do once she finished college. Then, Ella Wiebe, her class adviser, talked to her about nurses' training. And she asked Clara, who was older than most of the girls in her class, whether she had ever considered marriage. "I wanted to have a family, I told her. At that time, that was my main aim. 'But at this time,' I said, 'I don't see any clear leading.'"

But she did feel led to enter nurses' training at Bethel Deaconess Hospital once her college work was finished. And for her last year in college, she determined to live on campus, a bold step for her family, even though she was twenty-five at the time. "My parents held on to me real much. I really had to work up a storm to be able to go and stay on the campus."

Getting away from home deepened Clara's appreciation for her home and her parents. "When I did break away, that was the time that prepared me for my later breaking away which took me so very far."

Amid the Farewells an Introduction

The shape of Clara's breaking away took form when Orie Miller came to Kansas in May 1941 for a meeting of the MCC executive committee. The needs of the Mennonite refugees from Russia who had gone to Paraguay were a matter of urgent concern.

The meeting closed on a Saturday, and Orie, along with P. C. Hiebert, the chairman of MCC, decided that instead of going to church on Sunday, they would scour the Kansas countryside for a doctor for the Mennonites in the Paraguayan Chaco. When they came to Halstead, Dr. Rudolph Unruh recalled the letter he had received from Dr. John R. Schmidt in Baltimore. He sent the two men to Newton to see Dr. Herb Schmidt. When Miller and Hiebert told their need to Herb, he at once sent a telegram to his brother.

The following morning, as John returned to his hospital assignment after a weekend vacation, Herb's telegram about the need for a doctor for the Chaco colonies was waiting for him. As soon as he read its message, he knew what his answer would be.

Turning to his friends on the hospital staff, he said, "I'm going to Paraguay." They were stunned. Many had never heard of the place before.

As soon as Orie received word of John's readiness to go to Paraguay, he took John to Washington to secure the needed papers for the trip to South America. They also agreed that he would serve for one year and would receive forty-five dollars per month plus room and board. Plans were made for both Orie and John to leave for Paraguay by ship in ten days.

For John, this meant a hurried trip to Kansas to visit his parents whom he had seen only once in the three years he had been in training in Baltimore. Parents, neighbors, and especially Elder Unruh rejoiced in the news that John was going to aid the Mennonites who had come from Russia. They wished him well.

But amid the farewells came an introduction. When Herb went to make his rounds at Bethel Deaconess Hospital, he took his brother along. While standing around a patient's bed, Herb introduced John to a student nurse, Clara Regier.

Shortly after that, Mariam, Herb's wife, invited Clara to join her and the two brothers on a visit to nearby

Wichita. For John and Clara, it was their first date.

The meetings were quite casual. Clara did have a boy friend, though the relationship had not been going well. As John left for Paraguay, neither John nor Clara knew whether they would see each other again.

Sad Settlers in a Home Faraway

The ocean liner trip in June 1941 from New York to Rio de Janeiro became a time of orientation to Mennonite Central Committee for John as Orie Miller told him more about the crises being faced by the Mennonite settlers.

Paraguay, in lower South America, is a landlocked country divided by the Paraguay River. Almost all of its people live on the eastern side of the river. The land to the west is a large unpopulated wilderness, so flat that rainwater has no place to drain.

This great blank space on the map is called the Chaco, a name that means wilderness. Its forests have hard and durable woods, the most notable of which is the tree called the quebracho (or, ax-breaker) from which tannin, a chemical for curing hides, is extracted and of which Paraguay is the world's leading supplier.

Almost in the center of this great empty region were two Mennonite colonies—Menno and Fernheim—almost 400 miles northeast of Asunción, the nation's capital, by river boat, railroad, and road.

The Menno people had come from Canada in 1927 because they wanted isolation. Their 3000 people who lived in forty villages wanted to be separate from the world in order to maintain their own churches, schools, and German language.

But the Fernheim people came reluctantly in 1930 with the assistance of MCC because no other country would receive them. These 2000 people scattered in twenty villages had fled the oppression of the Soviet Union. They would have preferred to make their homes in Germany or, at least, to go to the United States or Canada, but the presence of trachoma, a most contagious eye disease that causes blindness, at times barred them from these countries.

They called their new settlement Fernheim (home faraway), expressing the heavy sadness with which they came to their wilderness settlement. A portion of the Fernheim colony did leave the Chaco in 1937 to cross the river and set up a settlement called Friesland in the more populated and developed eastern part of Paraguay.

Back with His Own People

At Rio, Orie with his son Albert and John with his cabin mate Dr. Cordier took a plane to Asunción. John shipped the trunk with his books, equipment, and most of his clothing by boat, expecting it to catch up with him in ten days. The ten days turned out to be six months.

With Orie Miller at his side, John made the long trip to the Chaco. Not usually subject to homesickness, John began to dread the day that Orie would return to North America and leave him alone with a strange people in the green sea of grassy clumps and thorny scrub trees.

Their journey ended at Filadelfia, the chief town of the Fernheim colony. Here the settlers had built a small hospital with a fairly complete supply of surgical instruments brought from Germany. But finding a doctor willing to live in their isolated community had been more than they could do.

It was the month of July and it was wintertime in this country south of the equator. A strong north wind had driven the temperature up to 104 degrees. Orie had long since left him and, overwhelmed by the work that had to be done and the failure of his baggage to arrive, John was sitting on his bed in the little one-room hut that was his home.

One of the colony ministers looked in the door, and, seeing him holding his head in his hands, said, "Just as I thought. If this is winter, you're wondering, what the summer will be like. Believe me, the summer will be no worse."

In fact, John found the summers not much different than they were in Kansas. Gradually, he found the Chaco to be quite livable, and even a happy place to be.

Coming into the hospital kitchen one day for his lunch, he found the cooks serving ammonia cookies, just like the ones that his Mennonite grandmothers in Kansas had made for him as a boy. And then he knew where he had landed. After living for almost eight years in the strange atmosphere of a medical school and a big city hospital, he was back with his own people.

Finding Ways to Operate on the Frontier

John needed every bit of inventiveness that he had to cope with the limitations of a frontier community. To treat the anemia of those worn out by disease and malnutrition, he needed to prescribe iron for their diets. To get that kind of iron, he went to the local blacksmith shop and heated rusted iron until red hot. He collected the reduced iron on a tin plate that he had cleaned and then prepared it further with mortar and pestle for ingestion. He found the results "very effective."

The settlers felt that much of their ill health was due to the rigors of the Chaco climate. Actually, John found the weather to be the source of good health rather than disease. Poor eating habits such as relying too much on starchy foods caused many of their ills.

In order to do surgery, John had to train his own anesthetist. He found a grade school teacher and gave him a quick course in the necessary procedures. Though the young man had never seen a surgical operation before, he learned quickly. "He did very well," says John, "but I had to keep my eye on his business as well as my own."

But he found a number of cases that required surgery more complicated than he was willing to tackle with only the help of his anesthetist trainee. So he asked MCC that his brother Herb be allowed to come for a few weeks to help with some major surgery.

Herb came in November 1941 and John gathered together the people most in need, some from the distant Friesland colony across the river. During Herb's two weeks stay, the two brothers performed over thirty major operations and many minor ones, often doing three in the forenoon and one in the afternoon.

The hospital's twelve beds were soon full, so after the first few days, patients were sent to private homes to recuperate. "This was no doubt," says John, "the greatest number of Mennonites to be operated on in one place in so short a time."

It was also the beginning of Herb's personal involvement in Paraguay and the life of the Mennonite colonies. He has made frequent trips to Paraguay over the years and involved himself in the development of the settlers in the Chaco.

All but Engaged by Slow Mail

Soon after coming to Paraguay, John wrote a casual letter to Clara Regier. She answered just as casually. After a letter had been written, it took almost four months until an answer could be received.

It was on Christmas Eve 1941 that Clara and the young man she had been dating in Newton broke off their relationship. She had eight long weeks to ponder the meaning of that separation. Then she received a letter from John in Paraguay—his first really serious love letter. He had written it on the night before Christmas.

After a few more letters, they were all but engaged to be married. John was ready, but Clara wasn't quite sure.

John left Paraguay late in 1942, not expecting to return, though he left most of his books and medical equipment behind. With a suitcase in each hand, a souvenir pelt under each arm, and a big black hat on his head, he made his way overland to the west coast of Chile, and took a ship headed for New Orleans by way of the Panama Canal and Cuba.

Arriving in New Orleans, John announced his arrival in a telegram to Clara at Mercy Hospital in Kansas City where she was spending a few weeks as part of her training program. The train to Kansas City was overcrowded and running late.

"When I got off the train, I put my suitcases into lockers and looked for a phone to call Mercy Hospital," says John. "I know I looked like a real bum by this time, not having shaved or washed for at least two days, and with a big old black hat and a walking cane.

"As I came to the phone, I noticed a lady there looking rather dejected. I don't know whether I really knew or the Lord led me, but I asked her, 'Are you Clara Regier?'

"So, here we were, past midnight in the busy Union Station in Kansas City."

Meeting John after the long separation was a bit unsettling for Clara. His presence seemed so different than the impression his letters had given her. "I had to get used to it, because I was used to the letters. I had a real struggle there."

But the Lord answered her prayers during the days of their visit in Kansas City. "The first time we were in church together and I heard him sing, I thought, 'I can go through life with this voice, without any doubt.' "

A Wedding Trip to Paraguay

But it was back to writing letters for a little time longer, as Clara continued in nurses' training and John took a job in Albuquerque, New Mexico. However, it soon became clear that a young Mennonite doctor could hardly find a satisfying career anywhere in the United States during the early 1940s. "People would always point at you and say, 'What's that young doctor doing out here? He ought to be in the service.' "

John knew that the military life was not for him. But it was either that or overseas service for the church. Clara hoped to go to Europe and P. A. Penner, a missionary friend of John's father and Herb's father-in-law, wanted them to come to India to work in a leprosy hospital there.

But at the time, the need seemed greater in Paraguay. MCC had not been able to find another doctor for Fernheim after John left.

Clara graduated from the school of nursing on August 20, 1943, and five days later, John and Clara were married. They left the following day for a three-year term in Paraguay. "I asked John what to take. He said, 'We don't need much. The people have everything there.' "

So, they each left with a suitcase and nothing extra. The allowance for the young couple would be seventy dollars per month plus room and board.

On their way to the Chaco, they stopped overnight at the breakaway colony of Friesland in East Paraguay. As soon as it was known that the doctor had come, people began to gather for medical help. Though he had no equipment or medicine, John received them in the shade of a tree and gave what help he could.

"I had to think of Jesus going around healing," says Clara. "I had a very high opinion of my new husband."

On their first morning in Filadelfia, wagons started rattling up to the little hospital long before dawn. People from every village had come to welcome Dr. John back and to confront him with all the ills accumulated during his absence of almost a year.

Clara's first task was to take notes on the consultations with the first patients, but this seemed impossible, for John was talking to the people in Low German, a dialect unfamiliar to the Prussian Mennonites from the land east of Newton, Kansas, whose only German was High German. "It's a twist of the tongue that's hard to get," says Clara, "but I did understand it very soon."

The colony leaders wanted to build a house for the doctor and his new wife, but until that could happen, the young bride and groom lived in the same little one-room hut that had been John's home during his first term.

But during those early days in Fernheim, most of Clara's work was outside her home. Seven village girls were chosen for the first nurses' training class. Teaching materials were limited. Clara had the use of a set of encyclopedias covering the complete medical field—thirteen big books which John had brought for his first term—but the material had to be translated into German first.

And from the beginning, the young girls had to do everything from helping with surgery to caring for the most severely ill. Typhoid cases needed careful isolation. Almost from the first day and almost before they had time to study, the young nurses had to learn about infection. "I didn't want any of them to get sick," says Clara, "so I really laid it on. They still tell me, even after all these years, how they came out of that class just feeling that they were crawling with germs."

Many of the surgeries were times of personal crisis for the new couple, as Clara would assist with the operation. "We were all on edge," she says. "John was nervous with the operation; nothing seemed to go right for him, and he was so brash with his statements. I was his new bride, and I was very upset because I thought, 'How can he love me when he acts this way?' That was one of the things I had to get over real quick."

Family Planning

"In those days," says Clara, "there was no talk of family planning. In fact, it would have been taboo. But I couldn't help it when these women came in with their tenth, eleventh, or twelfth baby, crying because they had another child and were so terribly overburdened.

"I'd take calendars into their rooms and circle the free period. And I would give the calendars along home with them, just hoping the preachers wouldn't hear about that."

John had a more direct approach to family planning counseling, according to one of the many stories told throughout the villages about the doctor at Filadelfia. Meeting poor parents whose family was growing much too steadily, John would say, "You'll have to learn how to sleep at night back to back, and you'll have fewer children."

Family planning had a more positive meaning for the doctor and his wife. Soon after arriving in the colonies, Clara found herself pregnant, which was a happy discovery because both wanted children and the beginning of a family could not be postponed. "I wasn't so young," says Clara, "and John told me that if he had to be responsible for the delivery, he wanted to have a child before I was thirty." And they did—with a few months to spare.

John Russell, their first son, was born in July 1944. "He was born in the middle of the coldest night in Paraguay with no heat in the delivery room. But I wasn't cold; just the rest were."

Then, a year and a half later, a daughter, Elisabeth, was born in the same delivery room at midday on the hottest day of the Paraguayan summer.

Helping Needy People

The Schmidts started a Bible class for their nurses and invited others to join them in their home. Clara gave piano and typing lessons. "That's what fulfilled us a lot," says Clara, "because we were needed, in whatever area you would look at."

John even received calls to serve as a veterinarian. And seeing the need to improve the quality of feed for dairy cattle during the dry season, he built a demonstration silo and filled it with silage.

In all this, they were helping to build a better community. But Clara was not quite satisfied. In dedicating her life to the Lord, she had had a vision of doing mission work, and their involvement in the life of the Mennonite people in Paraguay did not fit that expectation. "They had their churches and their preachers. This was not mission work. We were helping people who really needed us and it was a satisfaction. But still I never had my vision quite fulfilled.

"Later, when the Lord led us into the leprosy work, then he fulfilled this also in me."

The way into the leprosy work began with John's concern for the larger witness of the Mennonites in

Paraguay. He was pained to see the Mennonites holding themselves aloof from the people of the country. Many of them despised the Paraguayans, saying that the natives were still hanging by their feet from the trees and had yet to come down.

John often talked of a "thank you project" by which the Mennonites would serve the needs of Paraguay and express appreciation for the haven that had been given to them. The Mennonite Central Committee responded with support for such a venture as did some of the people of the colonies. Programs in hookworm control and in child feeding were begun in Asunción and in east Paraguay. Yet John did not find in these projects a response to equal the gifts that Mennonites had received.

Then a friend from the Disciples of Christ mission called attention to the country's need for help with leprosy treatment. It was the country's number one health problem with possibly 30,000 people infected. Treatment which was far from adequate was being given only in one government leprosy colony. Inquiries by members of the MCC team in Paraguay brought offers of support from several sides. The government promised land, the American Leprosy Mission and the Mennonite Central Committee would provide funds for building and operation, and the local Mennonites would also be involved.

As their term came to an end in September 1946, John and Clara left for North America with their two children, feeling that they had finished their work in Paraguay.

The Ulcer and the Miracle

They came to Freeman, South Dakota, in the winter of 1946, which after three years in the tropics struck them as quite severe. John opened a medical office on the second floor of a store building. Wearing a long fur coat that a thoughtful friend had donated, he went about making his calls. A round oak stove in the middle of the room provided heat for the office. But the nights were so cold that in the mornings when John reached for his coat hanging by the door, it was frozen to the wall.

The struggles of building up a new medical practice were complicated by John's failing health. Stomach ulcers that had been smoldering since the intense days of working his way through medical school finally flared up. He lived on puddings and baby food and he would often experience a real flare-up of ulcer trouble after shoveling snow when the old Ford got stuck in the snow while out on country calls.

Then came the opportunity to join Dr. Pankratz in Mountain Lake and so by the beginning of 1948, the Schmidts had settled down in Minnesota for what they thought would be a good long time. But even as they were finding new friends and building new relationships, concerns for old friends in Paraguay would not fade. They wondered often how the work on the leprosy program was coming along.

"We stuck our foot in it," says Clara, "because we asked what was happening to the plans that had been made for the thank-you project."

It was then that Orie Miller asked the Schmidts for their help. But it was clear that John could never return to Paraguay for any long-term assignment as long as the stomach ulcer was sapping his strength. So he decided on a test of whether they would go or stay.

John had been impressed with the skills of the doctors at the Mayo Clinic in Rochester, Minnesota, after having referred a patient from Freeman to their care. He wanted to see what, if anything, they could do with his case. In reporting his symptoms, he mentioned the possibility that he might go to Paraguay for another term of service. Thus, the Mayo doctors decided on a course they might otherwise not have considered.

They decided to operate, and removed four fifths of John's stomach. It worked. In six weeks, John was eating a popcorn ball and an apple that the children had brought home from a Christmas party.

"This operation had really been on the suggestion of going to Paraguay," says Clara, "and because he had been so miraculously helped, how could we turn it down?"

The Colony Model

To prepare himself for his new task, John spent ten days at the United States Marine Hospital in Carville, Louisiana, the only institution in North America devoted to the treatment of leprosy. Here John told of how persons in Paraguay afflicted with this crippling disease were often treated as criminals.

Most persons tried to hide the presence of the sickness as long as they could. When discovered, the police were often called and the poor victim would be shackled and led away under an armed guard to the government leprosy colony called Santa Isabella at Sapucay. Naturally, the colony became more like a prison than a center for healing.

Yet those in the colony may have been the lucky ones, for folk remedies could be horrifying. John saw a patient who had been seized by strong men and held over a fire so that the flames would lick the wounds. No screams, no matter how loud, could free the tortured soul from the terror which only compounded misery and infection.

In his discussions with Dr. Paul T. Erickson, the medical chief at Carville, John began to see that leprosy could be treated in other ways than in an institution or in a colony. The new sulfone drugs had made it possible to reduce the contagion of leprosy. This meant that persons with leprosy needed no longer to be quarantined but could remain in their own homes.

This was the beginning of a vision for an ambulatory leprosy treatment program. Instead of collecting patients in a hospital colony, medical workers would go out into the countryside to find the patients in their homes, examine them, and give them the needed medicines. From time to time, they would be visited to check their progress until they were healed.

The idea seemed worthy of a test and John wanted to give it a try. Dr. Erikson was excited about it and felt that it would work.

But the Mennonite Central Committee and the American Leprosy Mission resisted the new idea. For five years, they had been working with plans based on the colony model and they intended to stick with them.

They pointed out that the money that had been pledged was for a leprosy colony for 250 patients. The advisory committee members in Paraguay who had been chosen to work with John were all committed to the colony way of treatment. So Orie Miller decreed that the plans already made would be the ones that would be followed.

That seemed to settle the issue. John and Clara were resigned to going the colony route when they left for Paraguay in August 1951. Three new children were going with them: Wesley had been born in April 1947 in Freeman, David in October 1948 and Marlene in April 1951 in Mountain Lake. And their baggage included sixty-four crates of medical and electrical equipment and other specialized items for the building of a full-fledged leprosy colony.

Buying Land at Kilometer 81

Work had begun the year before to survey the 6000-acre tract of land near Concepcion which the government had donated to the Mennonites for their leprosy colony. Concepcion was on the Paraguay River, along the route that Mennonites often followed going from the Chaco colonies to Asunción. It seemed an ideal location.

But when the Mennonite workers inspected the land more closely, they found more than one hundred families living on the land, and some had been there for more than forty years. Since it seemed impossible to peaceably resettle these families, they decided to find another site.

An estate of about 3000 acres was found about fifty miles east of Asunción. It had both high and low ground and had a brook running through it. The Mennonite Central Committee purchased the land directly from its owner, a Frenchman.

The gateway to the new plot was at the stone marker that read Kilometer 81 on Route 2 which led from Asunción east to the Brazilian border. The site quickly became known as Kilometer 81 and continued to be called that even when formally named Centro de Salud Menonita (Mennonite Health Center).

John settled his family in Asunción until the house at Kilometer 81 at least had a roof. Having once studied engineering, he now found use for skills that had gone unused for many years. He drew plans for the first buildings, laid out roads and bridges, tested the soil, purchased building materials, and hired workers.

Old friendships in the Mennonite community had to

be renewed and conferences held with Mennonite leaders. New colonies had appeared in 1947 when 4500 Mennonites who had escaped from the Soviet Union during World War II settled in Neuland in the Chaco and in Volendam in east Paraguay. Canadian Mennonites began new settlements at Sommerfeld and Bergthal in East Paraguay.

Relationships with the government's ministry of health had to be cultivated. In 1950, the Mennonite Central Committee had received the consent of the government to operate a leprosy program. But this agreement referred to the site at Concepcion which was later abandoned. Did that contract apply now to Kilometer 81? No clear answer was given for several years.

And before leaving the United States, John had asked whether a North American physician might work in Paraguay. Earlier, he had worked mainly in the Mennonite colonies which were communities apart from the regular stream of Paraguayan life. But the leprosy program would serve all Paraguayans. It would seem that such a service to the poor and neglected would be gratefully received, yet the answer was a long time coming.

Pacified with Cake and Coffee

While Paraguay directly needed a leprosy treatment center, every community preferred to have such a place at a distance from its own homes, lest a gathering of many sick and crippled people endanger its health.

The people of Itacuribi, the town nearest to Kilometer 81, had dreams of developing their city into a tourist resort. They were sure that a leprosy colony would ruin their plans.

In fact, the minister of health secretly promised them that the Mennonites would never lay one brick on top of another. But it was not long until signs of building activity began to appear on the Kilometer 81 site.

One Sunday afternoon when John was gone a truck loaded with men came down the lane from the highway. They said they would allow no further building. Clara and the Mennonite workers who were with her tried to explain in the little Spanish that they knew that the houses being built were for workers and would not be used for leprosy patients.

After allowing the men to inspect the premises, they invited their unexpected guests to have coffee and cake. The men became less hostile and finally seemed satisfied that the Mennonite program would be no threat to them. They left with the rocks they had brought for the battle they had expected to fight.

Later, it was learned that someone had even gone to seek the help of President Stroessner to put an end to the Mennonite project. But all the president would say was, "I wish the Mennonites would build a leprosy hospital in every corner of Paraguay."

Finding the Hidden and Afflicted

The strong resistance of the neighbors to a leprosy colony made it more desirable to test other ways of treating leprosy, so building plans were modified. Instead of large pavilions to house many patients, it was decided to build only several smaller guesthouses to shelter only a few patients: those most seriously crippled, those in need of intensive care, and those without homes.

The rest would be treated in their homes as John had originally envisioned. But finding the patients was not easy. John and his medical workers had to comb the villages and farmhouses, traveling often on horseback because the area had few roads.

They found first those leprosy sufferers who had just been deserted by their families and left to die. Such was the fate of Ramona Candida who was one of the first patients discovered by the Schmidts, just as they were beginning to doubt that they would ever find any of the hundreds of victims they knew existed.

They found Ramona, full of sores, lying on a pile of rags in the dark corner of a hut attended only by her small son who brought her bits of food that he could find. She could only move one arm to reach the jug of water at her side. She was so near starvation, and so reduced to skin and bones, that it was difficult even to give her an injection.

Ramona was brought to a half-finished guesthouse at Kilometer 81, and because no other nurse was willing to assume her care, Clara took on the task. All of Ramona's clothing and bedding had to be boiled and her young son was taught to build and tend the fire under the caldron to boil the water. Clara had no place to keep her isolation gown and would hang it on a door in the unfinished building only to have the wind blow it away at night.

But after seven or eight months, Ramona's strength returned. And Clara wondered, "How does she feel? We've taken her out of her misery, given her food and clothing. But, really she doesn't understand. How can we tell her of the Christian love that we have in our hearts for her?"

Freely Given Work

The building continued and other patients came. Workers were needed to help the patients, to work in the kitchen and laundry, to work in the clinic and pharmacy, to work on the farm and in the gardens, to teach school, and to do the hundreds of other tasks that needed doing. Where would they all be found?

John and Clara set out to visit the Mennonite settlements and remind them that the leprosy program belonged to them. "If once this was an MCC project with colony representatives," John said, "it is now the project of the different Mennonite colonies of Paraguay and we are your co-workers."

The several settlements delegated members to serve on the Kilometer 81 committee. And every year, on the first Sunday in May, Mennonite congregations in Paraguay gave a freewill offering.

But the most important contribution was the volunteer service which they gave through *Christlicher Dienst* (Christian Service), an organization of voluntary workers who came in a steady stream to Kilometer 81 to help at first with the building and then with the medical service and evangelistic program of the mission.

The first group of twenty came in 1952. Some gave their time freely for three months, others for six months or more. They worked without pay, receiving only their travel, room, board, and work clothes while on the job.

Over 500 people have given voluntary service at Kilometer 81, often thirty people at one time. For many of these workers, most of whom were young people, the work at Kilometer 81 gave them a chance to apply their faith in a practical way.

"I'm not interested to have you build castles for us up here," John would tell each group of volunteers. "If the work at 81 has helped you to make your Bible knowledge more meaningful, that's what I want."

Sharing Faith and Life

From the beginning, Kilometer 81's workers formed a small Mennonite community of German- and English-speaking people in an area where the rest of the people spoke one of Paraguay's two official languages, either Spanish or Guarani. Even before patients came regularly to the medical center for treatment and even before a missionary able to speak the local languages was appointed, the Mennonite community at Kilometer 81 began to share its faith as best it could.

The first opportunity came with the first Christmas. The Paraguayan custom was to prepare a display of the nativity scene at each home using clay figures of animals, shepherds, and the holy family bought in the market and set up outside the home, sometimes under a grape arbor.

How do Mennonites observe Christmas? The people in the community wanted to see their nativity display.

Under Clara's leadership, a Christmas festival was planned. Songs in Spanish were rehearsed, cookies were baked, stuffed animals were sewn, and passages from the Bible were chosen for reading.

The program was a success and more. Four hundred people came and before the night was over, the hosts lost control over the crowd.

"It was very dumb and we had to learn a lot of things," says Clara, "but that was really our first mission thrust."

As the health workers went from village to village looking for patients and carrying medicines for those under treatment, they also distributed tracts and sometimes held religious meetings in the homes and communities visited.

Eventually, a chaplain was appointed by the Mennonite congregations; Johann Regehr came to Kilometer 81 in 1956. He had been trained in a seminary in Argentina and was able to preach in Spanish. At that time, Kilometer 81 had no chapel, but Sunday services for the resident patients were begun in the hall of one of the patient guesthouses.

One of those who attended those services was Ramona Candida. Before the spread of leprosy in her body had been checked, she was crippled and partially blinded. But her life had been spared and she had a home among people who cared for her.

But Ramona gave no evidence of a response until one Sunday at a church service. "Then she got up in her crippled condition,"says Clara, "took her pillow and put it on the floor and made her confession of faith. It was a great day."

The Ministry's Doctor

The leprosy work began slowly because government recognition was slow in coming. John wasn't licensed to practice medicine in Paraguay and the value of a leprosy treatment program that did not colonize its patients was uncertain.

The Mennonite Central Committee hoped that John might be licensed as a physician recognized by the government. John, however, felt that the large investment in time for language study and the need to take endless examinations would take too much of his time.

In talking to one Paraguayan doctor, who later became the dean of the country's medical school, John was told that such a medical license would really have little value.

"What do you want a permit in Paraguay for? We as doctors stand behind you, and that's all you need," the doctor said.

In 1956, the health ministry took note of the home treatment methods for leprosy and issued regulations for such an ambulatory program. One of those regulations had special meaning for Kilometer 81; that was the requirement that the work be done under the supervision of a physician licensed in Paraguay.

The person appointed by the health ministry to do that supervision was Dr. Eduardo Rodriquez, who became Kilometer 81's chief supporter and promoter among medical and government circles. He visited the program regularly and became thoroughly familiar with the work that was being done.

Yet John had one objection to the arrangement and that was the government's demand that Kilometer 81 pay the salary of the doctor appointed by the ministry of health. He felt that the work of the Mennonite leprosy program was of such value to the country that the government should have carried the cost for the doctor they had chosen.

"This is supposed to be a mission," he said. "They are supposed to appreciate this. They aren't supposed to draw money from us for doing this."

He took his case to the Mennonite Central Committee and after a lengthy discussion as to whether the fifty dollars per month should be paid, the MCC administration told John, "You pay the money." He did, but always under protest.

Home Treatment Accepted

John's decentralized method of treating leprosy soon proved itself a great advance over older methods of housing all patients in an institution. Where plans had been made for a colony to treat 250 patients, the Kilometer 81 program was treating over 500 leprosy patients in their homes by 1957.

As the number of patients increased and the burden of visiting people in their homes grew heavier, outstation clinics were established. All who were to come to these scattered clinics were asked to come for their treatment rather than depending on someone to come to them. "People don't appreciate it if they don't have to do something," said John, "so let's make it possible for them to come to a center."

The Mennonite Central Committee and the American Leprosy Mission eventually gave their support to a strategy that they had first resisted. "So far as I know," said O. W. Hasselblad, president of ALM in 1967, "John Schmidt ... was the first to try such a venture and it has become the basis for leprosy-control work throughout the world today. It virtually eliminates the need for the 'settlements' of several decades ago."

In fact, the ALM was ready to take a firm stand against the colony pattern and called instead for an integrated medical program. Every effort, said Hasselblad, should be made to avoid the development of an institution for housing large groups of leprosy patients. "Such colonies," he said, "have often caused as much crippling through long-term institutionalization as the disease itself."

Ambulatory Evangelism

As Kilometer 81's treatment for leprosy has used an ambulatory approach, so also has its evangelism. The major carriers of the gospel have been the patients who have become Christians as a result of their contacts with the Mennonite leprosy program and who have gone back to their home communities and joined congregations there or formed their own fellowship of believers.

The Christians among the small group of patients living at Kilometer 81 have often involved themselves in a witness to other patients. Dona Hosafina, a German lady, who is now over 90, and who once had leprosy, lives on the station in a house which her congregation

John and Clara Schmidt with an anniversary picture gift.

built for her. She makes the rounds among the patients reading the Bible to them. "I'm glad when the doctor orders footbaths for the patients," she says, "because then they can't run away when I come and read to them from the Bible."

It was Dona Hosafina's daughter Amalia, who worked with Clara for many years in doing mission work in the villages and communities nearby. Amalia, a dwarf and once a leprosy patient herself, repeated the Bible stories in Guarani that Clara told in Spanish.

Out of these activities, a congregation was organized at Boqueron, where the members pitched in to build a chapel. But for Clara, the gathering of the believers was sometimes accompanied by a bit of awkwardness. "When I had converts," she says, "then the German preacher didn't believe very much in women preachers, so they had to come to him first before he would accept them."

Thankfulness for a Family

Clara filled the gaps in the Kilometer 81 program, doing the things that would have been left undone otherwise.

For many years, the hospital's office was in the Schmidt home. Clara had to fill in as a bookkeeper, practicing a craft for which she had never received any training. "It started real simple, just keeping a monthly account and sending in a report and getting a check.

"But I got into a real bad place. We felt a monthly check was lost, but my books couldn't bear it out—my wonderful bookkeeping! So then I had to learn bookkeeping from the MCC bookkeeper in Asunción, Margaret Braun. She got me started on a system."

Clara was also housemother for the mission and editor and publisher of the mission's newsletter, *Im Dienste der Liebe.*

During all this time the young Schmidt family was growing. Mary Lou was born in March 1957 during the family's home leave in Kansas. But their household often included other children who needed a home for shorter or longer periods. Among these were Cris and Josie Acosta, a brother and sister from the Paraguayan community, who were taken in by the family in 1964 and have been part of the family ever since.

The rigors of being foreign workers in a developing country did not leave the Schmidt family unscathed. The separations for education in distant places were painful. In 1961, the three oldest children stayed behind in Kansas to go to high school. "If a mother's heart was ever torn, it was when that plane took off," says Clara. "That was a hard time."

But harder times were yet to come. The growing up years were not always smooth and there were times of deep water and difficulties to endure. But the family weathered the storms and has become stronger. "We're real happy for all our family," says Clara, "real thankful."

New Ideas Bursting Out All Over

Where John had once been the innovator in leprosy treatment showing the way for the American Leprosy Mission, the ALM's integrated program began to call for changes, sometimes before John was ready for them.

The ALM wanted to try new methods at Kilometer 81 that had been tested at its other centers in other parts of the world. They proposed a program in physiotherapy and chose Eleanor Mathies, a North American nurse working in the Mennonite colonies, to go to India and Ethiopia to receive special training for the work at Kilometer 81.

John questioned the value of such a program, fearing that patients might expect miracles. Of what value, he wondered, is physiotherapy to the Paraguayan peasant? "This fellow with the crippled hands will never use a typewriter. But he can hold a spade. He is going to be promised a lot of improvement. If it doesn't come and his hand is still partly crippled, he is just going to be unhappier than he was before."

He had a similar concern about the proposed introduction of plastic surgery which was the specialty of Dr. Franz Duerksen, a Mennonite physician born in South America, who received special training with the support of the American Leprosy Mission.

But John was quick to recognize the contributions that others had to make. He takes pride in the work that is now being done in physiotherapy and in restorative surgery at Kilometer 81.

The Growing Witness

After the Schmidts had been working for some eight years at Kilometer 81, Elder Jacob Isaak, one of the leading ministers in the Mennonite community, made a confession to John. "For at least four years," he said, "I wasn't at all convinced that you would make a go of this leprosy work or that it deserved support."

He had seen other North American programs and had seen other workers come and go. He felt that the leprosy work was just another project in that series. "He just didn't have faith that any North American was going to stay with it," says John.

But the Schmidts persisted and so did their co-workers who joined them. The leprosy program became one that no one in Paraguay could ignore. Little by little, the Mennonite community increased its involvement through voluntary service, through financial support, and finally by asserting itself in the shaping of policy. And as policy questions were studied, John's role in the program was put to the test.

People looking at the leprosy program after years of giving little attention to it found things they didn't understand; others heard reports from persons in the government who had once opposed the program. As these items were circulated in the Mennonite communities, uneasiness grew and charges made against the leadership.

Hans Niessen was selected by the Mennonite community to go to Kilometer 81 and review the concerns with John and bring back a report. Niessen proved to be a real peacemaker; John calls him a lifesaver. "We had a conference with him," says John, "and he did us a real service. I'm very greatly indebted to him."

John affirmed that the Kilometer 81 program belonged to the Mennonites of South America. "I always said it was their work to start with. Naturally, to get a work going, I had to be somewhat dictatorial in it, I guess, but I never did anything without conferring with the people. Now, I think, MCC got the idea that it was all my work because I didn't ask them too much."

But John had long felt the need to make a transition from the work that he and Clara had begun. "It was a concern of mine almost from the beginning: How will I get out of this thing? Am I building something that somebody else will never be able to take over?"

He saw this as the critical test of his leadership. If it was just the work of a person or a family, the work might well die with them. "We definitely didn't want this to be that kind of business because we felt that it was something that the Mennonites needed in Paraguay."

But the transition was hard. "It was traumatic to get out of it," says John.

Multiplied Opportunities

The chance to make the change presented itself in an invitation from Vietnam and in the person of Dr. Franz Duerksen. The relationship with Franz Duerksen and his family has been a long-standing one that goes back to John's first term in the Mennonite colonies. John had encouraged Franz in his choosing to go into medicine. And Franz had always shown an interest in the work of the church and especially in the Christian witness at Kilometer 81.

While still in medical school in Argentina, Franz spent some time at Kilometer 81. While there, he told John, "When you need somebody to take your place, remember me."

And John said, "I sure will do that."

So it was that John turned to him when he felt the

appropriate time had come. "I pleaded with Franz Duerksen. I said, 'We have had a good time with the Mennonites in this work, but the time has come for us to get out. You can salvage this thing because ALM has real confidence in you.' "

Duerksen did take on the medical program at Kilometer 81 late in 1971, bringing his skills in surgery to the healing of many leprosy patients and guiding the treatment program into a new era of growth and witness.

And in January 1972, John and Clara found themselves in South Vietnam for a four-month term of giving medical assistance to the leprosy treatment centers in a war-torn country that left the needs of many unmet. Their tour of service was sponsored by the American Medical Association's Volunteer Physicians for Vietnam program with a special assignment given to Clara by the Mennonite Central Committee.

They returned to Paraguay to make their home in Tres Palmes, not to retire but to continue to serve the needs of the people, both Paraguayan and Mennonite. For the years have multiplied rather than decreased their opportunities to be of service.

The Lord Has Led

Tres Palmes is a new Mennonite colony just developing in east Paraguay. John became a member of the colony committee and he and Clara are members of the mission committee at work in the region.

"It's an area that's just opening up," says Clara, "felling the forest and building sawmills and with no doctor around. I guess we are still pioneers."

They have opened a small clinic near their home to serve the needs of many of the Paraguayan people who are not served by the colony's hospital.

Though their three daughters are now in North America, their three sons have made their homes in Paraguay. John Russell operates a ranch in the Chaco. David serves as a missionary in the Tres Palmes area. And Wesley, who studied medicine in Paraguay, took over the medical work at Kilometer 81 during the recent absence of Franz Duerksen who took leave to go to Canada for further study.

John and Clara see the potentials of Paraguay just beginning to open up. The Mennonite colonies have a major responsibility for the growing Indian population in the Chaco. "I could work with some of the people," says John about a ministry to the Indians. "It's not something where we should sit down and fold our hands and see what's happening but we should work with the people."

John sees new potentials in the Menno colony which was once closed to outside contacts. "Our work at 81 has given us an inside road into the Menno colony," he says. "They are sometimes more open to change than some of the Fernheimers are." And there will be opportunities to render service at the scattered clinics of Kilometer 81 and even at Kilometer 81 itself.

So prospects for more work and a new career in Paraguay seem just to be opening up for them. "All these things are tremendous in a man's experience," says John. "This whole movement of Mennonites to Paraguay and what's becoming of them—and now Herb staying out there! It's nothing that we have done, but it's an opportunity that we have."

"It's just the way the Lord has led," says Clara.

So the Schmidts have once again made a choice. They have found that for them it's best to be in Paraguay.

14. Pyarelal Joel Malagar

By
Marion
Keeney
Preheim

Mission work started in the village of Ghatula, India, in 1915. It centered around an orphanage. It was in this setting that Pyarelal Joel Malagar, later to be known as P. J. to his North American friends, was born on August 12, 1921. His mother served as a Bible woman for the mission. Each day, Monday through Saturday, she went from village to village to talk with the women about their faith and to teach the Bible to them. The mission employed as many as sixty women in this work. His father meanwhile taught in the mission primary school.

In these years the Malagar family lived in a two-room house provided by the mission for its workers. It had both a front veranda and a back one. Malagar vividly remembers his mother telling him Bible stories and his father illustrating parables and miracles through the drawing of sketches, sometimes during the evening hours by the light of a kerosene lantern.

When he was old enough he was sent to the mission boarding school in Dhamtari, which was the headquarters for the Elkhart mission board work. This was seven miles from Balodgahan where he and his parents were living at the time. He enjoyed school, but one day when he was nine years old, word came that his father had died. Missionary Ernest E. Miller took him home to be with his family.

The years that followed proved to be hard ones for them all. His mother received less than 10 rupees ($1.50) monthly. She would use this to buy a quantity of rice for 25 cents, which would last ten days. Milk was about five cents a quart. This left little money for anything else. They were helped by receiving free schooling from the mission, including meals while at school.

These years at school proved to be a time of real growth for Malagar's eager spirit. They began every morning at school with Bible classes, reciting passages like the Ten Commandments and the Lord's Prayer. He attended worship services and Sunday school regularly. Christian Endeavor came every Sunday afternoon with Bible quizzes competition, and storytelling.

The Impact of Singh's Influence

When Malagar was 17 years of age an evangelist named Bakhat Singh held revival meetings in their community. Malagar vividly recalls this period: "When Singh came to Dhamtari he impressed me so much with his emphasis on the Bible, his faith in God, his sacrifice, and his consecration. He repeatedly appealed to people to bring their own Bibles to the services, to read them, and to believe in God. The first thing he did was to share his own conversion experience. This was a striking experience for me. He was a man who had been converted at a great cost. He came from an Orthodox Sikh family in the Punjab. When he became a Christian his parents disowned and avoided him. He was not allowed to even step into their house. Since his wife lived with his parents this meant he was also cut off from her. At that time he was studying engineering, but when he was converted he decided to become an evangelist. Wherever he could go to preach the gospel, he went. That was how he came to our area."

It was through Singh's visit that Malagar accepted Christ. He says of this, "I cannot explain how I got converted, but the manifestation of it was obvious to me. The hostel boys used to have short evening prayers at 9:00, but after the revival we continued up until midnight studying the Word and praying together.

We who had had a conversion experience did not understand what had happened. Our Bible teacher in high school was J. D. Graber. It was he who helped us to understand our experience. He told us about the new birth, the conversion experience, repentance, and how the Holy Spirit works within us. Because of this conversion experience many of us felt we should leave to become evangelists. We needed counsel. Sam King, who was principal of our high school, once came at midnight and saw that we were all still in prayer. He thereupon began to provide counsel to us. A number of boys did leave the school, but I continued on." He graduated from high school in 1940 and spent the following year in village evangelistic work.

Beginning Christian Work

This was both challenging and difficult. He says of it: "I remember once I had to walk a distance of some 30 miles on foot with old Deacon Sadhuram. We had our things in a bullock cart and just followed the cart walking on foot. Once we left in the morning and arrived close to midnight at a village thirty miles away. The next day we did work in that village. Then we would move on to a new village. At each place we talked to the people about their salvation and the kingdom of God."

Malagar tells another story which happened that

year: "I had a similar experience of walking another 30 miles with a young man who was also an evangelist. By the time we arrived at our destination we were dead tired from walking all day. We had no food. But God had prepared a sumptuous meal in a Muslim house, though we did not know it at first.

"What had happened was that a certain Muslim man had heard that we had come and sent for us to come to his home. We did not believe him to be serious about this and didn't go. Then he sent for us a second time. So we washed up and went. There we found he had fried rice, mutton curry, and a lot of other things to eat. Soon the day's fatigue was gone. The next morning he provided us with tea. He also sent his servant to clean the house in which we were to live and helped us to get settled. He did all these things even though we were just two young men. For a time we went out from that village on foot every day for a radius of 12 miles, preaching in the surrounding villages."

Malagar did not forget the vocational counseling he had received in high school—that he should continue his education. He spent the next four years, from 1941 to 1944, at the South India Bible Institute in Bangalore. Soon after, on January 1, 1945, he was ordained by missionary George A. Lapp.

Following his ordination he began working as an evangelist and as assistant pastor to missionary J. W. Kaufman in Maradeo. The church had five families, all of whom were farmers. Malagar recalls many experiences from this time, including the following: One day one of the village women became seriously ill. He felt that he should walk to the missionary doctor's home to find help, but the village headman said to him, "Don't go there." Everyone knew that panthers lurked along the path he would walk, which was close to the river and the forest. But Malagar said, "No I must go call the doctor. This woman is in trouble." He went and returned safely. The people were surprised that he was not hurt. "I feel I could not have done it by myself," Malagar told them, "God protected me. I would not be fulfilling my job unless I helped that woman." Another time a pregnant woman came to see him at night in deep pain. He again took the same road to call the doctor for help.

In the village of Maradeo, which included about 700 acres, lived an old man who was both headman and landlord. He had been a former headmaster of a high school and was well educated. He had also become a Christian through the evangelistic work of Singh, but he was anti-missionary and critical of church people. Then he began coming to Malagar's house at 4:00 a.m. to pray and study the Bible together. Gradually his heart changed toward the missionaries and the church.

The Maradeo church celebrated the love feast every Sunday. During this experience they shared and talked together. They studied the Bible. Soon one of the results was that everyone began to tithe. In that way they were able to help Mennonite students in different colleges and send small Christmas gifts to all Mennonite students they knew who were away from home. Malagar says of this, "It was a great experience. It helped me to see people giving and helping."

Pastor and Evangelist

In January 1946, P. J. Malagar moved to the Drug Church, 56 miles west of Dhamtari, where he served both as pastor and evangelist. A unique experience he remembers from this time is bicycling 21 miles during one night to a village where the Edwin Weavers were having an evangelistic camp. They had planned baptisms for the following day. A huge crowd did show up, but only one person came forward to be baptized. He was an illiterate farmer from a low caste. To his dying day this man never renounced his faith but testified to it wherever he went.

Malagar's pastoral work in Drug was not without its problems. He was young and single, and lacked experience. There were problems of discipline, of two families feuding, and of young people with marital problems. But he worked hard to help them all as best he could, while also carrying on evangelistic work in the villages. On Sundays he preached and worked in outlying congregations.

There was a Christian library with a free reading room in the city of Drug. Malagar saw this as an opportunity to witness and went there to dialogue with the people who came to read. Many times it was a point of contact for him to invite people to his home. He talked with lawyers, farmers, and students. Sometimes a Muslim would come and he would talk with him.

After a year at Drug, Malagar attended Hislop College at Nagpur, where he was a student leader and active in the Student Christian Movement. In connection with this he attended the Trienniel Convention of the SCM at the Christian College in Tambram, Madras State. Later that year he served as student pastor in Nagpur at a church called the "1840 Church" because it had been built in that year.

To Goshen College

Late in 1947 Sam King came with the special message that the mission was choosing Malagar to study at Goshen College in the United States. The Council of Mennonite Colleges was offering him a foreign student's scholarship. He accepted the invitation and came to Goshen in June of 1948, where he was able to attend the Mennonite World Conference, as well as speak at the youth rally held during the conference. For several months before the college opened he stayed with J. D. Graber, who was now home from India. Then he moved into "Eighth Street House" where foreign students and others lived.

When school opened he registered in the seminary, not in the college. His tests showed that while he had little knowledge of American literature and some other subjects, he did score high in Bible areas and consequently became a Bible major. During the following two years he completed his last year of college and two years of seminary work, earning both the Bachelor of Arts and Bachelor of Theology degrees.

In reflecting upon his Goshen studies he fondly remembers some of his teachers like Harold S. Bender, J. C. Wenger, Guy F. Hershberger, Ernest E. Miller, J. D. Graber, and Howard Charles. He sensed a special interest in Anabaptist history and theology and felt a great deal of gratitude to Harold Bender, whom he considered his primary "mentor." For the first time in his life he was confronted with the whole range of the believers' church way of life and thought.

In commenting on this time Malagar remembers that Mennonites were still conservative in their dress and speech. Once he went out to preach at a conference. The minister he was staying with noticed that he was wearing an ordinary suit and tie. He thereupon called on some women in the area and overnight they turned Malagar's open coat into a plain collared coat. In introducing him at the conference the minister said the people should give their money to save the heathen and not for them to wear ties and open coats. But Malagar observes that he has seen many changes since that time. Through the years he has come to appreciate the real Mennonite concern for nonconformity which is much deeper than outward things like dress or food.

While in the United States Malagar traveled extensively in behalf of the work of the Elkhart mission board. It gave him the opportunity to see much of the country, from California to Florida and Virginia. He was even able to get to Canada for several mission meetings. In these meetings he always reported about the church in India and its growth. He also shared his own pilgrimage of faith and told about his own family background. Frequently he also accompanied quartets and choirs, giving the talk for the groups.

By 1950 he was ready to return home. The Goshen College Church provided him with a traveling scholarship to accompany other Mennonite college students through Europe. They visited all the countries where Mennonite churches existed—England, Holland, France, Germany, Switzerland, and Italy. They also visited refugee camps where people were still suffering the aftermath of World War II. They stayed in homes where house and barn were attached together in the old traditional European pattern. This gave him an added feel for the European tradition of Mennonitism.

From Europe Malagar went on to Palestine. He had asked J. D. Graber to give him the privilege of seeing the Holy Land. He traveled from Damascus to Jerusalem in a taxi and was received by Geraldine and Myron Ebersole who were working with Arab refugees in Jericho. They served as his hosts during his four-day stay, which included the celebration of his 29th birthday. And then he returned to India, landing in Bombay.

Marriage and Further Studies

On reaching home his first concern was to get married to Satyavati P. Das, a trained schoolteacher. She was teaching at the Garjan Memorial School where M. M. Good was in charge. M. M. Good and missionary J. N. Kaufman had arranged the marriage for him. Miss Good acted as god-mother for Satyavati who was an orphan girl. The Malagars were married on November 10, 1950. Ernest E. Miller preached the sermon and performed the ceremony at the Balodgahan Church. (The Malagars now have two sons and one daughter.)

With his fresh education and experience Malagar did much praying about what he should do next. He asked the mission and conference for permission to start work in a new area where there were no churches. In June 1941 he went forty miles south of Dhamtari to the town of Kanker. He found, however, that there were a number of Christian families living there. He began immediately to organize a house church. His veranda served as a Gospel Center where he distributed literature. People could come from 4:00 to 8:00 p.m. to read. Thus he made contact with the people.

In the meantime things were changing fast on the mission field. Missionary E. I. Weaver, who was serving the conference as bishop, was leaving the country. At his request the Annual Conference decided to elect their first Indian bishop. On May 8, 1955, P. J. Malagar was ordained to that office.

Because of this new work he found it necessary to move to a more central place. He went back to Balodgahan where he was both bishop and pastor. He was also in charge of all the institutions at the station—the mission rice farm, the schools, dispensaries, and a home for the aged. Already in 1952 the mission board had merged the work of the Indian Conference so Malagar, as bishop, was also responsible for funds and personnel. Nearly every Sunday found him visiting different churches.

Jan Gleysteen Photo

Pyarelal Joel Malagar

In 1960 he registered at Serampore Theological Seminary for the Bachelor of Divinity degree under the tutelage of Theodore Essebegger. For the next two years he had no direct church responsibility in order to complete his studies.

MWC at Kitchener

In 1962 he came to his second World Conference, which met at Kitchener, Ontario. At that time the mission board was thinking of changing overseas missionary structures and wondering how their work could be related to that of the Mennonite Central Committee and the Indian churches. They had thus far had an organization called the Mennonite Relief Committee of India, composed mostly of missionaries from the different Mennonite groups. Whenever an emergency arose MCC would work with them. But the mission boards and MCC felt that the churches in India were strong enough to have a church organization for their own relief work. At a luncheon meeting in Kitchener it was decided to ask Orie Miller, MCC executive secretary, to visit India to discuss this concern with the church conferences.

Orie Miller did travel to India for this purpose. Together with MCC director Vernon Reimer he traveled to most of the churches and spoke at the conferences. As a result of these meetings a special organization called the Mennonite Christian Service Fellowship of India (MCSFI) was organized in February of 1963. P. J. Malagar was asked to serve as director of the new organization. A constitution was worked out and a job description for the director was defined.

Right from the beginning they spelled out that they would not disturb the work of the conferences, but that MCSFI would relate more on a fellowship basis to develop a program of evangelism, peace education, relief, and voluntary service. From that time to the present P. J. Malagar has been engaged in this kind of work with MCSFI. He says of it, "I felt very glad to do this because I felt an acceptance by all the conferences and churches. We have come together for many meetings."

Malagar remembers some of the conferences and meetings he has planned over the years. He helped plan the first all-Indian Peace Conference which was held in Dhamtari. Five large all-India retreats for young people have also been held. Once he helped organize an all-

India college students' camp. In 1977 a women's conference was held with over 200 women coming together for a first-of-its-kind conference. Pastors have been brought together for retreats. Some of Malagar's best contribution in his work has been his ability to organize seminars, retreats, conferences, and consultations.

It has also been Malagar's role as director of MCSFI to serve as a bridge between it and MCC. The work of MCC in India is organized in such a way that the Indian churches do not necessarily need to involve themselves with it, but MCC is willing to share both finances and project involvement when it comes to an emergency. Thus MCSFI has been in the voluntary service program of MCC right from the beginning. In 1963 they sent two volunteers to the General Conference work for the East Pakistan Christian Council. In 1965 a famine broke out in Bihar Province in India and Indian volunteers worked there with MCC. Volunteers also served in flood affected areas in 1978.

Malagar recalls a particular time in 1970 and 1971 when over one million refugees came to India from East Pakistan, now Bangladesh. Some 86 young people from the Indian Mennonite churches were involved in serving meals, providing fresh water, and taking care of the incoming flow of refugees. It was during the rainy season and they had to wade through mud and slush everywhere. The tents of the refugees had to be put on bricks and wooden planks to keep them off the wet ground. Babies were dying. Eventually an international team of nurses came to help care for these people.

During this crisis Malagar's organizational gifts again came to good use. Agency people from all over, including MCC, were working around the clock. Nurses walked from tent to tent in rubber boots to reach the people. MCC workers were providing materials to shelter the people as they came into the camps. A tent had to be used as a place to store medicines. Many of the people who came from Bangladesh were extremely emaciated. Some became sick and died of cholera. Volunteers often could not eat all day while working, because it was not safe to eat there. They just drank tea.

Even though MCSFI is an independent organization, Malagar has been involved with MCC directors in many projects. He recalls some of his experiences with them. One time he was traveling with Edgar Metzler. They had first class train tickets, but they could not get into the car. Thus they went to the third class car and slept on the floor of the train all night. He also worked with Vernon Reimer, Neil Janzen, and more recently Bert Lobe. One Sunday morning Bert Lobe, John Wieler of MCC Canada, and Malagar visited a cyclone affected area. As a result of this visit they were able to secure 80 volunteers from the Indian churches to work in clearing up the debris over a three-week period. Three medical teams came. Malagar himself drove one of the medical teams from Dhamtari to the disaster area, a distance of over one thousand miles.

"Our church people respond to disasters in a quick way," says Malagar. "They can't give much, but they have held special Sundays for Vietnam, Bangladesh, and recently for South India. This money all went to the MCSFI office and we spent it."

Through MCC the MCSFI has also been close to overseas work. They sent their first volunteers to Vietnam Christian Service, a couple named Devadoss, who set up a laboratory in the hospital at Nhatrang. During a second period of service the same couple worked in Saigon. MCSFI has also worked closely with MCC in the Bangladesh program.

Witness and Growth

These involvements also led to other things. MCC and the Council of Mission Board Secretaries helped to develop an organization called the Asian Services Conference, which was to work together in responding to human need. Malagar became involved in this in 1970 and was appointed executive secretary. In that capacity he helped to convene the first Asia Mennonite Conference, held at Dhamtari in 1971. This organization has also sent a worker to Bangladesh. A second Asian conference was held in Indonesia in 1980.

Malagar was also involved in setting up international workcamps, first begun by missionaries from Japan. It seemed to him that reconciliation was desperately needed between Koreans and Japanese who had been traditional enemies. During the first work camp they had an experience where the Japanese broke down and said to the Koreans, "We have made a mistake. We want to overcome it with the love of Christ. We want to love you." A work camp was held near Calcutta in 1971, in connection with the Asian Conference. A new hospital was being built and the youth in the work camp gave considerable aid to cleaning the hospital and arranging the furniture. In 1977 the Tenth International Reconciliation Work Camp was held in the Philippines, some 100 miles northwest of Manila. The eleventh work camp was held before the convening of the 1980 Asian Conference.

As though all of these involvements were not enough, Malagar has had others as well. He has served as moderator of the annual conference of Mennonites from 1955, except for a few years. As bishop he has served as chairperson of the ministerial council of reference which interviews new candidates for ordination. He served as chairperson of the church growth committee for the Mennonite Church in India's annual conference. He also served as liaison for theological education for the Mennonite church's board of governors in connection with Union Biblical Seminary at Yeotmal.

P. J. Malagar has been particularly active in the area of peace. He works with the Fellowship of Reconciliation, the Ghandian peace movement, the Christian Peace Conference, and other historic peace churches. He has served as president and now vice-president of the working committee of the Fellowship of Reconciliation in India. It has been a new experiment in India to deal with the peace position. He says of it, "Our churches in India are not as much confronted with the peace question as you are in the United States and Canada, but we are really making a start in this whole area."

He also became involved in literature and radio work, serving as chairperson of the Mennonite Literature and Radio Council from 1956 to the present, and as chairperson of the Peace Commission for that group. From 1967 to 1971 he edited a monthly newsletter called *Shanti Sandesh* (which means peace messenger) for the Council. He has also served as editor of the church paper *The Mennonite Newspaper* for about eight years. From 1971 to 1977 he served as executive secretary of the Mennonite Economic Development Association of India (MEDA), and had served on the Mennonite Agriculture Development and Relief Association.

Thus throughout his lifetime P. J. Malagar has given himself to the work of the church, and to many causes related to it, to further Christ and his kingdom. Who could ask for more to do in a lifetime than he has done!

15.
Harry and Olga Martens

**By
Shirley B.
Souder**

It was 1945 in the West Indian island of Puerto Rico and the end of World War II. But it was by no means the end of suffering for thousands of women and men, boys and girls. The hopelessness of the poor was evidenced in the country and in the city ghettos. At that time the city of San Juan had the second worst slum in the world.

Squatters settled at points along the shoreline for stretches of eight to ten blocks. Here the tide came in and the tide went out. This land was free. But it was not without cost. The price paid by the poor in the absence of garbage and waste disposal systems was disease. Hookworm was rampant. The protruding stomachs of many children told of the malnutrition suffered as a result of inadequate diets. Mothers and sisters frequently were seen picking lice from the heads of young children.

There seemed to be no future for these people. Many adults were unemployed. American plantation owners underpaid their laborers. Among the rural poor, men, women, and children toiled in the fields in the hot sun. Many oxen could be seen pulling plows.

Because ships were committed for military use, it was difficult to export sugar. Consequently, much of the sugarcane grown on the island rotted. Little flour was available for bread, the staple of the people. The poor were hungry.

It was just this confrontation with the plight and misery of the poor that deeply touched the lives of Harry and Olga Martens. For the first time this couple from rural Kansas came face-to-face with poverty as they labored in Puerto Rico. Working in the La Plata Valley near Aibonito, Harry was the director of Civilian Public Service (CPS), an alternative to military service. Olga worked as dietitian. The CPS unit included about fifty men and women who were involved in educational, recreational, and health programs, as well as a heifer project.

But to Harry, all these efforts seemed so small. One day Harry complained to Dr. S. C. Yoder, a former president of Goshen College who came to visit the unit, "We're doing the best we can. But it's just, it's just so little! In fact, you might as well send me to the Pacific Ocean with an eyedropper and tell me to drain it!"

The comment which followed made a significant impact on Harry's life. Dr. Yoder responded, "Harry, it's wonderful for people like you to have this kind of compassion and love. But let me give you a little counsel here. You remember when our Lord was on earth. He fed *some* of the hungry. He healed *some* of the sick and opened the eyes of *some* of the blind. But when he left, there were some sick, some blind, and some hungry left. And there will be some left after you and me. Don't take it all. But," Dr. Yoder continued, "don't ever use the excuse that the poor you shall always have with you. You have a job to do! Do your part and God will bless it."

That then became the vow of Harry and Olga—to do

their part. This was the beginning of a shared dream. And so they mused, "Well, now, we don't have much money. We never will have great landholdings. We just have ourselves. And that we can give. We can't put ourselves in the offering plate, but we can offer our services."

The vision of giving one tenth of their time in service was born. It became an incarnation of love as Harry and Olga served members of the human family from Gulfport, Mississippi, to Puerto Rico, from Mexico to Central Europe, from the Middle East to Bangladesh, from Canada to South America.

The Expansion of Harry's World

Harry Martens was born on August 31, 1911, in McPherson County, Kansas. The eldest in his family, he played on the family farm with his two brothers and two sisters. They enjoyed fighting in the hayloft. And when their parents were not home, these pranksters rode the cattle and broke in young horses.

Harry worked hard on the farm too. Early every morning he was in the barn milking the cows. In the heat of the afternoon Harry followed the horse-drawn plow in the field. One day while plowing, lightning struck from behind. Frightened, the horses ran away.

It was with great determination that Harry began to study at nearby Bethel College in 1933. His father, a successful and aggressive farmer, thought that it was unnecessary for Harry to go to college. After all, a college education wasn't needed to become a successful farmer. But it became obvious to both father and son that unmechanical Harry would never become a successful farmer, for the imagination of this growing boy invited him far away from the farm. And even though his mother could not understand Harry's inclinations, she continued to pray that God's will would be done.

Harry often thought, "It doesn't matter how small and how unimportant a little boy I am out here on the Kansas farm, I can do something, somewhere, and somehow that will make a difference in the world."

Perhaps it was the persistence of this dream that gave Harry the determination to complete college despite some unexpected odds. Hardly six weeks after beginning his freshman year, Harry developed severe eye problems which a doctor later called trachoma. Before long he was unable to read anything. Words disappeared as he tried to focus on them on a printed page. And as the words, so the familiar faces of family and friends became strangers to Harry.

This was the biggest test in his life. "How could God allow this to happen to me, and at such an important time in my life?" Harry questioned. He heard the Bible read. He prayed. "What have I done wrong?" he wondered. "God has deserted me. And of all places and of all times when I need God most, it's now as I'm getting ready for something worthwhile." Although this was a time of much sadness to Harry, he learned from it how to understand and to care for other people who were suffering and unhappy.

Harry's dream of involvement in international relations was stimulated during these college years. History professor E. L. Harshbarger and Bible professor A. E. Kreider strongly influenced him. Harry served as president of the International Relations Club and the Student Christian Movement. This latter involvement took him to Estes Park, Colorado, for two summers. Here, as well as at other student conferences, he met many world-minded people—Kagawa of Japan, T. Z. Koo of China, William Temple of England, Kirby Page, E. Stanley Jones, John R. Mott, Howard Thurman. The boundaries of Harry's world stretched beyond the farm, beyond Bethel College, beyond Kansas, beyond the United States itself.

In the Footsteps of Olga's Parents

Named by her father after the Russian empress who had been kind to the Mennonites in Russia, Olga Reimer was born the second of three children and the only daughter on September 3, 1913, in Harvey County, Kansas.

Her father, a stern yet loving man, was an ordained deacon, and her trailblazing mother was a leader in the Women's Missionary Movement. It was not unusual for Olga to go along with her parents on weekend visits to persons widowed, lonely, and ill. And perhaps following her parents' example, Olga later learned how to befriend that refugee child in Amman, that aging woman in Puerto Rico, and that lonely foreigner in America.

Education was greatly valued in this family. And so it came as no surprise that Olga chose teaching, or perhaps teaching chose Olga, as her vocation. After all, at some point in their lives all members of Olga's family were teachers.

A love for poetry was instilled in the child Olga by her mother, a favorite being a poem which teaches that time counts.

I have only just a minute,
Just 60 seconds in it.
Forced upon me—can't refuse it,
Didn't seek it, didn't choose it;
I must suffer if I lose it
Give account if I abuse it.
Just a tiny little minute
But eternity is in it.

This poem was like a planted seed which took root and sprouted in the industry of Olga's life. The flexibility and adaptability of this many-gifted woman becomes obvious in the potpourri of her roles—from wife and mother to founder of kindergartens in the Middle East, from hospital dietitian in Puerto Rico to "funeral director" in Mexico, from caterer to the Vanderbilts in New York City to proxy CPS overseer in Gulfport, Mississippi, from country schoolteacher in Kansas to nursery school director in Elkhart, Indiana.

A Partnership Is Formed

Although Harry and Olga had become acquainted before attending Bethel College, they really discovered each other during their college days and during those summer months at the YMCA youth camp at Estes Park, Colorado. Imaginative and idealistic Harry met his practical counterpart in Olga, a creative and determined young woman, an elementary education major. In her Harry found delight and encouragement during his difficult Bethel years. It was Olga who gave him enthusiastic support for continuing his higher education. Likewise, the mission-mindedness of Olga's family fostered his own growing interest in mission.

Harry and Olga were married on May 29, 1937. It was a happy but busy weekend indeed. For on Thursday Harry graduated from college, the following Saturday Harry and Olga married, and the next Tuesday Harry began work at Bethel College as director of the Student Office. This initiated Harry's more than twenty years of service to Bethel as dean of labor, dean of men, business manager, and assistant to the president.

During this time Olga taught in Kansas schools for several years. The births of their son Duane in 1941 and daughter Delia in 1947 introduced an exciting dimension to life, that of parenting and nurturing their own children. An active volunteer, Olga directed much energy into the Bethel College women's auxiliary.

Those Bethel years were not without interruption. By the end of 1939 war had already broken out in England, threatening Harry's immediate educational plans. But determined, Harry and Olga left their plainland Kansas home in 1940 eastward bound for New York City where Harry pursued graduate study in personnel administration at Columbia University. Or, as Olga says, "I got the education—Harry received the degree." For during that year, Olga was Harry's eyes as she read page after page of his textbooks to him.

It was this New York City experience which taught Olga how to fly. For to live and to work here was like being tossed out of the safety of her Kansas nest, far away from the protection of her dearly-loved mother and the security of her close-knit family. And Olga did fly. She became exposed to the worlds of the Fosdicks and the Vanderbilts and that of movie stars as she served dinners and parties with stunning efficiency. Here she developed a sense of independence and self-confidence unknown to her before.

CPS Days, 1943-46

World War II had intensified by the time of Harry's graduation from Columbia University in 1940. Leaving New York City, Harry began managing a number of farms operated by Bethel College. As a farm worker he was eligible for a deferment. However, a strong believer in nonviolence, Harry refused this deferment from non-military service despite the opposition of many friends.

"I won't accept a deferment. I can't do it," Harry said firmly to the President of Bethel College. "Look at all those young men younger than I who have been called and have had to go and serve for an indefinite time. No, I can't accept a deferment."

And so, against the will of everybody excepting his wife, Harry volunteered to direct CPS work. He was accompanied by Olga and their son Duane on these assignments which extended from January 1943 to October 1946. As CPS director and regional director in the Midwest and the East Coast, Harry could test and implement some of his earlier youthful dreams. Here Harry gained experience as peacemaker, reconciler, administrator, camp minister, diplomat.

Many young Mennonite, Amish, Quaker, and other draftees in the base camps that Harry directed were unhappy about being drafted. Many lacked the understanding of their wives and families. Consequently, some wives left their husbands; others threatened separation. It was Harry's duty to counsel with the wives and parents of these young men—to attempt to create understanding and peace in families, to ease the troubled minds of the draftees.

Harry confronted a frightening experience on such a family visitation across country. One angry man told him, "If that son-in-law of mine sets foot on this yard, I will shoot him on the spot. I would rather shoot him than any of those innocent Japanese or Germans we shoot over there. This guy is guilty!" He continued threateningly, "If we are not willing to stand up for our country, that's yellow in my books and I'm going to let him know it!" As he said this, Harry noticed a gun standing nearby. And this was simply one of many challenges that Harry faced as he confronted the prejudices of people against conscientious objectors.

Gulfport, Mississippi, provided Harry and Olga further opportunity to interpret the Mennonite way of peace to the local community—a way of peace that interrupts the turmoil of war, a way of peace that ends the violence in interracial relations. Olga assisted in the opening of the Gulfport camp. For a while she was the only woman in this CPS camp. After being in Gulfport only six weeks, Harry was called on an emergency CPS assignment to Florida. Later he was transferred to the CPS unit in Puerto Rico. During this time Olga remained in Gulfport to assist in the administration of the development of the camp. It was she who was unexpectedly asked to address a large Methodist congregation as to the reason for the CPS unit in Gulfport. After Olga's response the pastor of this uninformed congregation commented, "You sounded too apologetic. My Bible says that we are to go into all the world with the gospel of love. You are doing just that. You have no need to be apologetic."

Earlier while in Colorado, Olga had related to the wives of CPS men. She had taught these Amish and Mennonite women such tasks as grocery shopping. Olga had heard their complaints that they had no money for food and clothes for their families. She was a woman who listened. Traveling alone with Duane, Olga had interviewed many CPS wives. On the basis of these interviews, Olga had then made a recommendation to the CPS administration requesting allowances for these women, a recommendation which the administration did approve.

Now, several months after Harry's earlier departure from the United States, Olga and Duane were reunited with him in Puerto Rico. But while Puerto Rico provided the setting for this reunion, it created a greater distance between this small family and their families in Kansas. The pain of separation became most apparent with the death of Olga's father. Unable to return home, Olga was comforted by friends in Puerto Rico. The people brought her a black dress to wear immediately, since it was the custom in Puerto Rico to dress in black while in mourning. Olga had seen her Puerto Rican friends rolling in the dirt and tearing at their hair while grieving. And now she was expected to set an example of how a Christian accepted death. At the time of her father's death, Olga was assisting with embalming on the island. Indeed, Olga was confronted with death and well acquainted with grief.

Beginning Needlework

A woman almost daily passed the Martens' home, her body haggard and her face worn, the struggles of life so evident in her form. "How are you?" Olga frequently asked. Repeatedly the response was heard, "Struggling with life."

And perhaps it was out of Olga's own struggle that she compassionately responded to the unhappiness of Maria, a runaway girl in the local community. In befriending Maria, Olga invited her into the Martens' home. Olga gave the girl linen to embroider, promising to pay her for her work. In the tradition of the local women, Maria beautifully decorated the linen with a finely embroidered pattern. After this, other women sought Olga, eager to earn money too. In a San Juan department store Olga purchased a bolt of linen. Not knowing what the market for the needlework would be, Olga and Mary Lauver, another MCC worker, daringly undertook this project of helping poor women earn money through this local art.

While visiting the CPS unit in Puerto Rico, Mrs. Edna (J. N.) Byler discovered the fine needlework of these women. Taking the embroidered linens to the United States, she spoke to women in Mennonite churches. Mrs. Byler showed them the embroidery, telling them about the women who made them. The needlework began to sell. Orders were taken when the supply was gone. This was the beginning of the MCC Needlework Project in 1946, the by-product of a Puerto Rican girl's struggle with life.

Harry and Olga found their Puerto Rican experience to be truly a struggle with life, a struggle with death, a struggle to live in peace as brothers and sisters in the CPS unit, a struggle to give effectively of their talents to people in need. And it was out of this struggle that Harry and Olga decided to give one tenth of their time in service.

Vocations and Avocations

This commitment of one tenth of their time became the avocation, or second vocation, of Harry and Olga. It was their response of thanksgiving for God's gifts to them—the gifts of love and forgiveness, family and friends, food and shelter.

The seven years of avocation with MCC punctuated the many more years in their respective vocations—Harry as administrator and Olga as teacher. After leaving Bethel College in 1959, Harry and Olga moved to Elkhart, Indiana. Here Harry was assistant to the president of Mennonite Biblical Seminary for the next ten years. Between 1970 and 1976, Harry became known as "Pocketbook Pastor" in his work with Mennonite Foundation as Estate Planning Consultant and Central Regional Manager. Again Harry could be heard talking about good stewardship—not only of one's time, but of one's "treasures" too. In 1976 Harry "retired," but he continued to be a wise steward of his talents as he joined forces with Mennonite Biblical Seminary as General Consultant and Director of the MBS Associates.

Elkhart Truth Photo

Harry and Olga Martens

Characteristic of these years for Olga was kindergarten teaching at Jimtown, Indiana, from 1959 to 1966. In 1970 Olga became the director of the nursery school of the First Congregational Church in Elkhart, Indiana.

And so, Harry and Olga brought the strengths and skills of their vocations to their avocations of service. The partnership which was born in 1937 was maturing like that seedling that grows into a sturdy oak tree. It was as a team that they ministered in Central Europe, in Mexico, in the Middle East, in Bangladesh, and in South America. Part of this team was not always visible in these countries. Nevertheless, Olga's presence as partner was evident in her mothering and fathering of Duane and Delia at times of Harry's absence from the family.

Harry Alone in Central Europe, 1952-1953

Harry was thankful that Mennonite young men did not have to fight during wartime. Instead, as CPSer's these men could work in fire-fighting, mental health, dairy testing, soil conservation, and sanitation work. But in most of these situations, there was little or no apparent danger to these men's lives. Harry thought, "We should do more than that. Many young men go abroad with no assurance that they will be coming back alive."

And so, in 1952, in the ongoing aftermath of World War II, Harry volunteered to go to Europe. "After all," Harry continued, "there is something that I *can* do. There is something I *must* do. Our faith is to be lived."

This proved to be a difficult decision for Harry and Olga, however. Earlier plans to travel to Europe together changed because of personnel shifts. The days just before Harry's departure were tense. Quite unexpectedly Olga's mother had a heart attack and died less than twenty minutes later in Harry's arms.

"Now what should I do?" Harry questioned. "I'm ready to call the whole trip off!" Even his suit had been shipped ahead to Europe, causing Harry to borrow a suit for the funeral.

"No," Olga said, "Mother is gone. Now I feel all the more that you must go. You go." She considered further, "I'll go as far as Pennsylvania and I'll find something to do in MCC headquarters and stay there."

A Difficult Parting

That then became the plan. But the hour before Harry's departure from New York City was one of the longest and most difficult hours of his life. He had decided to favor his family with a tour of the ship *U.S.S. United States*, a big new liner on which he was to sail. This was the vessel's second voyage. Two hours before departure, the Martens family boarded the ship. Not unlike many Kansans, they never had been on a big ship before. After a delightful time together on board, the family gathered in the ship's cabin for a word of prayer and thanksgiving.

The time to say good-bye had come. Eleven-year-old Duane became very sad. He threw himself on the bed, clung onto the rail with both hands, and said, "Dad, I'm going with you." Five-year-old Delia now sensed that something very unusual was happening. She asked questions and started to cry.

Harry was not going to leave this way. Giving a quick good-bye to his wife and daughter, Harry knelt by his son and gently pleaded with him. "Many soldiers had to go. They didn't want to go. And they went out there to fight. I'm going to bind up the wounds, son. Somehow we must pay a price too." Finally, Duane said, "All right, Dad. This one more time."

As father and son came to the gangplank, two police guards escorted the child down the plankway. As they reached the bottom, Duane broke away from the guards, running into his father's arms. With further persuasion, the distressed child was again escorted down the gangplank. As the gangplank was drawn up, water separated Harry from his waving family.

Harry seriously asked, "Where is my loyalty? Is it with my family or with somebody out there that I don't even know?" He questioned further, "God, what am I to do?" During this agonizing struggle, Harry came close to refusing the trip. But the time of the ship's departure arrived. Tugboats moved the vessel out of harbor. Harry watched the waving hands disappear into the fog.

While in Europe for three and one-half months during 1952 and 1953, Harry's assignment was, in part, a response to needs resulting from the destruction of World War II. He worked closely with the Pax programs in Germany, Greece, and Holland. While in Germany and Greece, Harry wrote the first guidelines for the Pax program. Not only was it his job to write the rules, but to interpret and to implement them as well. Another part of Harry's assignment took him to Yugoslavia. His task was to explore the possibility of a Christian witness in a communist country.

While visiting Pax men in Germany, Harry saw the celebrations among refugee families as the last rafter of a newly-emerging house was nailed into place. A house was soon to become available to a refugee family which had lost their home during the war.

Not only did Harry meet people who were suffering because of the war, he also met that part of himself that hurt inwardly at the separation from his family. That first Christmas away from home found Harry with about seventy fatherless children, war orphans. Since he couldn't spend this special day playing with Duane and Delia, he comforted his sadness by sledding and ice skating with these orphaned children, and brought joy to their depressed spirits.

You Take Them

Orie O. Miller, executive secretary of MCC, commissioned Harry to find a way to save the MCC agricultural development program in Greece. All odds were against the survival of this program. Harry spent ten days in Athens negotiating with government officials.

Across the room in the Office of Agriculture, the Minister of Agriculture sat in his overcoat, rubber boots on his feet. There was no heat in the room and Harry sat shivering in the cold. Money was tight. Recently 2,600 government workers had been laid off. Now Harry presented his case. It was a tough one. He asked for funds to help run MCC's program. Before leaving Athens, Harry was assured of the necessary funding and equipment. Why was this decision made when the end of this program seemed inevitable? Apparently most convincing testimonies had arisen from among the local people—people who knew the importance of keeping this program, people who were partners in the MCC witness.

While Harry was visiting Greece, a lady sent word for him to stop at her cottage. On receiving the message once, Harry ignored it. He received word a second time and ignored it. The third time Harry said, "No, it's not that I'm not interested. But there's a limit to what I can do. The time is short and there is much that I have to do yet." This woman persisted. Finally, Harry went to her house. It was an extremely humble home with dirt floor. A candle dimly lit the room. In a tin can nearby the woman found some hot water. She served Harry tea.

The plea of this woman was that the Mennonites should stay in Greece and continue their agricultural program and witness. With the help of an interpreter, Harry learned that she was distressed because her country's young people were getting nowhere. "For generations we have suffered. Is there ever going to be an opportunity?" Even in this darkness a faint light seemed to flicker. That was the Mennonite presence.

As Harry was taking leave, he looked up. There in the darkness four little eyes caught his attention. Two children. He casually commented, "Well, now, I wouldn't mind taking them along to my home."

To Harry's displeasure, this comment was translated by the interpreter. The woman made a quick dash for Harry. She took hold of him and said, "You take them! You take them! Please!"

After a long time Harry replied, "You look to me like you have the same kind of love my mother had for me. You can't give up those children. How can you do it?"

"Oh," she said, "oh, yes, I can. I'll tell you why. If I could send my children to your land, your land of freedom, your land of plenty, and your land of opportunity, and maybe to a Christian home, like your people over here, what more could I do for my children? Please take them!"

This was a deeply touching encounter which further convinced Harry of the misery many people were suffering. It confirmed the plenty that people saw in America. But it witnessed as well to the way of love exemplified by the Mennonites working in Greece.

During this European trip Harry saw the devastation caused by the worst flood known to Holland in four hundred years. Thousands of dams and dykes had broken. Houses were buried under ten feet of water. The North Sea had reestablished its boundary—the waters did not recede. A small number of Pax men helped initially during the emergency. But greater resources were needed to reclaim the sea-buried land and to rebuild the washed-out towns.

While Harry was in Europe, Olga struggled to be both mother and father to the children in Akron, Pennsylvania. Having lost the presence of both mother and husband, Olga at times felt lonely. As she counseled and mothered homesick and discouraged young MCC workers, listening to each story, the harshness of her own losses gradually lessened.

Teaching captured her attention two days weekly as Olga commuted about seven miles to Lancaster classrooms. She also tutored a German-speaking immigrant family in the English language. And as a "floater" in the MCC office, Olga worked in the clothing center, in the orientation classroom—wherever she was needed.

Trips to Mexico

The Old Colony Mennonites were the first Mennonite settlers in Russia. They later migrated from the Chortitza settlement to Canada in search of greater cultural and religious freedom than was evident in late nineteenth-century Russia. Then in 1922 about 6,000 Old Colony Mennonites in Canada migrated to the San Antonio Valley in Mexico. Desiring greater freedom than Canada allowed, they wanted the privilege of establishing and operating their own schools without government interference.

Life in Mexico, however, wasn't without difficulty. The year 1951 marked the onset of a four-year drought. These Old Colony Mennonites, by now 18,000 in number, were chiefly farmers. They lived in small villages between two mountain ranges. During these rainless years, crops failed and animals died of thirst.

Without rain farmers were unable to farm, losing their main source of income. It was a struggle for life.

At nighttime it was not uncommon to spot blazing fires dotting the open fields. Women picked cactus, burning off the thistles. This cactus was then fed to the animals. Inside the cactus was moisture that might keep the animals alive another day.

Among these Mennonites, it was believed that this suffering came from God. The bishop opposed any kind of dole or relief. "After all," the bishop said, "it must be the Lord's will that we suffer, so we're going to suffer willingly."

In response to the problems of drought, hunger, and disease, Harry Martens made several trips to Mexico in 1952 and the following years. His first trip, which preceded his Central European assignment, was to negotiate with government officials in Mexico City for visa privileges for MCC personnel. This was necessary in order for help to come to the Old Colony Mennonites.

Help finally did come to these drought-stricken, desperate people. Several carloads of flour were shipped from Kansas, and well-drilling rigs were sent from Nebraska. Flour was doled out to the people from a storeroom. Fearing their bishop's displeasure for accepting relief, Old Colony Mennonites frequently drove by the storehouse in their buggies. Passing by perhaps five times, they finally halted their buggies. Entering the storeroom, they said, "We're at the end. We're not supposed to come, but we have no choice." Trading their last hen for flour, they could now bake bread for the family for a few more days. At times parents pleaded, "Would you please take our children. Keep them a month, or two, or three, until this terrible drought is over. Just keep them so they will be fed. We can't stand to see our children suffer."

During these visits Harry made negotiations for the closing and reopening of a government hospital. He successfully untangled the matted political red tape. The hospital was reopened. A later trip to Mexico involved a search for additional territory for the Old Colony Mennonites.

On two of these trips Olga and the children accompanied Harry. The children went to a school where English wasn't spoken. Only German or Spanish could be heard.

Olga became involved in church work. Many young women in this church felt alone. Some didn't understand the German sermons or hymns because they spoke only Spanish. Olga met with these women. They were hungry for fellowship.

One night as Olga was speaking to this women's group, the meeting was interrupted by the message that a prominent and wealthy businessman in Cuauhtemoc had died. The women knew about Olga's work in Puerto Rico preparing bodies for burial. Consequently she was asked to provide this service now. The next day was a Catholic holiday and so a casket had to be bought yet that night. Word of the funeral was carried by wagon to friends and relatives. Within the next twenty-four hours Olga's flexibility and skill were strongly evidenced as she assumed responsibility for the funeral preparations. A hand-sewn handkerchief with a crocheted edging was the elderly grandmother's token of gratitude for Olga's willing service.

Mennonite Disaster Service

Growing up in tornado and flood-ridden Kansas, Harry quickly became aware of the frustration and inefficiency of uncoordinated volunteer services in disaster areas. Many times carloads of volunteers arrived at a site early in the morning. Midafternoon still found these volunteers unassigned to work tasks.

The present witness was ineffective. It was time for Mennonites to become organized on a national and international level. Harry shared this vision with other Mennonite leaders. And out of this vision Mennonite Disaster Service was born. At the beginning, Harry served on the Executive Committee. He later became executive secretary on an unpaid basis.

During the summer of 1956, Harry and his family traveled from coast to coast, introducing to the North American Mennonite people the importance of MDS. The idea caught like fire. For this was a way that the lay person in the local congregation could demonstrate the love of Christ in responsive self-giving to that neighbor in need. Truly that smallest act of kindness is much when God is in it.

Called to the Middle East Crisis, 1967-1969

After Palestine was partitioned in 1948, Arab refugees moved into the warm Jordan Valley on the West Bank. The Six Day Israeli-Arab War in June 1967, however, caused thousands of Arabs to flee from the West Bank of the Jordan River, a refusal to live under Israeli occupation. Over 55,000 Arab refugees settled in tents along the arid East Bank, living in tent cities. They were part of a larger Arab population, numbering over 500,000, which lived along the Jordan's East Bank in huts and sheds. Later Israeli shellings drove over 100,000 Arab refugees inland to the hills of Amman. They faced a cold, wet winter in these seven tent cities. Their flimsy tents provided pitifully inadequate protection against the wind, rain, and cold that faced this homeless people.

This was a time of crisis—a time inviting forth such

persons who could be reconciling agents among peoples that knew no peace. MCC identified Harry and Olga as such a caring team. A man with keen administrative ability, Harry had shown an unusual capacity to sort out major problems from minor ones. He increasingly was assigned to crisis situations with the responsibility of responding to immediate emergency needs, laying the groundwork for future MCC involvement. Gifted with humor and the ability to communicate his sincerity, Harry was able to gain the confidence of otherwise mistrustful persons.

Before going to the Middle East, Harry and Olga were briefed by government and relief organization officials in Washington, D.C., and in Geneva, Switzerland. In Rome the Martens met with a special United Nations representative to the Middle East for a briefing.

Seating himself in a chair, this lanky representative was silent for a while, and then he said, "Well, I understand that you are going to Jordan."

To this Harry responded, "Yes."

"Uh ha. Well, it's going to be tough," the representative added.

"I had assumed that," Harry replied.

"It's going to be very, very tough. In fact it's going to be so tough that after you've been there a month or so, you will say that there's just no solution to these problems." These comfortless words added to the fears already growing within Harry and Olga. But after a long pause, the representative most advisedly said, "Well, let me just give you this little hint as to how you should do this. You will know that the big problem is made up of many small problems. Even though at the moment there is no solution to the big one, the little ones have solutions. You work at the little ones and we'll finally get to the big one."

This proved to be wise counsel as Harry and Olga immersed themselves in finding solutions to some of the "little" problems—the needs of the homeless Arab refugees. Although interested in long-range development programs, as MCC relief director in Jordan, Harry was responsible for directing relief distributions of food, clothing, blankets, tents, and medicine. Tons of clothing bales and thousands of Christmas bundles came from MCC. These were distributed among the refugees. Blankets, quilts, sheets, school supplies, soap, processed beef—all were sent to Jordan at Harry's request.

Harry became friends with these people. Although the refugees knew that Harry wasn't an Arab, they closely identified with him as a friend. Slowly confidence was built.

On snowy nights Harry went among the people, giving them warm blankets. On one such night the tents were leaking because of the heavy snow. Everything inside the tents was wet. It was late at night. Faster than by radio, word traveled that dry blankets were coming. As Harry struggled to take the blankets to the chilled refugees, they came running from all directions. Six inches of wet slush covered the ground. Having walked bootless for most of the day, Harry's feet were by now nearly frozen. He slipped. And as he fell, Harry noticed that the people who were crying for blankets had no shoes on their feet. As a result of this experience he felt a closer identification with the people. Harry learned that although he was not poor like these refugees, he could know with them what it means to be poor in spirit.

It was important that someone give evidence of caring. "Is there anybody in the world that knows what's happening to us?" the refugees asked. "And if they do know, do they care?" As Harry and Olga responded to the comfortless, the discouraged, and those hopeless, again and again they were embraced and kissed. The refugees had discovered these human kin who had not forgotten them.

Caring for the Children

While in the Middle East, Olga lost no time. Separated from her children during this twelve-month assignment, she focused her energies on the refugees in whose midst she lived. At times she worked twenty hours a day. Within three months of her arrival Olga had established a mother-child center.

Observing the number of pregnant women who had fled to the Jordan's East Bank, Olga realized that these women had no clothing, diapers, or blankets for the expected infants. Olga cabled Akron, requesting a prompt shipment of layettes. Despite the scarcity of supplies, a few pairs of scissors were found. Russian-made material was found too. Renting one room, Olga and a young refugee woman started the center. Here an expectant mother was taught how to sew a gown for her baby's layette. A layette included a gown, a blanket, and diapers. At the baby's birth, each mother received a second layette, shipped already-made from Akron. Recognizing the merits of that first center, Olga helped to open several more mother-child centers. Arab women whom Olga had trained directed the centers.

Olga quickly discovered that although there were schools in the tent cities for children six years and older, there was nothing for the kindergarten-age child. These children, consequently, were underfoot frustrated, despairing, with unemployed parents and grandparents in overcrowded tents. A tent with floor space of fifteen feet by twenty feet often housed fifteen people. Standing outside his own tent, an Arab boy could see neighboring tents squatting closely by his family's tent. He couldn't count all the tents within a stone's throw. And there were so many more heavily dotting the hillsides. In one camp alone there were up to 30,000 people living in tents.

Many children and their families were happy that kindergartens were started in the tent cities. In each of the six kindergartens begun by Olga, one hundred children could attend. In the beginning classes were held inside two large tents, two shifts in each tent with twenty-five children attending each shift. Remembering well the stories that their parents and grandparents had told them again and again, these boys and girls easily remembered the lessons that they were taught in kindergarten.

The children had fun teaching Olga how to count in Arabic. She, in turn, taught them how to count in English. To sing and to dance together was always a delight. At times gusty winds tore the tent, uprooting the stakes and dusting students and teachers with sand. The wintertime was very cold. The children shivered without shoes. Then it was hard to work or play.

Despite these difficulties, kindergarten was a place where the children could receive love. They happily returned home, showing the family the fruits of their day. The family enjoyed hearing them talk about their school day.

While in the United States and absent from her little friends, Olga continues to provide their school supplies. She still makes kindergarten kits, sending the kindergartners crayons, scissors, pencils, glue, and construction paper in a large drawstring bag.

When not teaching in one of the kindergartens, Olga assisted with the needlework project and organized women's activity centers. A woman who cared about other women, her concern ministered to the needs of these her sisters. Likewise, Olga allowed the lives of these women to deeply touch her own.

One day a young woman came to a mother-child center in Jordan, her face deeply marred—this woman obviously a ravaged victim of the napalm bomb. Very, very slowly, but finally her layette was completed, despite the fact that she had only one hand with which to sew.

"Such an unjust exchange," Olga sadly thought. "A piece of flannel in exchange for the destruction caused her by the American-made bomb. And it's an American now who wants to give her this flannel."

The Ugly American

In 1967 to 1969 when Harry and Olga worked among the Arabs in the Middle East, it was not a popular time to be identified as an American. After all, the United States was helping the Israelis by sending ammunition to Israel, which was used to fight the Arabs. And so Harry and Olga had to prove themselves not as Americans but as Christ's loving people. On occasion anger was directed against Harry and Olga because they were Americans. When in the presence of Arab friends, Harry and Olga were safe.

There were times, however, when Harry and Olga were among people who didn't know them. On one such occasion Harry was walking alone down an unfamiliar street. The street was wet with snow. An angry mood filled the air. The cold, gusty wind and the wet, falling snow merely reminded this people anew that here they were a people dispossessed of their homeland, with little or no food, and without blankets to comfort them in the bitterness of this foreign wintry cold.

As Harry walked down the street, donned in hat, someone shouted, "Johnson!" Lyndon B. Johnson was the United States president at the time. From among the people, snowballs were hurled. Gradually a crowd of men gathered, following him. As the fervor of the mob rose, Harry continued to be pelted with snowballs. Stones were planted in these angry weapons. Finally, one knocked Harry to the ground. Immediately he was surrounded by a sea of faces that glared down at him. Speaking rapidly in Arabic, the crowd clearly communicated a spirit of hatred. Folding his hands across his chest, Harry looked up at the faces in the crowd. He tried to speak.

Then quite unexplainably, the line of men was broken as two middleaged women undauntingly moved toward Harry. Taking his hands, they led him away from the disturbed crowd. With hasty speech they addressed each other, speaking just as quickly to the onlooking mob. After gaining a safe distance from the threatening scene, the women departed, their identity unbeknown to Harry.

Walking with the Mighty to Help the Poor

The Martens went out of their way to be responsive to people from all walks of life, whether ambassador or refugee. They openly accepted relationships with people in influential political positions. Fouad Atella, an Arab Christian and world-renowned attorney, and his wife, Lydia, proved to be delightful and helpful friends of the Martens. As a result of this rapport, Harry and Olga gained entrance among officials who otherwise would have remained strangers to them. Frequently after a long day of hard work among the Arab refugees, Harry and Olga could be seen at night socializing with government officials, embassy personnel, and ambassadors.

These relationships with high government and church officials were most important during the Martens' second assignment in the late 1960s. Harry's role was primarily that of reconciler and negotiator. And his assignment was to contact persons in the highest positions in the church and government. He was to share with them MCC's concern for peace. Traveling from Damascus to Beirut to Jerusalem to Cairo to Amman, Harry met with officials.

Harry could be heard asking groups of Christian leaders, "What would you say if we were to visit Golda Meir tomorrow?" Or, "What would you tell Nasser if you had the opportunity?" "What would you wish me to say?" These were not impossible dreams. For during this time, Harry had audience with King Hussein of Jordan and Anwar Sadat of Egypt.

Upon returning to the United States, Harry confronted government people—Senators and Representatives, United Nations officials and members of the State Department. Again his plea was for reconciliation in the Middle East.

These attempts at peacemaking were recognized in 1968 as King Hussein decorated Harry for his work as Middle East Commissioner for MCC. In 1969 the U.S. State Department awarded Harry the Lane Bryant Volunteer Award for his work as MCC director in Jordan.

In Suffering Bengali, 1972

In 1972, less than three years after returning from the Middle East, Harry found himself traveling further eastward to war-torn and typhoon-stricken Bangladesh. Because Olga had a teaching assignment in Elkhart, Harry responded to this emergency alone.

Bangladesh, "the land of the Bengali people" formerly

known as East Pakistan, is a country officially born in 1972. With help from India, the West Pakistani army was defeated in December 1971. This ended a most bloody revolution against the West Pakistani military rule.

Bangladesh is a land of contrasts. A country about the size of the state of Arkansas, it has a population of 75 million people. Compare this with Arkansas' population of less than two million people. Characterized by green rice paddies, coconut palms and banana trees, rickshas, wooden plows drawn by bullocks, fertile soil, and rivers decorated endlessly with sail boats, paddle boats, and cargo-carrying barges, Bangladesh is a country pained by throes of widespread poverty.

Harry had encountered poverty before in Puerto Rico, Mexico, Greece, and the Middle East, but never had he seen so many people in such a large area so poor. In a little over a year, these people were victimized by two disasters which took their toll in over one million lives. In November 1970 a typhoon ripped through this land only to be followed by a brutal war. Nearly ten million Bengalis fled to India. But unlike the Arab refugees, the Bengalis were able to return to their homeland, to their villages and neighbors, to their thatched huts. Over two million Bengalis were left homeless, however. And so Harry traveled to Bangladesh for two months to show these survivors of typhoon and war that somebody cared.

In the Kalishpur camp there were 41,000 detained Bihari people who built little huts around an old abandoned schoolhouse and a few other buildings. Harry's first trip into this area was in a Red Cross jeep. After the jeep had been parked, Harry went to see the director of the refugee camp. On returning a few minutes later, Harry and the director found the jeep surrounded by several hundred weeping and shouting women and children.

The director finally said to Harry, "You foreigners, I know you want to help. Maybe we can find a way." He continued, "But I doubt if this is the time because these people have not had any rations for four days. All they are living on is the little they might have saved from the days before. And they're desperate!"

With this, Harry and the director tried to walk toward the jeep. Harry's shirt was torn by a woman who was screaming, begging, shouting. Although they finally got to the jeep, they were unable to go anywhere. The women stood in front of the vehicle, blocking it.

Getting the director's attention, Harry said, "Now look, this is serious. I just cannot take this. You tell them that whatever it takes, we're going to see that they get food of some kind within twenty-four hours, if there is any earthly way to do it. We'll employ a commercial plane to fly food from India. Whatever is necessary, we'll do it!"

Harry told the director to interpret these words to the people. He told him once. The director didn't do it. And then twice, and he didn't do it. By the third time Harry was provoked. He said, "Now look, this is getting us nowhere! Promise the people that we'll do all in our power *now*, not tomorrow, right now!"

Finally, the director replied, "I'm sorry you didn't understand them. You didn't know what the people are asking. You thought they were asking us for rice or for bread. But they weren't. They were asking for poison."

This desperation and misery deeply disturbed Harry. Within the twenty-foot by thirty-foot abandoned school-house he discovered about ninety elderly people with no beds, nothing, except burlap sacks which clothed their bodies. They waited for death. When the food didn't reach, they were the first to go unfed. Then there were the small children. Mothers gathered groups of six, seven, or eight children and laid them in the hot sun, hoping that the sun would heal them. They were suffering from cholera and smallpox. Before Harry had left the camp a number of children had already died. To encounter death was a daily experience, an hourly occurrence.

Confused as to what to do and looking for answers, Harry sought a church. He was directed to an English service. The service had already started by the time Harry found it. On entering the church, a timely refrain greeted him.

> *Grant us wisdom, grant us courage for the facing of this hour.*

Harry's courage was renewed. As he left he was again more willing to trust God.

One of Harry's first tasks was to find out what volunteer agencies were working in Bangladesh, where they were located, and what they were doing. In that way they could work together and divide the work.

A major MCC project was rebuilding houses. Many of the Bengalis' thatch-roofed homes had been destroyed by the typhoon or the war. And now 250,000 houses were needed. The Bengalis did virtually all of the work. They cut lumber. Hard wood was used for building the structures. Tin was imported from Japan for the roofs.

Although these Bengalis who were involved in reconstruction were poor people, they were not the poorest among the poor. Harry was shocked to hear that in those poorest Bengali families, there was rejoicing when a cripple was born. A people formerly without a source of income, they now foresaw this child as a legitimate breadwinner for the family. In the future their crippled child would shuffle his way across the street to beg for money.

With the burden of such knowledge Harry worked among the people. And with the burden of this awareness he wrote an article entitled "I'm Afraid to Come Home," which he sent to the United States. With this burden he returned to North America to address those wealthiest members of the world's family.

Harry and Olga made the practice of traveling throughout the United States and Canada when they came back from their service assignments. As they traveled, Harry and Olga confronted North American congregations with the reality of the disparity between the world's rich and the world's poor. Harry and Olga repeatedly made this invitation:

> *Let's join in the war for survival—the war against hunger. Let's do our part to close the gap between those who have and those who do not have.*

To the Jungles of Brazil, 1974

It was homecoming for Harry and Olga. Again they entered the little Mennonite chapel at La Plata. This was the first Mennonite church building in Puerto Rico which had been built twenty-eight years earlier when Harry and Olga were involved in CPS activities on the island.

This return visit was part of a seventy-day assignment to South America during the summer of 1974. Harry's major task was to review the needs of the Indian tribes and Brazilians resettled in the Amazon River Basin. His secondary assignment of reviewing all major MCC programs in South America took them to Puerto Rico, Colombia, Bolivia. Paraguay, Uruguay, Argentina, and Brazil. Olga's role was to evaluate the self-help programs and their possibilities in these countries.

During this trip Harry and Olga became personally acquainted with many MCC workers. In Bolivia the Martens bumped along a rugged road in a pickup truck with seven other "Northerners" toward their destination, a two-room schoolhouse which also housed two Teachers Abroad Program (TAP) teachers at its far end.

Walking through the classrooms, the Martens noticed its simple furnishings—desks and benches made from halved tree trunks, supported by tree limb legs. The group gathered in TAP teacher George Reimer's small living quarters. Here they joined together for their regular, biweekly Bible study and prayer meeting. Since the host had arranged a meal with several villagers at the home of a nearby farmer, the ten followed a narrow path to the hut.

Strong tree limbs framed this wall-less hut, its roof made from palm branches. A handmade hammock hung overhead for the baby. Crude tables and tree-stump benches were borrowed from neighbors in preparation for the coming of these guests.

Seated around the tables, the group spontaneously began to sing a song of thanksgiving. Peanut soup was served by the aged mother. In place of bread or crackers, two bowls of home-dried corn were set on the tables. Quietly the group ate as they sat there in the lean-to, hammock in corner.

The aged mother said, "We are very poor, but we are not lazy. We work hard. We simply have not had the opportunity."

The presence of Christ was felt in their midst. His message resounded within each person: "For God so loved the *world* that he gave his only begotten Son...." Kisses and embraces were the benediction on the "communion" of these brothers and sisters, Bolivians and North Americans.

Harry and Olga met the elderly missionary couple, Pastor and Mrs. Giesbrecht, while in Paraguay. As a young refugee, Pastor Giesbrecht had come to Paraguay. He felt a need to do something for the local people, especially the Indians. Although he wanted to volunteer as a missionary, his home church at first refused involvement or support.

Independently then, Giesbrecht began to work with the Lengua Indians in 1935, without knowledge of the language or culture of this tribe. Ten years later, the planted and watered seed began to sprout. The testimony of the first Indian Christian touched the lives of his tribe's people. This was the beginning of the Yalva Sanga Indian Congregation.

Now thirty years later, Harry and Olga participated with over five hundred Indians in the annual harvest festival of this congregation. In the midst of these celebrations, the fruits of their land could be seen as a reminder of God's goodness and spiritual blessing.

Missionary Giesbrecht so aptly said, "Through these years we had only *small capital* but a *great God.* We worked and trusted in his mercy."

The focus of the Martens' assignment was the Amazon River Basin in Brazil. This vast area of jungle, approximately three fourths the size of the United States, was the hunting and gathering territory of many Indian tribes. But in contrast to the mountainous coastlands, this jungle interior was relatively unsettled.

A goal of the Brazilian government was to encourage Brazilians to settle in this inland jungle territory. In the 1950s the capital of Brazil was moved from coastal Rio de Janeiro to inland Brasilia. The biggest incentive for resettlement is the building of the transcontinental highway. Spanning the continent from coast to coast, this highway is to include a network of secondary roads that will provide entrance into the Indian hunting grounds.

These questions were posed to Harry, "Does the mission board or MCC have a responsibility to the Brazilian Indian? If so, what is it? What should be the relationship of these agencies to the already-present Wycliffe Bible Translators?"

And so, answers to these questions were sought as Harry and Olga lived in the river basin among the Palikur Indian tribe and the Satere Indians. They observed the Wycliffe Bible translators as they struggled to translate "the Lord is my shepherd" in light of the fact that these Indians did not know the meaning of "shepherd" or "sheep."

As Harry and Olga saw the Wycliffe missionaries' concern for the Indian people, they developed a profound respect for their work. A supportive role to the Wycliffe Bible translators was absent, however. And this became Harry's vision and recommendation for Mennonite agencies—to provide agricultural, educational, medical, and social services to these Indian tribes, freeing Wycliffe translators to do their translation work.

This need was expressed by Wycliffe Bible translators who lived with the Satere Indians. They sent this message with Harry as he left for the United States.

Dear Brothers and Sisters:
We beg you for the love of Jesus that you might send someone to help here in Satere land. Indians are turning to Christ but we just do not have time to finish translating the Bible for them and also to help them in farming and medicine and education. They number 3,000 and we hardly have time to do our job anymore. Please.

A Team Ministry of Love

One day while on an Asian assignment, Harry was quietly walking along a wooded path at early dawn. Hearing a favorite melody, Harry remembered when Olga and he had helped to introduce the same song to Christians in the Middle East. His reminiscence was interrupted by these words which echoed in broken English.

We are one in the Spirit,
We are one in the Lord. . . .
And we pray that all unity
May one day be restored.

We will walk with each other,
We will walk hand in hand. . . .
And together we'll spread the news
That God is in our land.

We will work with each other
We will work side by side. . . .
And we'll guard each man's dignity
And save each man's pride.

Indeed, these words tell the story of Harry and Olga. Even though they never were ordained as ministers, Harry and Olga learned that as lay people they could be ministering and caring persons. Offering the gift of themselves, they believed that a little is much when God is in it. During the course of all their travels they said, "Out of our own strength we can do little. God is the source and the enabler of our strength."

Whether rich or poor, refugee or government official, Bengali or Brazilian, Arab or Jew, Harry and Olga recognized these people as brothers and sisters in this their human family. While in the United States, Harry and Olga demonstrated this as they opened their home to children and youth from Puerto Rico, Mexico and Holland, Jordan and Bangladesh.

As Harry and Olga talked and walked and worked among the rich and the poor, the meaning of the love of Christ was expressed. In thankfulness for God's love to them, they responded in love to others. And out of the brokenness of their own lives, Harry and Olga could respond in self-giving to their suffering brothers and sisters.

They will know we are Christians
By our love, by our love.
Yes, they'll know we are Christians
By our love.

The
Authors

Dyck, Clara K., a nurse and college teacher turned free-lance writer, lives in Winnipeg, Manitoba.

Patkau, Esther, former missionary to Japan, is presently serving as assistant pastor of the First Mennonite Church in Saskatoon, Saskatchewan. Her biography of J. J. Thiessen grew out of her MA thesis work on his life and thought, submitted to the Lutheran Theological Seminary in Saskatoon.

Preheim, Marion Keeney, former MCC worker in Algeria, is a homemaker and writer living in Newton, Kansas.

Prieb, Wesley J., is professor and director of the Center for Mennonite Brethren Studies at Tabor College, Hillsboro, Kansas. His biography of P. C. Hiebert is part of a book-length writing assignment presently in progress.

Shelly, Maynard, a former pastor, editor, and MCC worker in Bangladesh, is now a free-lance writer living in North Newton, Kansas.

Sider, E. Morris, is professor of History at Messiah College, Grantham, Pennsylvania. One of his writing projects presently is a book-length manuscript of the life and work of C. N. Hostetter, Jr.

Souder, Shirley B., MSW, is serving as a social worker in Lagrange, Indiana. Her biography of Harry and Olga Martens was written while attending Goshen Biblical Seminary and working part time with the Institute of Mennonite Studies.

Wiebe, Christine, formerly of Hillsboro, Kansas, served for a time as MCC volunteer at Akron, Pennsylvania, and is presently on MCC assignment at the Marymound School for Girls in Winnipeg, Manitoba.